The
HIDDEN

GW00372847

of
Devon & Cornwall

Front Cover: St Michael's Mount
by
Graham Lewis

Acknowledgements

The Publishers would like to thank the following for their
assistance in the production of this book:
Elaine, Deborah, Kelly, Administration. Graham, Joanne,Production.
Peter , Kevin, John, Research. Gerald, Joanna, Writing.
Julian,Clare. and finally,
Simon at Scorpio for the maps.

OTHER TITLES IN THE HIDDEN PLACES SERIES
(ORDER FORM AT BACK OF BOOK)

Ireland

Scotland

North Wales

South Wales

The Welsh Borders

Northumberland &Durham

Lake District

Yorkshire

Lancashire, Cheshire, I.O.M

East Anglia

Somerset, Avon, Glos, Wilts.

Dorset, Hants, I.O.W.

Thames & Chilterns

TheHeart of England

The South East

Printed & Bound By Guernsey Press C.Islands.
Copyright M & M Publishing Ltd. 118 Ashley Rd .Cheshire. U.K. WA14 2UN

Foreword

The Hidden Places Series

is an established collection of travel guides which cover the U.K and
Ireland in 16 titles.

The aim of the books is to introduce readers to some of the less well
known attractions of each area whilst not ignoring the more
established ones.

We have included in this book a number of hotels, inns,
restaurants, various types of accommodation, historic houses,
museums, and general attractions which are to be found in this part
of the country, together with historical background
information.

There is a map at the beginning of each chapter with line
drawings of the places featured, along with a description of the
services offered.

We hope that the book prompts you to discover some of the
fascinating "Hidden Places " which we found on our journey , and
we are sure the places featured would be pleased if you mentioned
that our book prompted your visit.

Safe Journey.

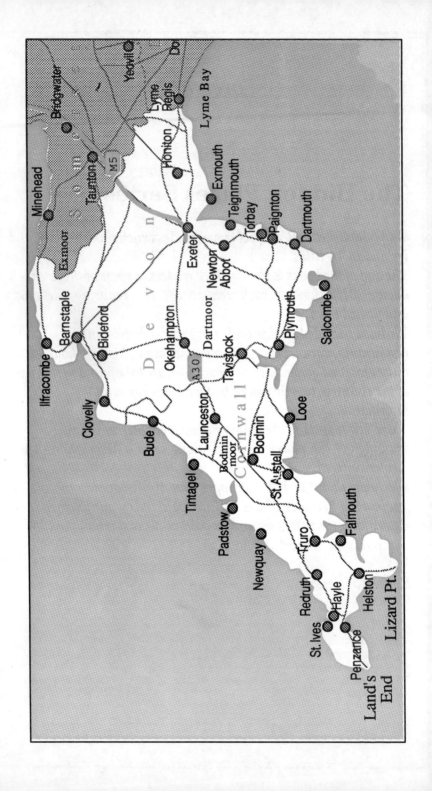

THE HIDDEN PLACES OF
DEVON & CORNWALL

CONTENTS

CHAPTER ONE

EAST DEVON

Honiton High Street

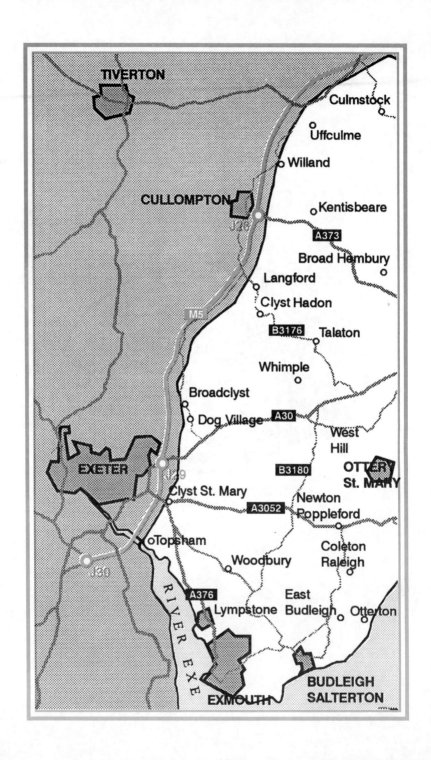

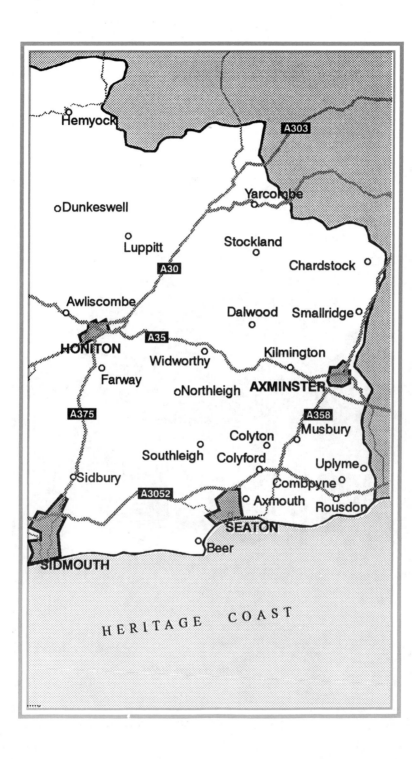

Honiton High Street

CHAPTER ONE

EAST DEVON

Honiton to the Blackdown Hills

HONITON. The main centre of east Devon, is a delightful little town in the valley of the River Otter which could be described as the 'gateway to the far southwest'. The settlement was once a stopping place on the *Fosse Way*, one of the ancient Romans' four royal roads of Britain, which connected Exeter with Bath, Cirencester and the east coast at Lincoln. Honiton's long association with overland travel has had a significant effect on its character; the main feature of the town is its wide, ribbon-like High Street which for centuries carried horse-drawn coaches, and later the busy A30 trunk road, from the South West peninsula to Salisbury and London.

In the late medieval period, Honiton was an important market town and centre of the woollen industry; indeed, the first serge cloth in Devon is said to have been manufactured here. However, it is for another material that the town is perhaps best known: Honiton lace. Lace-making is thought to have been introduced to east Devon by Flemish immigrants at the time of Elizabeth I. By the end of the 17th-century, the industry employed around 5000 people, most of whom worked in their own homes making fine 'bone' lace by hand. (At that time, local children from the age of five went to 'lace schools' where, along with a basic education, they were instructed in the intricacies of lace-making.) However, the introduction of cheaper machine-made alternatives towards the end of the 18th-century almost wiped out demand for the traditionally-made fabric until a lifeline was thrown to the industry by Queen Victoria when she insisted upon Honiton lace for her wedding dress. This ensured a small but enduring revival and today, traditional handmade lace can still be found in local shops.

A series of devastating fires in the mid-18th-century destroyed most of the older buildings in Honiton, with the result that the town now has the pleasant, unhurried atmosphere of a Georgian coaching town. (This relaxed atmosphere was enhanced by the opening of a much-needed bypass in the 1970s.) One building which survived the flames stands near the centre of the main street, the part 15th-century **All Hallows Schoolroom;** after having been used as a school for three centuries, it is now an interesting local museum which houses a unique collection of traditional lace.

Another pre-Georgian building, **Marwood House,** can be found at the northeastern end of the High Street. It was built in 1619 by the second son of Thomas Marwood, one of Queen Elizabeth I's many physicians who achieved notoriety by curing the Earl of Essex when all others had failed. Marwood Sr. then lived on to the extraordinary age of 105 and was buried in St Michael's, Honiton's former parish church.

Tucked away in the High Street is **WINEWORLD** - definitely a place for those who appreciate the fermented juice of the grape. Jonathan Sing is your expert guide to the wines on sale here, and the aroma that assails you as you enter the premises is sure to get your tastebuds working.

Due to the relatively small size of the shop you feel transported into an 'Aladdin's Cave'. Jonathan has a vast knowledge of his wine selection with over eight hundred wines in stock at any one time. Many of the wines on show are top medal winners and as an independent wine merchant Jonathan can obtain more or less anything you require. His claret selection alone averages 60 winners at very competitive prices, as he often buys bin ends and bankrupt stock. Jonathan greets all his customers with a smile and is delighted to offer advice when you come to make your selection. You will also find an interesting selection of well priced wooden bowls turned by Joe &Roy who assist Jonathan at the shop.

Wineworld, 83 High Street, Honiton, Devon. Tel: 01404 43767

Standing on a hill to the south of the town, **St Michael's churchyard** is worth a visit for its striking views over the rooftops to the Blackdown Hills. Inside, there are some noteworthy 15th- and 16th-century features, although sadly the original rood screen was destroyed in 1911 when the building was gutted by fire. Honiton's present parish church, St Paul's, was built in the 1830s in mock-Norman style; it stands beside All Hallows Schoolroom in the High Street. A couple of buildings on the outskirts of the town are worth a mention: **St Margaret's Hospital** to the west was founded in the middle ages as a refuge for lepers who were refused entry to the town. In the 16th-century, this attractive thatched building was reconstructed as an almshouse. To the east, an early-19th-century castellated toll house known as **Copper Castle** can be seen with its original iron toll gates.

AROUND HONITON

To the north of Honiton lies an irregular diamond-shaped area of countryside whose northern edge is bounded by the M5 and the Somerset border. This area of gently undulating farmland is seldom visited by the casual visitor, yet it contains some delightful rural settlements and isolated farms. Unlike the rolling hills which characterise much of the rest of Devon, here the landscape is a high, flat-topped plateau which is cut into long fingers by a series of attractive south-flowing rivers. On the northern edge of Honiton lies the National Trust-owned **Dumpdon Hill**, an 850ft steep-sided outcrop which is crowned by a sizable late-Iron Age hill fort. Both the walk to the summit and the views over the Otter Valley are breathtaking.

On the A373, just outside Honiton, you will find **GODFORD FARM**. Set in the glorious rolling Devon countryside, in a river valley, this is a working dairy farm. here, Sally Lawrence provides comfortable Bed and Breakfsast accommodation in the listed 17th century farmhouse.

There is a family bedroom with private bathroom, and a twin room with a shower room. guests are well looked after, and have their own lounge with colour T.V and open log fire for those chilly evenings. Also on the farm, there are 2 self - catering cottages, each sleeping up to 4 people. Both cottages are well equiped and have all the facilities you would need on a self- catering holiday.

Godford Farm, Awliscombe, Honiton.
Tel: 01404 42825

LUPPITT. The remote hamlet of Luppitt lies three miles further north and is reached by way of some tortuous winding lanes. The settlement lies at the bottom of a steep valley and occasionally can be cut off for days by winter snowfalls.

The mainly 14th-century **Church of St Mary** is believed to stand on the site of its Saxon predecessor; though twice restored, some fine internal features remain, including an extraordinary hand-carved font, thought to date from the 10th-century, and a beautifully engineered oak cradle roof.

DUNKESWELL. The village of Dunkeswell, two miles to the northwest of Luppitt, lies in the heart of the Blackdown plateau. Its church of **St Nicholas** contains a carved Norman font depicting what is believed to be one of the earliest representations of an elephant in England. The remains of a 13th-century Cistercian abbey can be found two miles further north on a site now occupied by the Holy Trinity church, a Victorian afterthought.

Before rising to the crest of the Blackdown Hills on the Somerset border, the land descends into the valley of the River Culm. Though it seems unlikely today, this was once a major centre of the woollen industry.

HEMYOCK. Means summer streams in celtic, was once the terminus of the Culm Valley Light Railway, and has an interesting place of interest in the shape of Hemyock castle which is situated behind the church in beautiful grounds. It is privately owned, but there are opportunities for visitors to explore some recently excavated ruins, and picnic by the moat.

Hemyock Castle Tel: 01823 680745

CULMSTOCK, in the heart of the valley, was an important manufacturing centre and small market town where traders would come to buy fleece for spinning into thread, thread for weaving into cloth, or cloth for dying, fulling (a process of mechanical beating which thickened the fabric) and shipping to the main centres of population throughout Britain and the Continent.

A disused woollen mill and some 18th-century weavers' cottages can still be seen beside the river. The present-day population of Culmstock is little more than half what it was at that time; nevertheless, this is a pleasant community with a handsome 15th-century flint-built

Coldharbour Mill

church whose pride and joy is a velvet cope which was embroidered by the folk of the parish to celebrate the consecration of the church in the late 1400s; after having served as an alter cloth for centuries, it now sits in a glass case in the north aisle.

UFFCULME a couple of miles downstream, was mentioned in the Domesday Book, although in common with other settlements in this part of Devon, it seems it had no mill at that time (water powered mills were introduced to the area during the century following the Norman invasion). In common with its neighbours, this large village became an important wool-producing centre in the late-middle ages, and later it became known for its high quality serges. **Coldharbour Mill**, a museum to the south of the village, provides an interesting background to this golden age.

BRADFIELD, two miles to the southwest, is best-known for its part-Tudor, part-Jacobean mansion of the same name. The house has belonged to the Walrond family since the time of King John, and despite having been comprehensively restored in the 1860s, still retains many fine internal features, including an early-Tudor great hall with a hammer-beam roof, carved panelling and charming minstrels' gallery.

KENTISBEARE. An excellent example of a late-medieval church house, or Priesthall, can be found adjacent to the church in the nearby village of Kentisbeare. Remarkably well-preserved, this also has a minstrels' gallery, as well as its original oak-mullioned windows, buttery hatches and carved oak screens. Such church houses were forerunners of the modern parish halls and were used for meetings, feasts and community celebrations.

BROADHEMBURY. Swinging southeastwards back towards Honiton, the exceptionally pretty village of Broadhembury lies a mile to the north of the busy A373. Because it forms part of the estate belonging to the Drewe family, the village has been immaculately preserved. A single street of pristine cob and thatch cottages rises up towards the 14th-century **St Andrew's church** and its neighbour, the **Drewe Arms**, an attractive inn which occupies the former church house. Monuments to the Drewe family are much in evidence in the church, whose most famous incumbent was perhaps one Reverend Augustus Toplady, the author of the hymn *Rock Of Ages*. Though pleasant enough, the church interior may have been even more so had its Victorian 'restorers' not torn out and burned the medieval rood screen. The Drewe family still live at **The Grange**, a late-Elizabethan manor house which lies a mile to the southwest of the village. It was purchased from Dunkeswell Abbey in 1603 by Edward Drewe, a wealthy lawyer who already owned estates in the county at Killerton and Sharpham. Much altered in the 18th- and early 19th-centuries, the interior contains some exceptional plasterwork and wood carving, most notably in the oak drawing room.

One of the most impressive Iron Age hill forts in Devon lies close by at the end of one of the long spurs of land which characterise the Blackdown Hills. The massive earthwork ramparts of **Hembury Fort** once enclosed a seven-acre area including the site of an earlier Neolithic 'causewayed' camp. The fort continued to be occupied during the Roman occupation of Britain until the end of the 1st-century AD. On a clear day, the view from the top is spectacular, stretching southwards to the sea and westwards beyond Exeter to the Haldon Hills. The easiest ascent is from the east.

OTTERY ST. MARY. Five miles to the southwest of Honiton, is a pleasant little market town dating from Saxon times.

One of the most impressive parish churches in the whole of the Southwest can be found here, built in the 14th-century by Bishop Grandisson , who at the time was supervising the final touches to the refurbishment of Exeter Cathedral. It was constructed as the collegiate church for a small school for secular priests; the interior is unusually light and airy, and contains some exceptional features, including a square-faced clock believed to have been made around 1340 which once showed the phases of the moon as well as the time of day.

The vicar here for over sixty years during the 18th-century was John Coleridge whose youngest son, Samuel Taylor Coleridge, went on to become one of Devon's few prominent literary figures, with such works to his name as the *Rime Of The Ancient Mariner* and *Kubla Khan.*

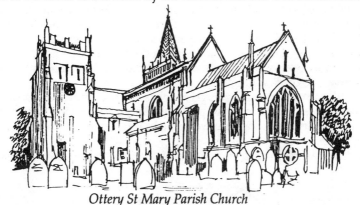

Ottery St Mary Parish Church

Despite some devastating outbreaks of fire, Ottery St Mary still contains some fine Georgian buildings, including an old wool manufactory by the River Otter which is a striking example of early industrial architecture. The town is famous for its Guy Fawkes celebrations which take place each year on the Saturday closest to November 5; these include the time-honoured tradition of rolling barrels of flaming tar through the narrow streets.

One of the few remaining Tudor mansions in the county, **Cadhay**, lies one mile to the northwest. This remarkable house is constructed around a rectangular quadrangle known as the 'Court of the Kings' whose four entrances are guarded by figures of Henry VIII and his offspring, Edward VI, Mary Tudor and Elizabeth I. (Open Tuesdays to

Thursdays, 2pm to 6pm in July and August, also Whitsun and August Bank Holidays.)

FARWAY Five miles to the east, and three miles due south of Honiton, the settlement of Farway contains some attractive thatched cottages, an early-17th-century country house-turned-school, Netherton Hall, and a part-Norman church built high up on a ridge. A remarkable series of Bronze Age barrows can be found on nearby Broad Down which mark the approximate course of the *faer weg*, the ancient ridgeway from which the village gets its name. Within easy reach lies the 189-acre Farway Countryside Park with its unique collection of deer and rare farm animals. (Open daily, Good Friday to end-September.)

Only 3 miles from Honiton and close to Ottery St Mary, just off the A30, you will come across **SKINNERS ASH FARM**. Skinners Ash is a family run rare breeds working farm with cattle, sheep, pigs, goats, and poultry. children are welcome to feed the animals and even collect fresh laid eggs from Henrietta, the hen. Others may prefer to take a pony ride, or just explore the farm and discover the different animals for themselves. The farm is situated in the Otter valley, and there are beautiful views and country walks to enjoy.

In the 16th century farmhouse, owners Jill and Brian offer bed and breakfast accommodation too. there are 2 large family rooms which can sleep up to 6 people. Alternatively, there is Bertie's Barn, a self- catering flat for 5 people. The flat is equipped to a very high standard, and comes with a 4 Keys Commended rating from the English Tourist Board. The farmhouse breakfasts will set you up for a days sightseeing, and evening meals can be cooked to order.

Jill can also prepare packed lunches and an aafternoons cream tea if you so desire. Meals can be provided for guests staying in the flat as well. Well behaved dogs are welcome in the farmhouse, but not in the flat.

There is plenty of car parking and a baby sitting service if necessary.

Skinners Ash Farm , Fenny Bridges, Honiton. Tel: 01404 850231.

This part of Devon is an ideal place around which to base a holiday, and there is an excellent choice of places to stay to suit every pocket.

PITT FARM is situated in the picturesque Otter valley in the centre of Devon. The attractive farmhouse is a thatched Devon Long House which dates back to 1566 with large beams and rooms and a well kept garden to sit in. The farm buildings and yard have their own separate entrance. George and Susan Hansford have a lot of experience in providing bed and breakfast accommodation and you will find their home to be very comfortable with very nice decor and a real feeling of space. There are six bedrooms, some with private bathrooms and all with tea/coffee makers. Sue offers traditional Farmhouse fare which is home or locally grown, a full English breakfast and Evening meals if required. Children's meals and baby sitting are available by arrangement. Open year round. ETB. 2-Crown Commended. From Ottery St. Mary: Take road to Fairmile and Pitt Farm is one mile on right.

Pitt Farm, Ottery St. Mary, Devon.   Tel: 01404 812439.

Just south of Ottery St Mary lies **FLUXTON FARM HOTEL**, a charming 16th century Devon longhouse with wonderful views over the Otter Valley owned and run by Ann and Maurice Forth.

The farm is delightful and full of character, with beams, open log fires and comfortable furnishings creating a cosy and relaxing atmosphere. The twelve guest bedrooms are all centrally heated and provide tea and coffee making facilities, and all but one are en suite. You can enjoy free range eggs with your full English breakfast - indeed, all the cooking makes use of the best of fresh local produce. As the hotel is licensed you can also enjoy a bottle of wine with your four-course evening meal.

The large lawned gardens are the perfect place to relax, and they feature a putting green and a small trout stream and pond. There is also a miniature railway line running round the garden. This is Maurice's great passion, and guests of like mind are welcome to bring their own engines with them.

Fluxton Farm Hotel, Ottery St Mary Tel: 01404 812818.

WHIMPLE. To the Northwest of Ottery St Mary and across the main A30 is the pretty village of Whimple.

Here, set below cider apple orchards, is an ancient rustic community, where horses are almost as common as automobiles. The village centre has a couple of village pubs - The Thirsty Farmer, is a large, friendly place, and the New Fountain is known locally for its good bar snacks, and evening meals at reasonable prices.

DOWN HOUSE is an Edwardian farmhouse, set in 5 acres of gardens, paddocks and orchard. there are splendid views across Whimple village to the cider country, the Tiverton Hills, and on a clear day, Dartmoor.

There are pleasant walks along the local lanes and footpaths and the more energetic will enjoy the Otter valley, the East Ridge leading to the sea at Sidmouth, and the coastal footpath from Exmouth to Lyme Regis.

Down House has recently been taken over by Joanne and Mike Sanders. They offer country house hospitality in the comfortable rooms which have all been designed in the style of Charles Rennie Macintosh, and named after famous cider apples. There are single, double, and family rooms (some en-suite) and all with hand basin, shaver point, hair dryer, trouser press, drinks tray and colour T.V. A traditional English breakfast is served each morning and afternoon teas are by arrangement.

Although the house is secluded and quiet, it is not remote. There is easy access to the A30, and M5. Exeter, Honiton, and the coast are all within 9 miles.

Down House, Whimple. Tel: 01404 822860.

LANGFORD. North of here at Langford, close to the B3176, is a fine place to stay. Bed and breakfast has been catered for at **NEWCOURT BARTON** for twenty nine years by Mrs. Sheila Hitt. You will find everything spotless in this traditional farm house. It's very quiet, set in the heart of the country where there are excellent opportunities for walking whilst being near to the sea. If you feel like something more energetic you can enjoy a game of tennis on the grass court; it's a good location for family holidays. There are two letting bedrooms with adjacent bathroom. The food is excellent with typical farmhouse breakfast and evening meal available by arrangement. ETB. Listed. Turn off the B3181 Exeter to Cullompton road.

Newcourt Barton, Langford, Cullompton, Devon. Tel: 01884 277326

STOCKLAND, five miles to the northeast of Honiton., has some attractive traditional stone-built cottages (the modern vicarage being the notable exception) and a delightful thatched 16th-century inn, **The Kings Arms**. The much-altered 15th-century church of St Michael was also thatched until two centuries ago. The remains of another Iron Age hill fort can be found one-and-a-half miles to the southwest on Stockland Hill, a prominence which is the site for another, more up-to-date, monument, a TV transmission mast.

YARCOMBE, further north,lies on the main A30. This interesting little village was originally known in Saxon times as 'Erticombe'. Interestingly, it was the estate of King Harold, who died at the Battle of Hastings. Elizabeth 1st later bestowed the estate to one of her favourites, Dudley, Earl of Leicester.

It was later sold on to the Drake family and Sir Francis Drake was later given the entire estate by the Queen. The village is, even today, still owned by descendants of the Drake family.

The skilfully converted Victorian village school in the hamlet of Yarcombe has been tastefully refurbished to offer the comforts and luxuries of a country house hotel, personally run by the resident proprietors, Jackie and Tony Rees.

All visitors to the **BELFRY COUNTRY HOTEL** will feel right at home from the minute they walk through the door, and in the two years since the hotel reopened many have returned again and again.The accommodation comprises six double rooms all having en-suite facilities. Each is individually furnished and comprehensively equipped and has beautiful views over the Yarty valley, but there is much more to the Belfry Country Hotel than somewhere to spend the night, and it is worth making a special visit to try the award winning **Chimes Restaurant.**

Jackie's home cooking , using fresh local produce, has gained an enviable reputation having already been awarded an A A rosette for its high quality. She can offer a table d'hote menu, which changes daily, and a superb a la carte selection. From starters right through to dessert you will be spoilt for choice, and every dish sounds deliciously tempting. To complement your meal, Tony has compiled a good selection of reasonably priced wines from which to choose . The restaurant is cosy yet elegant with a corner bar, open log fire, and the bell from which it takes its name still hangs between the chimneys.

The restaurant is open every night of the week to hotel guests and non- residents. To finish off a perfect setting, there is a comfortable lounge and and a pretty terraced garden. This is a peaceful, relaxing and friendly hotel of high quality, full of charm and personality. Situated on the borders of Devon, Somerset, and Dorset, it is ideal for touring, a short break en-route to or from Cornwall, and visiting the many National Trust properties, gardens, sporting activities , places of scenic beauty and coastal resorts close by. ETB 4 Crown Commended and AA 71%.

The Belfry Country Hotel, Yarcombe, Nr Honiton. Tel: 01404 861234.

WIDWORTHY lies to the south of the main A35, three miles due east of Honiton. Its part-14th-century **St Cuthbert's Church** is worth a look for its many elaborate monuments, many of which are to members of the local Marwood family. Among the several noteworthy houses in the parish is Widworthy Barton, a fine Elizabethan manor house standing adjacent to the churchyard which is noted for its period interior.

DALWOOD, on the opposite side of the A35 three miles further east, is the home of the **Loughwood Meeting House,** one of the earliest surviving chapels belonging to the Baptist Church. When it was built in the 1650s, the site was hidden by dense woodland, for at the time, Baptists were a persecuted sect who could only congregate in out-of-the-way locations. Under its quaint thatched roof, this charming little building contains a simple whitewashed interior with an early 18th-century pulpit and pews. In 1969, it was purchased and carefully restored by the National Trust. (Open all year round; admission by voluntary donation.)

SHUTE. Another National Trust-owned property lies a mile-and-a-half to the south in this village. **Shute Barton** is an exceptional example of a non-fortified late-medieval manor house which dates from the 1380s. Only two wings of the original building have survived, the rest having been destroyed in the 18th-century; however, a number of impressive features remain, including the great hall, with its imposing beamed ceiling, and the old kitchen, with its huge range capable of roasting an ox whole. Entry is by way of a Tudor gatehouse. (Open Wednesdays and Saturdays, 2pm-5.30pm between early-April and end-October.) Elsewhere in Shute, the village **church of St Michael** contains some unusual monuments, mostly to the Pole family, owners of Shute Barton; the memorial to Sir William Pole depicts the former Master of the Household to Queen Anne standing on a pedestal dressed in his full regalia.

MUSBURY is a small village on the Axminster to Seaton road. Just before this village you will find **LITTLE TRILL** and **LITTLE TRILL COTTAGES**

Overlooking some wonderful countryside and set in three acres of stunning gardens these five cottages, owned and run by Wendy and Henry Pountney, offer the very best in self-catering holiday accommodation. All well-equipped with the latest in kitchen appliances, charming decorations and central heating, they are super places to make your holiday base. B & B accomodation is available in the main house. Children and pets are also welcomed and a variety of old fashioned lawn games, such as croquet, will amuse everyone.

Little Trill Cottages, Musbury, Axminster Tel: 01297 34731

AXMINSTER. Nearer the Dorset border, the former monastic town of Axminster now benefits from a much-needed bypass. Founded in the 7th-century above an important crossing on the River Axe, the town has had a long and eventful history as a commercial centre. A Sunday market was founded here in the 12th-century and continued until the 19th. Two popular one-day agricultural fairs still take place today: one on the first Tuesday after 25 April and the other on the first

Wednesday after 10 October. Axminster is perhaps best known for having given its name to a type of high-quality carpet, although these were made in the town for a period of only eighty years between 1755 and 1835 (the old factory still stands to the northeast of the parish church). At one time, a church bell was rung every time a new carpet was completed, perhaps an indication of the poor productivity which led to the eventual downfall of the business. In recent years, efforts have been make to revive the carpet-making industry in Axminster with some success. The town also contains a surprising number of elegant 18th-century buildings, including a handsome coaching inn, the **George Hotel**. Lying three miles to the northeast of Axminster, the old ecclesiastical community of **Hawkchurch** belonged to Dorset prior to last century's boundary changes. The village once belonged to Cerne Abbey and its impressive part-Norman church contains some exceptional carved detailing.

Sidmouth and the East Devon Coast

SIDMOUTH. This genteel seaside resort lies at the point where the small River Sid breaches the soft local sandstone and reaches the sea. On either side, the bright red cliffs rise dramatically to over 500ft, creating a spectacular backdrop to the white Georgian and Victorian buildings of the town. Prior to the 1780s, Sidmouth was an attractive, but struggling, fishing village which faced annihilation following a series of unsuccessful attempts to build an effective harbour. However, this decline was reversed when the new fashion for bathing in the bracing waters of the sea arrived at the end of the 18th-century, a time when members of the leisured classes were unable to travel to the Continent because of the Napoleonic Wars.

Between 1800 and 1820, Sidmouth's population doubled as the aristocratic and well-to-do built substantial 'cottages' in and around the town; many of these have now been converted into impressive hotels such as the Beach House and the castelled Royal Glen. A number of less extravagant developments were constructed during the same period and given such flamboyant names as Elysian Fields and Fortified Terrace. In total, there are now almost 500 listed buildings in the town, and a stroll around the centre is likely to prove very rewarding for those interested in Georgian and early-Victorian architecture. The two bland 19th-century churches are the exception, although look out for the curious building known as the **Old Chancel** which was built in a glorious hotchpotch of styles from parts salvaged from the old parish church and elsewhere.

With its shingle beach, handsome buildings and refined atmosphere, Sidmouth provides an excellent base for a relaxing seaside break. Bear in mind, however, that the mood changes out of all recognition when the annual **Sidmouth International Folk Festival** comes to town. For one week in early-August, the streets and pubs teem with singers, dancers,

Sidmouth street scene

musicians and enthusiastic onlookers, and the atmosphere transforms from polite gentility to good-humoured revelry.

AROUND SIDMOUTH

SIDBURY, three miles inland, contains some noteworthy buildings, including the 16th-century **Porch House**, said to be one of Charles II's many hiding places during his flight from the Parliamentarian forces of Oliver Cromwell. The architecture of the village church of **St Giles and St Peter** spans almost a millennium and features a small Saxon crypt below the chancel which was only discovered in 1898; it is thought to be one of only six examples in the country. The 15th-century eight-sided font is extremely rare in that it retains its original lock, a feature dating from before 1560 when it was the custom to store holy water in the bowl. Above the village to the southwest lies **Sidbury Castle**, an Iron Age hill fort which offers some magnificent views of the coastline from Portland Bill to Berry Head.

Another good view can be had from **Roncombe Gate**, once a notorious rendezvous for smugglers transporting contraband inland from the coast.

WESTON. Near the village of Weston and conveniently located only 150yds from the National Trust Valley leading to the beach and coastal path, **LEIGH FARM** is a friendly, peaceful base for families, walkers, birdwatchers and nature lovers . The farm is very popular and visitors often return time and again - sometimes more than once a year. If you are lucky you may catch a glimpse of the badgers, deer, foxes, buzzards and many other types of wildlife which populate the surrounding fields. Four comfortable self catering, two bedroom, south facing bungalows and a self-contained cottage are available and all are equipped to very high standards. The bungalows all face south onto a well kept lawn with picnic tables. English Tourist Board rating 2-4 keys up to Highly Commended.

Leigh Farm, Weston, nr Sidmouth, Devon EX10 0P
Tel: 01395 516065 Fax: 01395 579582

Also in the village of Weston, is **HIGHER WESTON FARM**, a shining example of how a modern commercial farm can be run with a view to conserving the countryside and encouraging wildlife. In 1992 the farm won the Otter Trophy Award for Farming and Conservation and since then a number of innovative conservation projects have been undertaken. A very high standard of bed and breakfast accommodation is available in the farmhouse. The owner, Sandy Macfadyen, is a talented amateur painter and he often makes his studio available for his guests use. Other amenities include croquet and badminton. The farm makes an ideal base from which to explore the outstanding local countryside. The farm boundary is the coastal footpath which leads down to the secluded Weston Beach (no vehicular access). Most of the coast is National Trust owned being in the East Devon Heritage Coast Area, designated as one of outstanding natural beauty.

Higher Weston Farm, Weston, nr Sidmouth, Devon. Tel: 01395 513741

SOUTHLEIGH. Further along the ridgeway to the east, the great oval earthwork of **Blackbury Castle** stands above Southleigh, a scattered settlement with a charming part-13th-century flint-built church.

BRANSCOMBE. The coastal path offers some dramatic, if arduous, climbs and descents, and those looking for a less strenuous route to the sea should follow the road through Branscombe. The coastline here is some of the finest in Devon and Cornwall and should not be missed. The sheltered shingle beach is the permanent home to a handful of fishing boats and to the east, the ground rises sharply towards one of the great landslips which characterise this section of the Devon-Dorset coast. During a night-time storm in March 1790, a ten-acre slice of hillside broke away, slipping 500ft seawards and 250ft downwards, leaving a number of sharp pinnacles and columns in its wake. Today, a steep footpath snakes its way through the eerie gorge which resulted, and this can be included in a stunning 'round trip' walk along the cliffs.

Branscombe has no real nucleus, rather it consists of a number of scattered farmhouses and residences of varying periods, including late-medieval and Elizabethan; there is also a pub offering first-class food.

The church is dedicated to the little-known 7th-century Welsh saint, St Winifred, suggesting that the Christian heritage of the locality dates back to the Celts. Although little of the present building is thought to be pre-Norman, architectural features can be identified which span 500 years of the late-medieval period (details can be found in an informative locally-produced guide). The National Trust owns several buildings and farms in the village, including an old forge and a bakery, now an attractive tearoom and baking museum.

Between Branscombe and Beer, two miles to the east, the cliffs change suddenly from red sandstone to the distinctive white chalk which characterises much of the coastline of southeast England. The 420ft **Beer Head** is the first great chalk headland on the Channel coast, and it was in its remote bays and caves that smugglers landed and stored their illegal cargoes in the 18th- and early-19th-centuries. One infamous local law-breaker, Jack Rattenbury, wrote a remarkable account of his exploits in *Memoirs Of A Smuggler* which was published in 1837 when the author was 59 years old and had long retired from the trade. Local stories of ghosts and apparitions helped the smugglers to move their contraband inland without hindrance, the lane leading to Bovey House on the northwestern side of the village being a notorious haunting-place. This much-altered house was rebuilt in Tudor times for the Walrond family of Bradfield and contains some fine 17th-century plasterwork; it now operates as a hotel.

BEER is a charming fishing settlement turned select resort standing on a sheltered little bay. Its shingle beach is often littered with picturesque inshore fishing boats, their colourful appearance disguising the gruelling and often dangerous occupation of the fishermen. The village is perhaps best renowned for the building stone which bears its name: Beer stone was mined in deep quarries to the west of the village from Roman times to the late-19th-century. Soft when quarried, yet hard when exposed to the elements, this attractive pale stone has been transported as far as London and used in the construction of several important civic buildings and cathedrals, including Exeter, as well as in countless parish churches, country houses and domestic buildings throughout the locality (sometimes combined with knapped flints taken from around Beer Head).

In recent years, the underground workings have been opened to visitors during the summer months, providing a fascinating and rewarding testimony to almost 2000 years of the quarry workers' skill. The labyrinth of chambers has been described as a cathedral in itself, complete with roof columns and a series of side 'chapels' where stone was systematically removed. There is even a chamber, with tool marks still discernible, from which material was extracted to build the Roman villas of Exeter.

Surrounded by rolling farm and parkland, near the picturesque seaside village of Beer, you will find **BOVEY HOUSE HOTEL**

A 16th century manor house it originally belonged to the Abbey of

Sherborne before being taken over by the Crown following the dissolution of the monasteries. The most famous owner was probably Catherine Parr who was given the house by Henry VIII as part of her dowry. more than a hundred years later, another royal visitor was Charles II, who reputedly took shelter at bovey House following his escape at the Battle of Worcester. This part of the house's history is celebrated in the coffered ceiling of one of the bedrooms. in the centre of the ceiling is a large oak tree in relief, through the branches of which a man's face can clearly be discerned.

On the oval beams there are also figures depicting the Cromwellian troopers. It will come as no surprise that this room is known as the King Charles II Room, and the ceiling is a particularly fine example of a craft that Devon was noted for. At times the house stood empty and it was during these periods that Bovey House was reputedly used by smugglers.

There is evidence of a secret passage leading to the cliffs, and also a secret room, that was only discovered recently, but is now sealed off.

Today, the house has been tastefully modernised whilst still retaining many of its ancient and historic features, and offers a fascinating place to stay. There are 9 bedrooms and all but one are en-suite. The King Charles Room mentioned earlier is one of the bedrooms, and many of the others have four poster beds, all have T.V., drinks facilities and baby listening service. Downstairs there is an elegant drawing room for the exclusive use of guests - it was originally the site of the Medieval Hall, but is actually one of the newer parts of the house. The room has been decorated in the style of the 18th century and features an Adam ceiling and Delft tiled fireplace.

The Inglenooks bar is the oldest existing part of the house, and the huge fireplace dates right back to the 15th century. Offering its own menu, as well as a bar and fine selection of wines, it is popular with both locals and residents alike at lunchtimes and in the evenings. The dining room features Tudor linen - fold panelling and heavily beamed ceiling, and is an impressive and relaxing place to enjoy a meal. The chefs offer both table d'hote and a la carte menus and include fresh produce from the hotel gardens. Dining here, with full silver service, is a memorable experience.

Bovey House Hotel, Beer Nr. Seaton.
Tel: 01297 680241 Fax: 01297 680270.

SEATON. One mile further east, is a small seaside town which, before it developed as a resort, lay half-a-mile inland. Attractively framed by some impressive coastal scenery, much of the architecture is Victorian and Edwardian. The parish church of St Gregory dates from the 14th-century, and perhaps the most noteworthy feature of the town is the **Seaton Tramway**, a three-mile stretch of track running along the western bank of the River Axe to Colyton. Operated by an enthusiastic team of devotees, many of them volunteers, the open tramcars are popular with holidaymakers in summer and bird-watchers in winter; the latter benefit from being able to glide along the estuary, seemingly without causing disturbance to the local feathered population.

COLYTON. Those alighting from the tramway in **Colyton** will find an ancient and surprisingly attractive small town whose origins date back to the Celts. Throughout its long history, this has been an important agricultural and commercial centre, with its own corn mill, tannery, sawmill and iron-foundry.

Many of the older buildings are grouped around the part-**Norman church of St Andrew**, a striking building with an unusual 15th-century lantern and a Saxon cross which was recovered and restored after its broken fragments had been incorporated into the tower. Nearby, can be found the 16th-century vicarage and the **Old Church House**, a part-medieval building enlarged in 1612 and used as a grammar school until 1928.

Look out also for the **Great House** which was built on the road to Colyford by a wealthy Elizabethan merchant. Half-a-mile to the north of Colyton, **Colcombe Castle** contains some exceptional 16th- and 17th-century remains, including an impressive kitchen hearth.

Colyton's sister village of **COLYFORD** lies to the south and this charming village springs to life in September when it stages its annual festival.

Pippinfield Farm, Harepath Hill, Colyford, Seaton, Devon.
Tel: 01297 21521

PIPPINFIELD FARM is an ideal base for touring the Devon Coast. The house is south facing with views of the Axe Estuary; the pretty village of Axmouth lies beyond with a view of the sea at Seaton. Farmhouse bed and breakfast is offered by Anne and Barrie Spanton who are great fun and most welcoming. Bedrooms are en-suite and tea/coffee making facilities are provided. Full English breakfast is served and there's a three course evening meal if required. Home grown or local produce is used and special diets can be catered for. A comfortable lounge with television is available for guests. A farm shop sells home produced cider and a small suckler herd of cattle are kept, containing some rare breeds. ETB. 3-Crown Commended. Senior citizens welcome

St Andrews Church, Colyton

AXMOUTH. This brings us nicely to our next port of call, the delightful and historic village of **Axmouth** which stands a mile from the sea on the eastern side of the Axe estuary. This was once a much more important place than it is today. During Roman times, the harbour served as a main supply point for the occupying forces, standing as it did at the southern terminus of a branch of the Fosse Way.

Nowhere in Devon outside Exeter has yielded up more in the way of Roman remains. Even after the imperial ships sailed away, Axmouth continued to serve as a major commercial and military centre.

However in medieval times, a succession of coastal landslips and the unrelenting advance of a pebble bar across the mouth of the river left the village more or less high and dry.

Despite several attempts over the following centuries to clear the estuary and rebuild the harbour, Axmouth went into decline, an occurrence which, like Rye in East Sussex, had the fortunate side-effect of leaving many period buildings intact.

As a result, the present-day village is filled with an unusual

25

number of attractive cottages, farms and inns dating from the time of Elizabeth to Victoria. The church of St Michael also reflects Axmouth's past prosperity, having been built to an unusually large scale in the mid-12th-century and altered many times since.

A landslip even more spectacular than the one near Branscombe can be found at Dowlands Farm to the southeast of Axmouth. One winter's night in 1839, an eight-million-ton section of chalk hillside moved alarmingly seawards in what must have sounded and felt like an earthquake. The slip left a scar 150ft deep, 300ft wide and over half-a-mile long.

The coastal path now runs through this extraordinary chasm, though as it is a designated nature reserve, walkers should keep to the path. The tiny church of **St Mary the Virgin** in the hamlet of **Combpyne**, near Rousdon, was built in Saxon style in the 13th-century.

On the south wall of the nave, there is a rare 14th-century wall-painting of a ship confirming the congregation's long association with the sea. **Rousdon's** famous All Hallows School occupies a striking Victorian mock-Tudor mansion in the village.

A Roman villa was discovered near the Dorset border at **Uplyme** in the 1850s; the nearby Saxon manor belonged to Glastonbury Abbey from 774 AD until the Dissolution of the Monasteries in the 16th-century.

Sidmouth to Exeter

NEWTON POPPLEFORD.

LANGSFORD FARM, was built in 1874 and is situated in the picturesque village of Newton Poppleford. The courtyard of farm buildings have recently been converted into six self-contained comfortably furnished holiday cottages. A laundry room, childrens play area and outdoor heated swimming pool are also situated on site.

Only a short walk away from local shops, restaurants and pubs; and close to the East Devon Way Footpath, the River Otter and an RSPB nature reserve, the farm is ideally placed for a family holiday. Langsford Farm is situated on the left hand side of the A3052 on entering Newton Poppleford, heading towards Sidmouth.

Langsford Farm, High Street, Newton Poppleford, Devon. Tel: *01395 568249 fax:01395 568969 .e-mail langsford @ mail.eclipse.co.uk http://www.eclipse.co.uk/langsford*

Heading south from here past the village of Colaton Raleigh towards Budleigh Salterton along the A376 is a turning to

OTTERTON. The 330 acre working farm of **PINN BARTON** is where the Sage family have lived for the last 30 years.

Mrs Betty Sage is the proprietress of Pinn Barton bed and breakfast and gives a big warm welcome to all her guests, particularly children. Visitors have their own key and access at all times.

The sea is only two miles away where the beaches are clean and safe. There are lovely long walks along the cliffs and around the farm. The standard of accommodation is high with en-suite bedrooms, central heating, colour TV, clock radio, hairdryer and tea/coffee making facilities. Additionally, there are facilities for ironing and a fridge is provided for the use of guests.

An excellent farmhouse breakfast will set you up for the day and a good choice of eating places can be found nearby. Open most of the year - try a winter break at reduced rates. ETB 2-Crown Commended.

Pinn Barton Farm, Peak Hill, Sidmouth, Devon.   Tel: 01395 514004

Many of the older buildings in **Otterton**, are constructed of local red sandstone, including the tower of St Michael's parish church.

Nearby stands a manor house, now divided into separate apartments, which began life in the 11th-century as a small priory belonging to Mont St Michel in Normandy.

A village mill was recorded in the Domesday Book which probably stood beside the River Otter on the site of the present-day **Otterton Mill**. This handsome part-medieval building has been restored to working condition and features a water wheel driven by a powerful leat; the site now includes a craft centre, shop and restaurant.

Opposite Otterton on the western side of the River Otter lies the impressive, **Bicton Park**. The park is best-known for its landscaped gardens which were laid out in the 1730s by Henry Rolle to a plan by Andre Le Notre, the designer of Versailles.

There is also a formal Italian garden, a world-renowned collection of pine trees and a lake complete with a Victorian summer house known as the 'Hermitage'. On the more commercial side, there is a narrow-gauge woodland railway, an open-air exhibition of historic agricultural equipment, and a 'World of Tomorrow' feature, complete with interstellar travel simulator. (Open daily, 10am to 6pm between 1 March and 31 October.)

EAST BUDLEIGH. The A376 to the south of Bicton Park passes through **East Budleigh**, a delightful community of cob and thatch cottages with a little stream flowing beside the main street. This was once a prosperous small port and market town, and a much more significant place than its now bigger sister on the coast.

THE SIR WALTER RALEIGH INN on the High Street has an unknown history despite its rather illustrious name.

It contains evidence of a building which pre-dates by a century the birth of the Elizabethan adventurer whose name the inn now bears. Sir Walter Raleigh was born in a nearby farmhouse, Hayes Barton in 1552. When the call of the sea came, he set sail for the new world on his voyages of discovery.

Upon his return he introduced the potato and tobacco to England for which he is probably best known to this day. His exploits found favour with Elizabeth the first but with the accession of James I, his popularity waned and he was sent to the Tower. He was released in 1615 when he set sail for South America, a trip which led to disaster as upon his return he was executed.

Throughout Raleigh's travels, life continued at a leisurely pace in East Budleigh and continues to do so today. Visitors and weary travellers will find all their needs catered for at the Sir Walter Raleigh Inn. Here they can enjoy some welcome refreshment and even stay overnight.

The Sir Walter Raleigh Inn, High St .East Budleigh. Tel: 01395   442510

Hayes Barton, is a fine E-shaped Tudor house lying a mile to the west of the village centre. The Raleigh's family pew can still be seen in All Saints' Church, dated 1537 and carved with their (now sadly defaced) coat of arms.

The church also contains a series of over fifty 16th-century bench-ends which were carved by local artisans into weird and imaginative depictions of their trades. A small window in the chancel is a memorial to the naval officer who laid the first submarine cable under the Atlantic in 1858.

BUDLEIGH SALTERTON. The pleasant seaside resort of **Budleigh Salterton** takes its name from the salt-pans, or *salterns*, which were constructed near the mouth of the River Otter over 1000 years ago. Despite its early foundation, the town as we know it today developed in the last two centuries as a peaceful residential and holiday centre which is popular with those preferring the local cobbles to the sandy beach at Exmouth.

Several elegant late-Georgian and Regency buildings survive, and visitors should look out for **the Octagon** at the west end of the Parade which for a time was used as a studio by the painter, John Millais, the co-founder of the Pre-Raphaelite Brotherhood. An excellent view over Lyme Bay can be had from the summit of nearby West Down Beacon.

EXMOUTH. The two-mile long seafront at Exmouth, the first sandy beach in Devon, has attracted visitors from Exeter and beyond since the early 18th-century.

It is the oldest seaside resort in the county, and even before the arrival of the railway in 1861, the wealthy and fashionable arrived in large numbers to reap the benefits of the sea air and saltwater bathing. Originally a small fishing port formed from the parishes of Littleham and Withycombe Raleigh, the population rose dramatically between 1800 and 1900 from two-and-a-half to over ten thousand.

Much of this development was inspired by the Rolle family, owners of **Littleham Manor,** who were responsible for constructing some of the town's most elegant late-Georgian terraces, including **Bicton Place,** Louisa Terrace, and most notably, **Beacon Hill.** Sadly, architectural standards dropped during the Victorian period of expansion, but nevertheless, present-day Exmouth is a cheerful and unassuming seaside town with a lot to offer the casual visitor.

One of the finest seafront promenades on the south coast runs along the great sea wall, which was built in stages between 1840 and 1915. Somewhat surprisingly, the town was a target for enemy bombers during the Second World War, maybe because it was mistaken for Exeter, or maybe because it was an easy target. Many prominent buildings were hit, including the distinctive parish church of the Holy Trinity which was defiantly rebuilt with a large stained-glass window of Sir Winston Churchill.

Overlooking Exmouth Harbour is **THE KERAN'S HOTEL,** a small establishment with large appeal. Indeed this is no mean boast, Pat and Alfred Woods, the owners, have taken great care to ensure their small and intimate hotel offers all the comforts that guests expect from the larger and more impersonal hotel chains.

Prior to 1850 this was one of very few houses on the sea front at

Exmouth and Alfred is always happy to tell you of the building's interesting history.

As well as having seven modern and well decorated en-suite bedrooms, Kerans Hotel also has a bright and sunny residents lounge and a charming dining room that offers the best in home cooked English cuisine.

Adjoining the hotel is **Pilot Cottage**, a self-catering flat. This cosy cottage is roomy and comfortable and fitted with all the latest modern equipment to ensure that your stay is as relaxing and trouble-free as possible.

The Kerans Hotel, Esplanade, Exmouth Tel: 01395 275275

COURTLANDS CROSS. At **Courtlands Cross**, just off the A376 to the north of the town, stands the eccentric National Trust-owned property, **A La Ronde**.

This extraordinary 16-sided house was built at the end of the 18th-century for two sisters, Jane and Mary Parminter, to a design based on the 6th-century church of San Vitale in Ravenna.

The 8-sided central hall has a 60ft ceiling, an impressive staircase and gallery, and a number of unusually-shaped rooms radiating from the ground floor.

Many of A La Ronde's bizarre decorations and fittings, including a vast collection of rare and beautiful shells, were collected by the owners on an 18th-century Grand Tour of Europe. (Open daily, except Fridays and Saturdays, 11am to 5.30pm between early-April and end-October.) The Parminter sisters were also responsible for building the nearby group of buildings known as 'Point In View' in 1811. These attractive single-storey almshouses were built around a tiny chapel and are still occupied under the terms of the original covenant by 'elderly women of good character'.

TOPSHAM. Further north along the A376 and close to Exeter is the charming village of **Topsham** which was Exeter's gateway to the sea and at one time a place of great importance.

Lying at the head of the Exe estuary four miles to the south of the

A la Ronde

city, this delightful little riverside town contains some exceptional old buildings which have survived the town's decline and subsequent revival.

A port has existed on this ancient site since the days of the Celts, and the Romans used it as a main landing point, building a direct road to connect it with the royal forum in Exeter.

Topsham continued to grow in importance throughout the medieval upsurge in the wool trade, especially when a series of weirs prevented any kind of tidal access to the city.

The subsequent construction of the ship canal failed to herald the decline which was predicted, and the town continued to prosper, a fact borne out by some of the fine early-18th-century buildings in the town, most notably the gable-fronted **Dutch-style houses in the Strand** which were built from continental bricks brought in as ballast.

Once a thriving tangle of wharves, boatyards and chandleries, today the narrow lanes running down to the shore from the main street are filled with historic buildings of all descriptions.

Indeed, the entire old town has been designated a conservation area. The view across the broad estuary from the churchyard is outstanding, especially at high tide, and the old maritime inns are delightful places to visit.

WOODBURY. Inland, two-and-a-half miles to the east of Topsham, lies the high sandy ridge known as **Woodbury Common**. This is the site of **Woodbury Castle**, the strategically-important Iron Age hill fort which guarded the Exe estuary and the western approaches to the ancient east-west coastal ridgeway.

Almost half-a-mile in circumference, the remains of the great double earthwork ramparts offer some spectacular views over the surrounding countryside and coastline.

The fort gave its name to the nearby village of **Woodbury**, an ancient community which in recent decades has been a focus for new housing developments.

The part-medieval church of St Swithin contains a 15th-century Beer-stone font, a Jacobean pulpit and a number of interesting memorials. However, the building seems to have suffered more than most from the ravages of the Victorian church 'restorers' whose number included the infamous J. Loveband Fulford, the local parson and squire who took the now-legendary step of punching holes in the medieval rood screen so that his parishioners could see him more clearly.

Woodbury also contains an attractive manor house, **Nutwell Court**, which was mentioned in the Domesday Book and later belonged to the descendants of Sir Francis Drake's brother, Thomas.

Sadly, this building has also suffered greatly at the hands of a 'restorer', the wayward 5th baronet, who ended up having to virtually rebuild the place in the mid-18th-century following a series of disastrous piecemeal 'improvements'.

As well as standing at the head of the Exe estuary, Topsham also

Killerton House

stands at the mouth of the River Clyst, a river which gives its name to half-a-dozen villages and whose lower course roughly follows that of the M5. CLYST ST MARY. Lies two miles upstream at the eastern end of what is believed to be the oldest serviceable bridge in Devon.

Stretching for 200yds across a shallow water meadow, the five-arched causeway was built in the early-13th-century and then partially rebuilt about a century later when the two arches nearest the western bank were replaced.

The bridge then continued to carry the main Exeter to Exmouth road until a bypass was built in the late 1940s. Clyst St Mary's other claim to notoriety is as the site of the battle which ended the ill-fated Western Rebellion of 1549; as a parting gesture, the victorious Lord Russell set fire to every building in the village. CLYST HONITON. Now home to Exeter's airport, while a few miles further north, the remarkably well-preserved village of BROADCLYST. Stands on the B3181, a world away from the roar of the nearby motorway.

The village forms part of the National Trust-owned Killerton estate which was given to the Trust in 1943 by the Acland family, its owners for almost two centuries.

Many of the ingredients of the archetypal Devon village can be found here: characteristic cob and thatch cottages, a row of early-17th-century almshouses, a delightful green and a traditional village pub, the Red Lion, which was once the old church house.

The church itself dates from the 14th-century and has an impressive 100ft tower. Like many of its contemporaries, the interior has suffered some heavy-handed Victorian meddling; however, many of the original monuments remain, including the imposing tomb of Sir John Acland which was erected in 1620.

Lying a mile-and-a-half to the north on the opposite side of the M5, the present Killerton House was rebuilt by the Acland family in the 1770s to a design by John Johnson.

Though not built on the grand scale, the house has a comfortable and airy feel, and upstairs, several of the rooms have been set aside for the Paulise de Bush collection of historic costumes which date from the 18th-century to the present day.

Killerton House stands within an area of rich rolling farmland. The beautiful 15-acre grounds rise behind the house towards the site of an early-Iron Age hill fort which lies hidden in dense woodland on the crown of Dolbury hill.

The slightly-acidic local soil is ideal for late-spring-flowering rhododendrons, azaleas and magnolias, and later in the year, the herbaceous borders offer a spectacular high-summer display. It is also worth making the short detour to the private chapel which was built in the 19th-century and now has a strangely eerie atmosphere. (House open daily, except Tuesdays, 11am to 5.30pm between early-April and end-October; grounds open all year round.)

From here it is a short drive down the M5 to Exeter and our next Chapter.

CHAPTER TWO

EXETER TO THE NORTH COAST

Chambercombe Manor

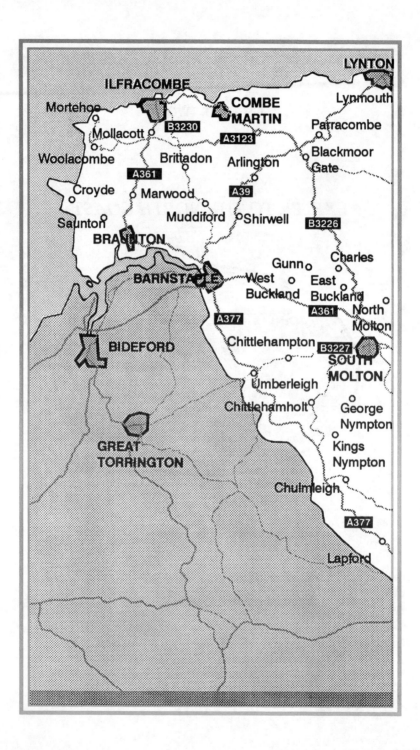

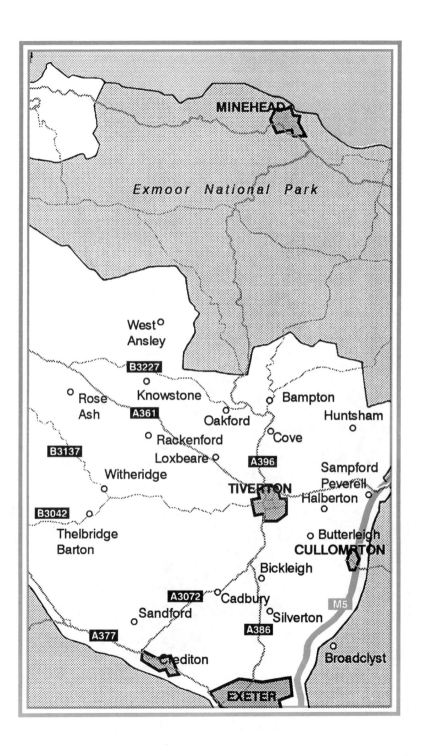

Exeter

CHAPTER TWO:

EXETER TO THE NORTH COAST

EXETER, The county town of Devon, has a population approaching 100,000, making it the third largest centre of population in the county after Plymouth and Torbay. It is also the capital of a vast rural hinterland which stretches from the Somerset border, across mid-Devon, to the Bristol Channel.

The city stands on a rise above the River Exe at what was once its lowest fording point. Protected by valleys to the north and south, and by the Haldon Hills to the west, a settlement has existed on this important strategic site since the days of the Celts.

The ancient Romans made *Isca* their southwestern stronghold, capturing it around 56 AD and constructing a military fort which they expanded into a city over the next century. Around this new regional capital, they built a massive defensive wall in the shape of an irregular rectangle within which the city remained right up until the 18th-century; several sections of the original masonry can still be seen today.

The Romans also built a number of important civic buildings during their near 400-year occupation, perhaps the most spectacular of which was the caldarium, or bath house, which was uncovered in the Cathedral Close in 1971. Another important Roman relic, a mosaic pavement, was discovered on the site of St Catherine's Almshouses in 1989.

During the Dark Ages that followed the departure of the Roman legions in the 5th-century, Exeter was twice occupied by the Vikings. William I then captured the city in 1086 following a siege which lasted eighteen days.

To defend their new conquest, the Normans built **Rougemont Castle**, the gatehouse and tower of which can still be seen in Rougemont Gardens to the north of the city centre.

The finest Norman legacy in Exeter, however, is undoubtedly **St Peter's Cathedral** which stands within its own attractive close to the west of Southernhay Gardens.

The original structure was built in the 11th- and 12th-centuries; however, with the exception of the two sturdy towers, the body of the cathedral was demolished in 1260 and rebuilt in Decorated style over the next ninety years.

Visitors entering through the magnificent west front are confronted by a light and harmonious interior which has one of the finest rib-vaulted ceilings in Europe. Internal features to look out for are the intricately-carved choir screen, the massive cathedral organ, the minstrels' gallery with its wonderful band of heavenly musicians frozen in time, and the 59ft bishop's throne which was hewn from local oak early in the 14th-century.

A remarkable astronomical clock can be found on the north wall of the transept. Dating from around 1400, its twin blue and gold faces indicate the phases of the moon as well as the time of day; its inscription, translated from the Latin, reads 'The hours perish and are reckoned to our account'. Further details on the cathedral and its history can be found in the guide available at the bookstall.

In addition to the cathedral, the centre of Exeter once contained over thirty churches, seven monasteries and several other ecclesiastical institutions. **St Nicholas' Priory**, in the lanes between Fore Street and Mew Street West, is an exceptional example of a small Norman priory. Now an interesting museum, visitors can view the original prior's cell, the 15th-century kitchens, and the imposing central hall with its vaulted ceiling and solid Norman pillars. (Open Tuesdays to Saturdays, all year round.)

Also worth making the effort to find is the 15th-century church of **St Mary Steps** in Stepcote Hill, the narrow cobbled thoroughfare which rises steeply from the site of the former West Gate. Inside, there is an excellent example of a Norman font with characteristic bands of carved decoration. However, the building is perhaps best-known for its remarkable 'Matthew the Miller' tower clock which was named after a medieval miller who conducted his life with such punctual regularity that the local inhabitants were able to tell the time of day by his movements.

One of Exeter's most rewarding attractions is its unique labyrinth of **Underground Passages** which were built by the cathedral clergy in medieval times to regulate the water supply and provide safe passage between the city's many ecclesiastical houses. Guided tours around this fascinating subterranean world are available all year round and are strongly recommended.

Another noteworthy structure dating from the medieval period is the picturesque **Wynard's Almshouse** in Magdalen Street which was built in the 1450s and restored last century.

Exeter's most impressive non-ecclesiastical medieval building can be found in the partly-pedestrianised High Street. The **Guildhall** was built by the powerful craftsmen's guilds in the late 15th-century, its splendid portico having been added a century later.

On occasion, the main chamber is still used for formal meetings of the City burghers, making this one of the oldest municipal buildings in Britain still in use. The oak-panelled hall is lined with fine portraits and coats of arms, and the striking exterior is faced with intricately-carved

St Mary's Steps

Exeter Quay

Beer stone. (Open Mondays to Saturdays, all year round when no official meetings in session.) On a smaller scale, the **Tucker's Hall** in Fore Street was built in 1471 for one of the city's most powerful wool guilds - the Company of Weavers, Fullers and Shearmen.

Inside, there is some exceptional carved panelling, a collection of rare silver, and a remarkable pair of fulling shears weighing over 25lbs and measuring almost 4ft. (Open Tuesday, Thursday and Friday mornings; Fridays only in winter.) Nearby Parliament Street, off the High Street, claims to be the world's narrowest street.

Exeter's importance as a centre of the wool trade developed throughout the Tudor and Elizabethan periods, with raw fleeces, spun yarn and finished cloth being traded in the market in considerable quantities.

Woollen products of all kinds were exported to the major cities of Europe, initially through Topsham downstream on the Exe, then later through a quay in the heart of the city, thanks to the construction of a ship canal in 1566 which was extended in 1675 and again in 1827.

Today, the five-mile-long waterway provides some fine, easy walking, and offers the added attraction of two pleasant, if extremely popular, canalside inns, the **Double Locks and the Turf Hotel.**

Following a long period of decline which began in the mid-19th-century, **Exeter Quay** underwent a dramatic revival in the 1980s when many of its old warehouses and maritime buildings were renovated and reopened as restaurants, shops and commercial units.

The **Custom House**, one of the most handsome 17th-century buildings in Exeter (and one of the first to be constructed of brick), can be found here. By the time it was completed in 1681, large quantities of sugar, rice, tea and other commodities were being landed at the quay, requiring an official presence of some consequence.

The Custom House was therefore constructed to an impressive standard, with fine plasterwork ceilings and balustraded staircases which are worth seeing. Visitors are admitted by arrangement with HM Customs and Excise, though casual visitors are generally welcomed.

Exeter Quay is also the location of the internationally-renowned **Maritime Museum**, the world's largest collection of boats. Exhibits include an Arab dhow, a reed boat from Lake Titicaca in South America, and the *Cygnet*, an eccentric rowing dinghy which was used to ferry guests to wild parties on her even more eccentric sister vessel, the *Swan*. (Open daily, all year round.)

The character of modern Exeter was much altered by the effects of World War II bombing, carried out, it was claimed, in revenge for the Allied attacks on the historic city of Lübeck.

The devastating raids of May 1942 destroyed much of the medieval and Georgian city, after which the Nazis are said to have boasted, 'Exeter was a jewel, and we have destroyed it.' Large areas of the old city had to be rebuilt in the 1950s, often in the form of modern shopping centres; however, some interesting small shops and wine bars are still to be found in the area around Gandhi Street, an old quarter which also contains the Exeter and Devon Arts Centre, worth finding for its pleasant café-restaurant.

A number of excellent museums can also be found in and around the city, including the **Royal Albert Memorial Museum** in Queen Street (local art and natural history), **the Devonshire Regiment Museum** in Holloway Street (military), and the **Rougemont House Museum** in the corner of Rougemont Gardens (historic costumes).

Around Exeter

Heading north out of Exeter either by taking the M5 or on the minor roads a place worthy of your attention is **KILLERTON HOUSE AND GARDENS**, as it is near the border with the previous chapter we make no apology for mentioning it again as it is well worth a visit. A National Trust property donated by the Aclands (probably the oldest family in Devon) in 1944.

It forms part of a working agricultural estate which covers 12 square miles of countryside and includes the village of Broadclyst.

The real glory of Killerton is the garden, first planted when the house was built, and never neglected since. A paradise for all with its rare trees and shrubs from around the world, flowering bulbs and colourful displays of magnolias, azaleas and rhododendrons, herbaceous borders and conifers.

Two curios of particular interest in the garden are the Ice House which stored forty tons of ice for the house, packed over five days by thirty men, and the Bear's Hut built in 1808 and used in the 1860s for a pet black bear brought back from Canada by Gilbert Acland.

The elegant 18th century house still retains a warm lived in atmosphere. The first floor of the house has displays of clothes from the last three centuries selected from the Killerton costume collection, the best collection in the south west. Killerton is open all year round, the house from mid-march to the end of October. Ring for opening times.

Killerton House and Gardens, Broadclyst, Exeter, Devon.
Tel: 01392 881345

SILVERTON. Stands on a low ridge above the east bank of the Exe. A settlement has existed here since early-Saxon times and indeed, this was once a thriving little market town which stood at the hub of a prosperous rural economy.

In the early 19th-century, however, a new turnpike road was built along the floor of the Exe Valley to bypass the undulating network of lanes around Silverton, sending it into decline. As a consequence, the centre of the village has retained an unusual number of cob and thatch buildings, some of which date back to the 16th-century.

Perhaps the finest of these, the **Church House,** is exceptional in that it is lies in the main street some distance away from the church.

The church itself was constructed in the 15th-century, for the most part of stone quarried from a local volcanic outcrop; its pleasant and airy interior contains some noteworthy features, including an original wagon roof, complete with brightly painted bosses, and a splendid 18th-century gallery with carved stone pilasters which spans the entire west end of the nave.

A convenient place to stay can be found within a mile of **Silverton**, just off the road to Broadclyst at **NEW PARK FARM** Set in 120 acres of mixed farmland, Mrs Gwen Hawkins offers traditional style bed and breakfast in the modern farmhouse. A warm and friendly atmosphere will quickly relax you and you will be sure of having a very pleasant stay.

New Park Farm, Silverton, Exeter Tel: 01392 861182

Tiverton and the Exe Valley

TIVERTON. Present-day visitors to the town may find it hard to believe that this pleasant provincial town was once the most important industrial centre in Devon.

A settlement had been founded by the Saxons on the wedge of land between the rivers Exe and Loman in the 7th-century which, two centuries later, King Alfred made reference to in his will.

By the time of the Domesday Book, the local agriculture-based economy had become well-established; however, it wasn't until the wool manufacturing industry was founded in the late 1400s that the town really began to grow, reaching its zenith in the 17th- and 18th-centuries, when locally-produced cloth was much in demand throughout Europe.

During Tiverton's golden age of wool-based prosperity, several local merchants and manufacturers became exceedingly wealthy, and it became a fashion for them to make extravagant charitable endowments, often in ways which would ensure their names lived on in perpetuity. Several such 16th- and 17th-century almshouses can still be seen around the town, including George Slee's in St Peter's Street, John Waldron's in Welbrook Street, and John Greenway's with its Tudor chapel in Gold Street.

Peter Blundell, another rich clothier from this period, chose to

Tiverton Castle

endow a school; **Blundell's Old School** was built in 1604 at the south-eastern end of town near the bridge over the River Loman, but was converted into residential dwellings when the school moved to a new location on the edge of town in 1880. Among the many influential people educated here was the author R. D. Blackmore, creator of the character John Ridd, whose education at Blundell's he describes in the opening chapter of *Lorna Doone*.

The 16th-century merchant John Greenway also paid for the reconstruction of the intricately-carved south side of **St Peter's parish church.** Decorated with sea-going merchant ships and a wonderful collection of heraldic animals and coats of arms, its impressive pinnacled façade should not be missed. Greenway also endowed the church's handsome south porch and south chapel, although much of the rest of the interior is Victorian. Monuments to several of the town's most noted benefactors survive, and there are also a couple of noteworthy 17th- and 18th-century paintings.

A great deal of damage was done to the older buildings in Tiverton by the great town fire of 1731. The Norman castle, however, suffered a different fate, having been deliberately dismantled by Parliamentarian forces following its surrender in 1645. Notwithstanding, several 14th-century remains have survived, including the main gateway, banqueting hall, round tower and section of the old chapel, and these have now been incorporated into a striking privately-owned residence. (Open Sundays to Thursdays, 2.30pm to 5.30pm between Easter and end-September.)

The castle and the parish church, with its striking red sandstone tower, stand on a rise above the river at the northwest end of town.

One of Devon's few noteworthy Georgian churches, **St George's**, can be found in the town centre. Consecrated two years after the great fire in 1733, it contains some fine period ceilings, galleries and other fixtures, although the pulpit and pews are Victorian. Elsewhere in the centre, there are a considerable number of handsome Georgian and Regency town houses, some made of brick.

Tiverton's informative local museum is also worth a look; it is situated in a former school building in St Andrews Street.

The last of the great woollen mills of Tiverton was established in 1816 by John Heathcoat, a Midlands entrepreneur who had been driven south from Leicestershire by Luddites, that irate band of hand-weavers who went around destroying labour-saving machinery in order to preserve their traditional livelihoods. Heathcoat founded a thriving and enduring textiles business which he passed on to his grandson, John Heathcoat-Amory. A profit-conscious mill-owning entrepreneur like his grandfather, Heathcoat-Amory built a large country mansion one-and-a-half miles to the north of Tiverton on a magnificent hillside site which was selected, so it is claimed, to give an uninterrupted view of the factory from the drawing-room window.

A quay on the southeastern edge of town marks the western end of the now-disused **Grand Western Canal**, the inland waterway which was built in a brave attempt to connect Topsham and the River Exe with Bridgewater and the Bristol Channel. Never fully completed, sections of the canal remained open for over 100 years until the 1920s. An attractive stretch running for twelve miles from the southeastern edge of Tiverton to the Somerset border has now been restored.

Whilst you are in Tiverton make sure to set aside time to visit the **Grand Western Horseboat Company** who operate traditional horsedrawn barge trips along this historic canal, which is now a designated Country Park. As you are gently pulled along by a heavy horse, wearing colourful harness, wildlife and aquatic plants gently nod to your passing. A trip with a difference for all the family.

Grand Western Horseboat Co.,The Wharf, Canal Hill, Tiverton. EX16 4HX . Tel: 01884 253345

Around Tiverton

Knightshayes Court was designed in the 1860s by William Burges, an architect known for his work on Cardiff Castle. It stands within 200 acres of wooded grounds, with a superb terrace, a formal garden set around a delightful circular pond, and an extensive network of woodland walks.

One of the garden's most amusing features is a topiary hedge which depicts a fox being chased by a group of galloping hounds. Much of the sumptuous Victorian interior has been attributed to J. D. Crace, notably the distinctive painted ceilings and wall fittings.

The house was given to the National Trust in 1972 by the original owner's grandson. (Open daily except Fridays, 1.30pm to 5.30pm between early-April and end-October).

LOXBEARE . A few miles northwest of Knightshayes.

Situated in a beautiful rural setting near the village , within easy travelling distance of all of the places described in this chapter and enjoying glorious views across the valley, **PRIMROSE LODGE** is an ideal place for year round family holidays.

Set on a working dairy farm, this Scandinavian pine lodge offers spacious self-catering accommodation for four to six people. The accommodation consists of a spacious lounge, a kitchen/dining area , a double bedroom, a twin bedroom, a bathroom with shaver point, a utility room and a second toilet with wash basin.

Primrose Lodge is fully furnished and superbly equipped with night storage heaters, an electric cooker, a microwave oven, a fridge/ freezer, an automatic washing machine and a colour TV. There is a lovely verandah with a picnic table and benches, a great place for a barbecue. Bed-linen and towels are included in the rent and parking is available for three cars.

ETB 3Keys Commended.

B & B accommodation is also available at the adjoining 300 year old

Knightshayes Court

farmhouse, **Lower Ingrams Farm**. Accommodation is of a similarly high standard and you can be sure of a warm welcome from Margaret and Ron, whose farm it is. Primrose Lodge is situated just off the A361, follow the signs for Loxbeare for two miles, Lower Ingrams farm is situated on the right hand side of the road.

Primrose Lodge, Lower Ingrams Farm, Loxbeare, Nr Tiverton, Devon.
Tel: 01884 881362

RACKENFORD. This lovely village has been associated with the wool trade for about one thousand years.

Today however, trade has declined, but many reminders of the village's past remain. **THE STAG INN** is one such reminder. Built in 1196, this Grade II listed, 800 year old inn is reputed to be the oldest 'tunnel inn' in Devon. A tunnel inn is so named because of the tunnel which links the front of the building with a yard in which the sheep were kept whilst the shepherd enjoyed a drink or stayed overnight.

The Stag Inn's tunnel has been carefully preserved and now forms the main entrance to the pub. The interior is no less remarkable, its Jacobean inglenook and panelling are exceptionally well preserved and are separately listed. This is a fine place to enjoy a good pint of real ale and some local gossip.

Interestingly the pub also has a resident ghost. Tom King, a highwayman, was once a friend of Dick Turpin, however the two argued over the daughter of an innkeeper, so Tom betrayed his infamous friend to the authorities. Tom's ghost is friendly and has been the subject of a number of careful scientific investigations.

The Well Room Restaurant occupies part of the original yard at the end of the tunnel and takes its name from the well which is now enclosed within the building. The pump is still in working order.

The food is simply excellent, and is largely based on fresh game and locally produced ingredients.

The pub is also able to offer fine accommodation for those wishing to stay a while in this charming village.

The Stag Inn, Rackenford, Tiverton, North Devon. Tel: 01884 881369

BAMPTON. North of Tiverton along the Exe Valley, this pleasant community was once a small market town and centre of the wool trade.

Now a quiet backwater, it possesses the remnants of an old castle and a much-altered 14th-century church with a wagon roof and some interesting tombs and internal detailing.

The village is liveliest during the last week in October when the streets are closed off, and sheep and cattle (though no longer Exmoor ponies) are brought down from the moor to be bought and sold in the autumn fair.

A local landmark in Bampton is the **BRIDGE HOUSE HOTEL** run by Brian and Val Smith.

Easy to find opposite the main car park and on the B3227, the hotel is a 250 year old building of character with stone flagged floors, beams and an open fire.

The Bridge House Hotel

Formerly " GibbingsTemperance Hotel and Cyclists Rest ", the Bridge House now, by contrast, has a well kept cellar but still caters for more active clients by arranging shooting , fishing , and riding trips, all of which is enough to work up a healthy appetite .

It is fortunate therefore ,that the hotel has a good reputation for food, where the 24 cover restaurant is very popular with the locals, always a good sign.

Here, in keeping with the sporting theme of the decor, guests can enjoy game in season, as well as salmon and trout. Whatever you choose, it will be well cooked and presented, accompanied by fresh vegetables .

There are 4 guest rooms available, and this would be an ideal place to stop for a good meal,or for a longer stay in order to take advantage of the many sporting activities available in the area.

The Bridge House Hotel, Bampton. Tel: 01398 331298

A traditional family run country Inn, dating from 1495, **THE EXETER INN** near Bampton has served in its time the wool, lime kiln and quarrying trades. Today this hotel and restaurant is popular with visitors to the beautiful Exe Valley. The accommodation is excellent and includes en-suite bedrooms, direct-dial telephones, colour televisions and tea making facilities. Stabling for guest's horses is also available.

The restaurant is renowned for its superb menu and weekend carvery, but it is likely to be busy so book in advance. The bar also serves a fine selection of light meals and real ales.

Whilst there, why not try your hand at one of the traditional pub games, such as shove ha'penny, table skittles, darts, crib or 'spoofing', a 3-coin game peculiar to this locality. Situated on the B3227 Tiverton/ Bampton road at the Dulverton roundabout.

Exeter Inn, Hotel and Restaurant, Tiverton Road, Bampton, Tiverton.
Tel: 01398 331345 Fax:01398 331130

EXBRIDGE, on the Somerset border, contains some interesting craft workshops and a good pub.

HALBERTON.   Three miles along the towpath to the east of Tiverton, the canal makes a broad sweep around the village. A large pond between the upper and lower sections of the village is fed by a 'warm' spring and has never been known to freeze over. The red sandstone church of St Andrew has some fine internal features, including a Norman font, a 15th-century carved pulpit, and a surprisingly massive rood screen with three door-holes and some fine tracery.

As well as carrying the Grand Western Canal, the shallow fertile vale to the east of Tiverton once carried the 'Tivvy Bumper', the branch-line trains which provided a shuttle service between the town and Tiverton Junction on the main London to Penzance line. (Railway enthusiasts can find one of the old tank engines on display near the site of Tiverton's former station.)

SAMPFORD PEVERELL.

Takes its name from the Peverell family who were once local Lords of the Manor. The 14th century castle which was at one time the family seat is now demolished.

Sampford Peverell is only five minutes from the M.5 and is easily found from junction 27. In the centre of the village is **CHALLIS,** a fine Victorian house owned by Mary & Graeme Isaac who offer very comfortable bed and breakfast accommodation.

The bedrooms have colour T.V., a hospitality tray, central heating and most have en-suite facilities. There is direct access from the half acre of garden to the Grand Western Canal where lovely walks and fishing can be enjoyed along the tow-path.

An ample full English breakfast is served with the option of an evening meal upon your return. There are two good local pubs in the village and the market town of Tiverton is only 6 miles distant.

Challis, 12 Lower Town, Sampford Peverell, Tiverton, Devon.
Tel: 01884 820620

CULLOMPTON. Four miles due south as the crow flies (or one junction away on the M5), is another small town with Saxon roots which grew in importance during the late-medieval upsurge in the wool trade.

The majestic parish **Church of St Andrew** reflects the town's former prosperity, having been constructed to a grand scale in the late15th and early16th centuries on the site of a pre-Norman collegiate church.

Built of an attractive combination of local red sandstone and pale Beer and Ham Hill stone, the building's 100ft tower dominates the surrounding townscape. Inside, the church is light and airy, thanks in part to its row of high clerestory windows, a rare feature in Devon. These help to throw light onto the magnificent 24-bay wagon roof, a marvellous example of carved vaulting and brightly-painted panels, which runs the entire length of the nave.

The church also possesses an impressive rood screen which is unusual in that it runs across the entire width of the building. As at Tiverton, Cullompton church has benefited from a series of benefactions from wealthy local clothiers, the most notable of which is the south aisle which was added by John Lane, a contemporary and rival of Tiverton's John Greenway.

The roof of Lane's aisle has some excellent fan tracery and outside, the carved façade is decorated with merchant ships and a wonderful assortment of objects symbolising the clothier's trade. Two sections of a rare medieval rood base can be found at the western end of the aisle; carved into gruesome representations of rocks littered with human skulls and bones, these heavy timber pedestals would once have held a tall crucifix in place behind the rood screen.

The heart of old Cullompton consists of a single main street which widens at one end to form a marketplace and has a series of lanes, or *courts*, branching off it.

In common with many other centres of population in Devon, the town has suffered badly from the ravages of fire, most notably in 1839 when over 250 buildings were destroyed in the Great Fire. As a result, the town's architecture is largely Victorian in character, although there are a couple of noteworthy exceptions: the much-altered Elizabethan Manor House, and the Walronds, an early-Jacobean house which is noted for its fine moulded ceilings and carved mantelpieces.

Comfortable and spacious B & B accommodation with central heating can be found near Cullompton in a Grade II listed farmhouse at **WISHAY FARM**. The rooms are very well appointed, accommodation with an en-suite facility is also available.

The traditional farmhouse food is excellent, the atmosphere is friendly and relaxed. From Cullompton main street turn right into Colebrook Lane, proceed for 2 miles. The farm is just past the next road junction.

Wishay Farm. Trinity, Cullopmton, Devon. Tel 01884 33223

BICKLEIGH. The lanes to the west of Cullompton lead to this picturesque village lying near the A396, three-and-a-half miles south of Tiverton. An ancient crossing point on the River Exe, the hills rise sharply to over 600ft on either side of Bickleigh Bridge, creating a skyline of exceptional beauty.

High above the eastern bank stands the much-altered village

church, largely 14th-century with a south doorway and font dating from two centuries earlier. Inside, there are a number of interesting 16th- and 17th-century monuments to the former local land-owning family, the Carews.

One of the most colourful characters to originate in Bickleigh was Bampfylde Moore Carew, the wayward son of the local gentleman-rector, who decided to live the nomadic life of a gypsy and was eventually elected their king.

After many misadventures, he was transported to Maryland, from where he escaped back to Britain, only to become involved in Bonny Prince Charlie's rebellion of 1745. When the Jacobite army reached Derby, however, Bampfylde decided against turning back to Scotland (and almost certain death on Culloden Moor), choosing instead to continue southwards towards Bickleigh where he resettled and ended his days peacefully in 1758 at the age of 68.

For centuries, the Carew family lived at **Bickleigh Castle**, a fortified manor house which lies across the river on the western side of the Exe. This largely-Tudor moated building was constructed on the site of a 12th-century Norman castle; in common with many such fortifications, however, much of the structure was demolished during the English Civil War to prevent its Royalist owner forming a troublesome pocket of resistance.

In spite of this, several remnants of the castle have survived, including a section of the great hall, the partly-reconstructed gatehouse, and a delightful little thatched chapel which dates all the way back to the castle's Norman foundation. (Open daily, 2pm to 5.30pm, between end-May and early-October.)

Bickleigh's other main attraction lies on the northern edge of the village near the Exe bridge. The **Bickleigh Mill Craft Centre and Farm** is housed in a restored working water mill and incorporates a number of traditional craft workshops, including those making handmade pottery, jewellery and hand-turned wood. The adjacent farm operates as a 19th-century Devon farmstead, with working shire horses, rare farmyard animals and a museum of rural history. (Open daily between April and December; weekends only between January and March.)

BUTTERLEIGH

Set in a magnificent position overlooking the beautiful Burn Valley, just a mile from the village is **FIG TREE FARM.**

The farm is a 25 acre smallholding and makes an idyllic rural retreat for those looking for that special break. Margaret Chumbley, your hostess, offers generous farmhouse hospitality in a friendly, family environment, and takes a special interest in ensuring that every guest's needs are met and their stay is as enjoyable as possible.

There are three guestrooms, two with a veranda overlooking the valley, and a comfortable guests lounge in the farmhouse, with self catering available nearby in a mobile home.

To set you up for a hard day's sightseeing, walking or cycling, 'free

Bickleigh Castle

cycle hire' available, there is a generous farmhouse breakfast for everyone, and a full evening meal menu with 'complimentary wine' makes for a perfect relaxing ending to the day.

Fig Tree Farm (B & B and Self Catering), Butterleigh, Cullompton.
Tel: 01884 855463

THORVERTON. On the opposite side of the Exe, two miles to the southwest of Silverton, is another village typical of this fertile undulating landscape. contains a surprising number of fine old buildings, many of which were constructed of Raddon stone taken from the now-disused quarry one mile to the west.

Those of particular note include **Jessamine Cottage**, with its Tudor entrance, **the old post office,** the **Dolphin Hotel**, and the thatched and colonnaded **Bridge House**, which dates from the 1760s and is now a shop. Little channels of water flow down the sides of Thorverton's unexpectedly broad streets to join a larger stream, known locally as the 'Jordan', as it crosses the green.

The parish church of St Thomas Becket still retains some impressive features, including its 15th-century tower, tall Beer-stone arcades, fine window tracery, and superb south porch whose fan-vaulted ceiling-bosses have been carved into whimsical representations of the Holy Trinity and four Evangelists.

NEWTON ST CYRES. The lanes to the west of Thorverton cross a number of small rivers before descending onto the A377 near this pleasant village of cob and thatch cottages which suffers greatly from being bisected by the main Exeter-Barnstaple road, a problem which has existed for so long that a cast iron bridge had to be installed earlier in the century to connect the local manor, Newton House, with the knoll on the opposite side of the road which supports the 15th-century parish church of St Cyriac and St Julia.

The traditional home of the Quicke family, Newton House was rebuilt of volcanic Posbury stone in 1909 on the site of a Georgian predecessor.

The church contains several striking memorials to the Quicke and the Northcote families, the most ostentatious of which is a 17th-century monument to John Northcote which portrays him standing between his two wives with his foot resting on a skull and his children kneeling at his feet, on the face of it a remarkable feat of self-glorifying chauvinism.

By contrast, a charming effigy of Sherland Shore can be seen in the chancel which depicts the 17-year-old boy leaning over a book-strewn table with his head resting casually on his hand. The ceiling of the south porch is worth a look for its roof boss depicting a sow suckling her young, a symbol which reflects one of the traditional methods for choosing the location of a new church: a pregnant sow would be set free in the parish and the church built at the spot she gave birth.

CREDITON. Three miles along the A377 to the northwest of Newton St Cyres, this busy town also has to cope with a surfeit of through traffic. The origins of this former market-turned-dormitory town date back to pre-Saxon times, although today, few of the buildings lining the broad High Street are more than 200 years old thanks to a series of devastating town fires in the 18th-century.

The town is still referred to locally as Kirton, meaning *Churchtown*, as this was once the preeminent religious centre in Devon. Indeed, this was the seat of the Saxon bishop of Crediton for 140 years before it was moved to the walled confines of Exeter in 1050.

That the bishopric should have been located here owes much to Devon's most eminent medieval son, St Boniface, born plain Wynfrith in Crediton in 680 AD.

After rising quickly through the ranks of the Benedictine Order, he became fired with missionary zeal and was granted papal authority to evangelise the Germans. Over the following decades he was successful in establishing Christianity in several German states and at the age of 71, he was appointed Archbishop of Mainz.

His many achievements included the founding of the great monastery at Fulda in Hesse, a religious community which became his final resting place after he was ambushed and murdered along with 53 of his companions in 754.

A minster was established at Crediton during St Boniface's lifetime which in 1150, was expanded into the collegiate church of the Holy Cross, the basis of the cathedral-like parish church that can be seen today.

Built of warm russet-coloured sandstone, this imposing cruciform structure was virtually rebuilt in the 15th-century when the clerestory was added. The interior contains a number of exceptional monuments, including those to Sir John Sully, a 14th-century comrade of the Black Prince who is said to have died peacefully at the age of 105, Sir William Peryam, a commissioner at the trial of Mary Queen of Scots, and John and Elizabeth Tuckfield, a family of well-to-do 17th-century clothiers.

The most spectacular monument, however, is that to that to Sir Redvers Buller, the Boer War general in command of the Relief of Ladysmith, which can be seen in the light of the clerestory windows high up on the west wall of the tower. The Lady Chapel at the east end of the church housed Crediton's famous grammar school from the time of Edward VI until 1859, when it was transferred to its present purpose-built site at the west end of the High Street.

A statue to St Boniface was erected in the gardens to the west of the church earlier this century; despite his veneration in Germany, it appears he had to wait 1200 years for recognition in his native town.

COPPLESTONE. Four miles to the northwest of Crediton. The impressive remains of a Saxon cross can be seen at the junction of the A3072 and A377 Barnstaple road at the point where three parishes meet.

An ancient landmark for travellers, the stone post, which was first recorded in the 10th-century, marks the spot where two ancient packhorse trails diverge. Standing almost 10ft high, the interweaving pattern of the original Saxon carving can still be made out.

CADBURY. Roughly midway between Crediton and Tiverton, it is possible to turn south off the undulating A3072 to reach this hamlet which takes its name from *Cada's burgh*, the Iron Age fort which once stood on the summit of the 800ft hill to the north.

On a clear day, the ancient ramparts offer some magnificent views over the surrounding countryside. Excavations on the site in the mid-19th-century revealed a vertical shaft from which several coins and items of bronze jewellery were recovered, suggesting this was once a holy place which remained in use throughout the Roman occupation. Standing in a more sheltered position above a narrow valley, the hamlet contains a simple 15th-century church with some noteworthy internal features, including a Norman font, a panel of early-15th-century stained glass, and an Elizabethan lectern.

FURSDON. A small estate lying to the east of the church has belonged to the Fursdon family in unbroken succession since the time of Henry III. Their late-Georgian house has a handsome colonnaded façade and is built on the foundations of an earlier manor house. Inside, there is an interesting assortment of artefacts which the family have accumulated over the centuries. (Open Thursdays and Bank Holiday Mondays only, 2pm to 4.30pm between Easter Monday and end-September.)

Another fine Georgian country house can be found at **Cruwys Morchard**, five miles to the west of Tiverton; the nearby church of the Holy Cross also contains some exceptional examples of early-18th-century woodcarving.

Barnstaple and the Western Fringes of Exmoor

Although geographically part of the same county, the towns and villages of North and South Devon are so psychologically remote from each other that they might as well lie at opposite ends of the country.

Thanks to the obstructive presence of Dartmoor, those living in south Devon simply do not venture north unless there is a very good reason to do so, and vice versa. As a result, the county offers wide differences in character and atmosphere, adding to its overall appeal.

BARNSTAPLE. This attractive town stands at the head of the Taw estuary at what, historically, was lowest fording point on the river.

It has been the most important town in north Devon since Saxon times, having been granted the status of a market town and borough in the 10th-century. Indeed, Barnstaple was recorded in the Domesday Book of 1086 as being one of only four boroughs in the county, by which time a mint had been operating in the town for around 100 years. Soon after, the Normans built a substantial fortification to defend their strategically-important acquisition, although nothing of this remains today except a sizable **castle mound**, 60ft high and 40ft across.

During the medieval period a wall was erected around the town and Barnstaple vied with Bideford to be the most important port and commercial centre on the Bristol Channel coast.

A bridge was first constructed across the Taw estuary in the late 13th-century, although the present 16-arched structure dates from around 150 years later; originally 700ft long but only 10ft wide, it has been modified and widened on a number of occasions since.

Barnstaple's great three-day fair, which still takes place each year in mid-September, has medieval origins, as do its regular Tuesday and Friday produce markets. These unpretentious gatherings take place in the Victorian **PANNIER MARKET** a wonderful 400ft-long structure resembling a glass-roofed railway terminus which is a delight to browse around.

Before the construction of the Pannier market, those with produce or goods to sell would bring them to Barnstaple in panniers or baskets, and line the sides of the High Street between Cross Street and Lower Boutport Street. Following the completion of the Guildhall in 1827, the Borough council undertok the redevelopement of the building, including the construction of a Pannier Market to replace the existing vegetable market.

Opened in 1855, the market, with a large glass roof supported by a system of wood and iron topped girders, eased the congestion whilst maintaining the tradition of people selling excess produce.

Today the market still thrives. Open 6 days a week it is full of stalls which display a great range of goods and with a bustling atmosphere, it is well worth a visit. On Mondays and Thursdays there is a craft Market, on Wednedays an antiques market, and on Tuesdays Fridays, and Saturdays the Pannier Market is open selling produce as well as plants, flowers, clothing, footwear, and many ther goods of quality and local interest.

Pannier Market, Civic Centre Barnstaple

Another feature of this historic market town is the quaint line of booth-like Victorian shops known as **Butchers' Row** which can be found opposite one of the main entrances to the market.

Barnstaple's High Street contains a remarkable number of noteworthy buildings, their true characters often being concealed behind modern ground-floor shop fronts. Many of them are in fact Georgian, including the somewhat austere **Guildhall** at the corner of the High

Pannier Market

Street and Butchers' Row.

Inside, there are some fine municipal portraits and an interesting collection of antique silverware.Like so many towns in Devon, Barnstaple was an important centre of the wool trade during the late-medieval period; however, unlike many of its rivals, it managed to hold on when the industry went into decline after 1600, thanks in part to a new trade importing raw wool and yarn from Ireland.

In fact, the 17th-century turned out to be something of a heyday for Barnstaple, and it was during this period that a celebrated school of craftsmen-plasterers became established, the work of which can still be seen around the town today, for example in the National Westminster Bank, formerly a Spanish merchant's house, at the south end of the High Street.

The 17th-century also saw the rebuilding of the spire on the parish church of St Peter and St Paul in an unusual lead-covered broach design. The body of the church dates from the 13th- and early 14th-centuries, but last century Sir Gilbert Scott gave it a heavy, solemn interior, a complete contrast to the likes of Cullompton or Crediton.

The area around the churchyard forms a tranquil oasis in the heart of the bustling town centre. The 15th-century **St Anne's chapel** and 17th-century **Horwood's almshouses** can also be found here, the former building later becoming the town's grammar school whose pupils included John Gay, the author of *The Beggar's Opera*.

As in other well-to-do commercial centres, the 17th-century saw a plethora of charitable endowments, including **Paige's almshouses, Alice Horwood's Maid's school,** and the **Penrose almshouses**, a delightful group of twenty dwellings set around a courtyard with a granite colonnade fronting onto Litchdon Street.

Another indication of the prosperity of this period can be found in **Queen Anne's Walk** on the old town quay.

This ostentatious open portico was completed in 1708 and was used by the Barnstaple wool merchants as an exchange. It was an 18th-century convention that a verbal bargain, if struck over the old Tome Stone, was rendered legally binding. In 1588, five ships sailed from the nearby quay to join Drake's fleet against the Armada.

One medieval industry to survive in Barnstaple is the manufacture of fine pottery. **The Royal Barum Pottery** (*Barum* being the ancient name for Barnstaple) was once located in the town centre, but now occupies a modern out-of-town site beside the road to Bideford.

Based on original Tudor designs and heavily-influenced by William Morris, the Victorian founder of the arts and crafts movement, the finished pottery features distinctive floral, fruit and animal motifs.

Visitors can view the manufacturing process taking place at certain times, and there is also an interesting museum, visitors' centre and a well-stocked pottery shop.

SUNNYMEAD HOUSE is a small guest house at **Newport**, on the outskirts of Barnstaple, owned and run by Ann Linscott and Sally Butler. Once on the main north Devon road, a new link road has enabled Newport to regain its original village character. Ann and Sally have gained a widespread reputation for the quality of their bed and breakfast establishment and they have been awarded the Guild of Master Craftsmen Certificate of Quality and Service.

A true home from home, with a warm and friendly welcome, this is a relaxing and peaceful place to stay. There are four bedrooms, all with a shower and some fully en suite. A ground floor room is particularly suited to disabled guests. There is also a full choice of English breakfasts and special diets can be catered for if Ann and Sally are advised in advance.

Sunnymead House, Landkey Road, Barnstaple Tel: 01271 328754

Around Barnstaple.

PILTON. On the northwestern side of Barnstaple, the A39 passes through the village, now a suburb but once an important settlement standing on a well-defended site to the north of the Taw estuary.

The church was originally part of a pre-Norman priory, and its somewhat stark interior contains some unusual features, including a 15th-century pulpit and a carved Tudor font set within a curious throne-like canopy. The streets of Pilton contain some handsome Georgian and Victorian buildings, but beware of the row of 'medieval' almshouses which were actually built in the mid-19th-century.

Barnstaple stands at the midpoint of the **Tarka Trail**, a 180-mile long-distance walk in the shape of a great figure of eight. The northern circle takes in parts of Exmoor and the North Devon coastal path. The trail takes its name from Henry Williamson's enchanting *Tarka The Otter* stories which were set in the valleys of the Taw and Torridge.

To the northwest of Barnstaple, the lanes between the A39 and A361 lead up from the Taw estuary into a very different landscape of high rolling farmland and wooded combes.

On the Bideford to Barnstaple road following the A39, and just half a mile from the Roundswell roundabout is the **CEDARS LODGE INN**, a delightful 18th century former Country House covered in Wisteria and with the original walled garden and orchard.

The house was extended and modernised by the Maskell family in the 1980s at which time they added a series of modern lodges providing self-contained private accommodation with en suite facilities, direct dial telephone, satellite TV and more.

The Cedars Lodge Inn creates a clever blend of traditional atmosphere with modern facilities, set adjacent to three acres of landscaped gardens. The huge orangery/ conservatory is quite delightful with an almost continental ambience and is used to serve all meals the year round.

There is a creative selection of a' la carte meals, carvery and home cooked specialities offering something to suite all palates.

The energetic can take advantage of the modern squash courts available to guests or, if you prefer, just relax with your aperitif on the terrace. With its superb facilities and so many of the renowned attractions of North Devon nearby, the Cedars Lodge Inn makes an excellent choice for a family holiday or business stop. Three crowns commended by the English Tourist Board.

Cedars Lodge Inn, Bickington Road, Barnstaple, N. Devon.
Tel: 01271 71784

MUDDIFORD. North of Barnstaple on the B3230 is Muddiford, and just outside the village you will find **BROOMHILL COUNTRY HOUSE HOTEL AND RESTAURANT** nestling in one of the most beautiful valleys in the county.

The hotel is an excellent example of a country house and it provides all guests with every comfort. This elegant Edwardian residence is wonderfully spacious; the number of bedrooms has been limited to eight to ensure that all visitors can experience a taste of gracious living.

All the rooms are en-suite, with colour television, full central heating, telephone and glorious views of the surrounding countryside. In winter there are roaring log fires in the public rooms to cheer up even the dullest of days.

The hotel and restaurant is owned and run by Zak and Beverly El Hamdou. Zak is the Head Chef and he has some 15 years experience gained from working in many of the world's top class establishments, including a five star hotel in Casablanca.

As well as the á la carte menu, the restaurant also serves a fixed price menu which offers excellent value. The food here is truly delicious and the choice is mind boggling. The extensive wine list also makes interesting reading. This really is an exceptional establishment and it is rare to find dishes of such quality outside the London area.

The hotel's amenities include a tennis court and sheltered swimming pool. The sloping terraced gardens, with their beautiful shrubbery and private trout stream set in five acres of wooded parkland, have to be seen to be believed. This is a hidden place of great beauty. With its delightful woodland setting, extensive grounds and top class food and wine Broomhill Country House Hotel and Restaurant is well worth a visit.

Broomhill Country House Hotel and Restaurant, Muddiford, Near Barnstaple Tel: 01271 850262

MARWOOD. The village is worth finding for its 14th-century cruciform church, a gem of a building with a superb intricately-carved rood screen, square-bowled Saxon font, 17th-century pulpit, and beautifully-carved set of bench ends.

Perhaps the most interesting feature, however, is the sundial set on the wall of the south porch which was made around 1760 by John Berry, a celebrated exponent of his craft who erected many of the finest sundials in North Devon.

This one shows the time of day in Paris, Berlin, Vienna and Jerusalem, as well as in Marwood, and also indicates the zodiac cycle. Nearby **Marwood Hill** is a delightful shrub-filled garden which is open to visitors daily, all year round. **Westcott Barton**, one mile to the northwest, is an impressive example of a large Devon *barton*, a self-contained manor farm with its own workshops and small mill. A lane to the north of Marwood follows the undeviating route of the ridgeway which once connected the Taw estuary with the sea at Ilfracombe.

BRAUNTON. Four miles to the west of Marwood, this sizable community is renowned as the largest village in Devon. Though in recent decades, it has taken on something of the character of a holiday resort and suburban dormitory, this is in fact an ancient settlement with a documented history going back to early Saxon times.

The substantial parish church is dedicated to St Brannoc, a Celtic saint of the type more often heard of in Cornwall, who landed here from Wales in the 6th-century. His bones are said to lie under the altar of the present 13th-century church, a story which might hold true, for the building almost certainly stands on the site of a Saxon predecessor.

As at Newton St Cyres, the church possesses a charming ceiling boss which depicts a sow suckling her young litter. According to legend, this alludes to St Brannoc's first attempt to build his a church on Chapel Hill; each morning he would arrive to discover the walls had been mysteriously dismantled until one day, he spotted a white sow farrowing in the valley below. This he interpreted as a sign: the church was built on the spot where she gave birth and the supernatural acts of vandalism ceased.

The scale of the present-day church, with its Norman tower and more recent broached spire, reflects Braunton's relative importance during the medieval period. The uncommonly wide nave has an impressive wagon roof embellished with a series of brightly-coloured bosses. Though surprisingly aisleless, the building contains an interesting small chancel screen, an exceptional series of carved bench-ends, some fine examples of Jacobean woodwork, and a number of striking monuments to the local gentry.

The adjacent church house was built with a double external staircase to allow direct access to the first floor from the churchyard or from the street; the lower floor now houses an interesting local museum.

Further afield, the old town centre contains some handsome Georgian, and older, buildings, several of which began life as farmhouses, their characteristic stone chimney breasts now facing the street.

What is arguably the district's most fascinating feature lies outside the built up area to the southwest. **Braunton Great Field** is one of the few remaining examples of the Saxon open-field strip system still to be farmed in Britain. Around 350 acres in total, the field was originally divided into around 700 half-acre strips, a furlong (220yds) long and 11yds wide, each of which was separated by an unploughed 'landshare' approximately 1ft wide. Throughout the centuries, many of the strips have changed hands, allowing them to be combined so that now there are only about 200 remaining. A medieval wall divides the southern edge of the great field from the now-drained Braunton Marsh, formerly an area of common grazing land. To the west, both the field and marsh are separated from the sea by a wide expanse of high sand dunes known as

Braunton Burrows, the southern part of which is a designated nature reserve noted for its migrant birds, rare flowers and insects. Beyond the dunes, lie the three-mile-long **Saunton Sands**, one of the most impressive sandy beaches in the West Country.

CROYDE. A very picturesque village and ideally located for beach or countryside. A little known spot it is well worth exploring . Baggy Point is a pleasant walk and marks the end of Croyde Bay. You will be rewarded with wonderful views. Also a good place for watersports.

Croyde's famous free house is **THE THATCH**; owned and run by Rock Barouh, this lively and popular pub stands in the heart of the village. Built between the 14th and 15th centuries, the Thatched Barn or The Thatch, as it was locally known, originally belonged to the Incledon Webber family, the Lords of the Manor of Croyde Hoe.

By the 1500s it was used by the monks of nearby St Helen's Priory as a barn for storage and for farm animals, and no doubt for brewing and consuming their own alcoholic beverages. Some time later the barn was converted into two cottages though a small barn was retained at the entrance end.

During the twentieth century the building has seen service as a tearooms, a shop restaurant and an arts and crafts centre and it was not until 1978 that it was converted, finally, into the free house it is today.

The Thatch is an inn in the true sense of the word. Weary travellers can take advantage of the excellent bed and breakfast accommodation in the tastefully converted bedrooms in the upstairs barn part of the inn. Guests are also treated to a mouth-watering menu of fresh bar snacks or four course meals and a wide range of traditional and keg beers.

The Thatched Barn Inn, Croyde Tel: 01271 890349

Six miles to the northeast of Barnstaple, the winding A39 passes the imposing National Trust-owned property, **Arlington Court**. This was the family home of a branch of the Chichesters from 1534 until the last owner, Rosalie Chichester, died without issue in 1949. (Perhaps the most famous postwar Chichester, Sir Francis, the air pioneer and first solo round-the-world sailor, was born two miles away at Shirwell.) The present house was built in 1822 to an unambitious design by Barnstaple architect, Thomas Lee; forty years later it was extended by the last owner's father, who also added the handsome stable block.

In 1881, the fun-loving Sir Bruce died, leaving Arlington Court, its 2775-acre park and a series of crippling debts to his daughter, then aged 15, who proceeded to live here for the remainder of her 83-year life.

Although unexceptional outside, the interior of Arlington Court is a testimony to the taste and preoccupations of Rosalie Chichester. More a museum than a mansion, there are displays of her personal collections of porcelain, pewter, shells, snuff boxes, and over 100 model ships, some made during the Napoleonic wars by captured French soldiers.

Probably the single most valuable item in the house, a watercolour by William Blake, was discovered after the owner's death on top of a wardrobe; it had been lying there for over 100 years, forgotten, and is now on show in the white drawing room.

Rosalie Chichester also turned the grounds of Arlington Court into something of a nature reserve. She erected an eight-mile-long perimeter fence to protect the native wildfowl and heron populations, and introduced Shetland ponies and Jacob sheep, some of the descendants of which can still be seen today.

The stable block became home to a unique collection of horse-drawn carriages, with rides being available to present-day visitors at most times. (Open daily, except non-Bank Holiday Saturdays, 11am to 5.30pm between early-April and end-October.) An interesting collection of over 500 species of birds, both indigenous and tropical, can be found in the 12-acre **Exmoor Bird Garden**, which lies beside the A399 Blackmoor Gate to South Molton road, four miles east of Arlington Court.

Although 70% of the **Exmoor National Park** lies across the Somerset border, a substantial strip taking in some of its highest and loveliest parts falls within Devon. The landscape consists of a high treeless plateau of hard-wearing Devonian shale which has been carved into a series of steep-sided valleys by the prolonged action of the moor's many fast-flowing streams, whereas the upland vegetation is mostly heather, gorse and bracken, the more sheltered valleys containing trees and cultivated grazing land.

The combes also provide shelter for herds of shy red deer which are free to roam, but seldom seen.

Easier to spot are the hardy Exmoor ponies, now almost all cross-breeds, which tend to congregate at roadside parking areas where pickings from holiday-makers can be rich.

Exmoor is crisscrossed by a network of paths and bridleways which provide some excellent opportunities for walking and pony-trekking.

Many follow the routes of the ancient ridgeways across the high moor, passing close to a scattered assortment of standing stones, hut circles, barrows and other prehistoric remains, including the mysterious **Shoulsbury Castle**, a four-acre Iron Age hill fort which was later used as a Roman military outpost. A magnificent view over mid-Devon can be had from the summit of Five Barrows Hill, itself a Bronze Age burial site, which at over 1600ft is the highest point on the Devon side of the moor.

MOLLAND. The southwestern fringe of Exmoor is littered with attractive rural communities. The church here retains one of the finest Georgian interiors in the county.

Its simple whitewashed-plaster interior contains some exceptional examples of 18th-century woodwork, including a complete set of box pews and an elaborate canopied three-deck pulpit which is crowned by a trumpeting angel. There are also several colourful monuments to the Courtenay family, traditional owners of the nearby manor farmhouse, West Molland. One incorporates a rare 'double heart stone', a block of stone fashioned into two chambers in which the hearts of a married couple were encased for all time.

Also in the parish lies Great Champson, the farm where, in the 18th-century, the Quartly family developed and maintained their celebrated breed of red North Devon cattle.

NORTH MOLTON. Though it is hard to imagine it today, this village, five miles to the west of Molland, was once a busy wool and mining town.

At intervals from Elizabethan times until late in the 19th-century, copper and iron were mined in the hills above the town and transported down the valley of the River Mole and on to the sea at Barnstaple. Evidence of abandoned mine workings still litter the district, and the remains of the old Mole valley tramway can be seen from Brinsworthy bridge.

The 15th-century parish church of All Saints reflects North Molton's former importance.

A striking building with a high clerestory and a 100ft pinnacled tower, it seems somewhat out of place in this slightly desolate place. Several noteworthy internal features have survived: these include a part-medieval pulpit complete with sounding board and trumpeting angel, a rood screen, some fine Jacobean panelling, and an extraordinary 17th-century alabaster monument to Sir Amyas Bampfylde, depicting the reclining knight with his wife Elizabeth at this feet and their twelve sons and five daughters kneeling nearby.

The church clock was purchased in 1564 for the then exorbitant price of £16 14s 4d; however, it turned out to be a sound investment for it remained in working order for 370 years before finally calling it a day in 1934.

A number of noteworthy buildings can be discovered around the churchyard, including the Tudor church house which was converted to a school in the 1870s, Court House, also Tudor, and Court Hall, the former home of the Bampfylde family (now the Lords Poltimore), which dates from Jacobean times, but was substantially remodelled in the 1830s.

EAST BUCKLAND. Is surrounded by beautiful countryside, and

there is a real 'hidden gem " here in the form of **LOWER PITT RES-TAURANT** which offers traditionally fine food in a superb country setting. The ambience is excellent and the atmosphere warm and relaxing. Set in a quiet hamlet on the edge of Exmoor the 16th century building provides an ideal setting for a memorable evening. Three en-suite double rooms of character are available for overnight guests. Rec. in all good food guides.

Lower Pitt Restaurant, East Buckland, Barnstaple, North Devon.
Tel & Fax: 01598 760243

SOUTH MOLTON. The River Mole reaches South Molton, a pleasant small market town which thankfully is now bypassed by the A361 North Devon link road.

This has been a focus of the local agriculture-based economy since Saxon times, and in common with many such towns throughout Devon, was a centre of the wool-trade in the late Middle Ages.

In the heart of the old town lies Broad Street, a thoroughfare of handsome Georgian and Victorian civic architecture which is so broad as to be almost a square.

Among the noteworthy buildings to be found here are the **Market Hall and Assembly Rooms,** the post office, the eccentric **Medical Hall** with its iron balcony and four Ionic columns, and the **Guildhall** of 1743 which overhangs the pavement in a series of arches. A narrow lane leads from Broad Street to the tranquil oasis of the parish churchyard.

The church itself has an oversized tower and has been much-altered since its completion in the 15th-century. Inside, the pulpit and font are excellent examples of the medieval stone-carver's art.

In the centre of the town an ideal place to eat or stay is the quaintly named**STUMBLES HOTEL AND RESTAURANT**, a combination of quality accommodation, top class cuisine and intimate restaurant, with comfort and friendly service a top priority.

Stumbles Hotel and Restaurant, 131-134 East Street, South Molton,
North Devon. Tel: 01769 574145 Fax: 01769 572558
The building has its roots in the 16th and 17th century when in part

is was owned by a baker whose bakehouse to the rear, now forms part of the accommodation and also encloses the attractive rear courtyard which is widely used in summer for dining and barbecues.

The imaginative menu which changes daily offers a mouth-watering selection of dishes, and in season, could offer Partridge or Pheasant and caters equally for vegetarian tastes.

You can dine in the friendly intimate restaurant and leave having made new friends. Eight luxury en-suite bedrooms are fitted with all the comforts you are likely to need including extra wide beds, television, telephone etc. It's no wonder visitors return here again and again.

On the northwestern edge of town, **Quince Honey Farm** claims to have the largest display of working honey bees in the world. As well as an interesting exhibition explaining the process of honey-making in detail, there is a large indoor apiary where colonies of bees can be observed going about their energetic daily business. (Open seven days a week, all year round.)

WEST DOWN, a beautiful old house, just three miles from South Molton was built in the early 1920's and is set in 30 acres of gently rolling countryside.

It offers a very high standard of B & B accommodation; all four rooms are comfortable, carefully furnished and have exceptional views. Additionally they all have central heating, en-suite bathrooms and are equipped with tea/coffee making facilities, remote control colour TV, hairdryers and many extras.

The dining room overlooks the well tended gardens and is a lovely setting in which to enjoy a full English breakfast and a four course evening meal prepared from fresh local ingredients. After dinner you can sit and relax in the comfortable lounge which has a large open log fire. Fishing and horse stabling facilities are also available.

West Down B & B, Whitechapel, South Molton, . Tel: 01769 550373

KING'S NYMPTON. The network of lanes to the south of South Molton connect a number of attractive settlements.

Take the B3226 from the A371 to Meethe (a village which no longer exists) and enjoy the beautiful drive past thatched hamlets and ancient forest and woodland along the Mole Valley with the river on your right.

Turn right from the B3226 onto a small road signposted 'George Nympton' and pass Meethe Gate, one of the few remaining scattered houses of Meethe. Turn right over a small iron bridge and climb a very narrow long steep hill to Great Oakwell at the top.

Here is **GREAT OAKWELL FARM** run by Betty and Ralph Cole from where there are glorious views over Exmoor and Dartmoor. Riding Stables are nearby or you can take your own Pony and use the Farm Stables and grazing.

The lovely old farmhouse is at least four hundred years old and full of character. There are two double bedrooms with television and a single bedroom which are tastefully furnished. The lounge is homely and comfortable and has television. The dining room has a lovely old Inglenook fireplace with domed bread oven and a wood burning stove to provide warmth and a welcome on the colder days.

Betty will provide you with an excellent farmhouse breakfast and an evening meal by request. Ralph will be happy to tell you about the history of the house which dates back in the records to King Harold.

Great Oakwell Farm, Kings Nympton, Umberleigh, Nth. Devon.
Tel: 01769 572810

King's Nympton has been an important place of worship since Celtic times and indeed, the grotesque carved roof bosses in the present-day parish church reflect this early link with paganism.

The church has an exceptional interior, with a set of 18th-century box pews, a painted chancel ceiling, and a superbly-carved medieval rood screen. The village also has a renowned plate collection, the finest pieces of which have been loaned to the Victoria and Albert museum in London. Elsewhere in the village, there is a charming thatched pub and an early-Georgian country house, **King's Nympton Park**, built of characteristic red brick.

SAMPSON BARTON COUNTRY GUEST HOUSE was, until 1970, part of a 250 acre farm. It still looks out over open farmland and the glorious surrounding countryside, but now has 2 acres of well maintained gardens including a pretty water garden.

The 17th century farmhouse is situated two and a half miles from South Molton within easy reach of Exmoor and the beaches of Devon. Veronica and Malcolm Knott have created a charming and relaxing atmosphere complimented by the huge open inglenooks and old oak beams.

Most of the well appointed bedrooms have full en-suite facilities. Veronica provides Full English breakfast and a four course evening meal from a good menu. All food is home cooked using local produce and the home cooked bread and 'unlimited puddings' make this a tempting long-term stay!

Sampson Barton Country Guest House, Kings Nympton, Umberleigh, North Devon. Tel: 01769 572466

CHITTLEHAMHOLT. **SNAPDOWN FARM** at Chittlehamholt, near South Molton, offers a self-catering holiday for nature lovers in twelve extremely well-equipped static caravans attractively set in sheltered paddocks.

This is a very safe place for children where a true appreciation of the country can be enjoyed. There is a 'badger set' in the farm woods with purpose-built hide for guests to observe them. Wild foxes and deer, buzzards and many types of birds may be seen.

Guests can help with milking the goats and feeding the goats and the pony. Children will enjoy the play areas, and near at hand you will find fishing, riding and marvellous walks.

This is not a commercialised site and you will need a car. Snapdown is within easy reach of the North Devon Coast and Exmoor.

Snapdown Farm Caravans, Chittlehamholt, Umberleigh, North Devon. Tel: 01769 540708

CHULMLEIGH. Has an outstanding church, its opulence reflects Chulmleigh's former importance as a market, wool and coaching town; however, the construction of a new turnpike road along the Taw valley in 1830, combined with the arrival of the railway 25 years later, heralded a decline from which it has never really recovered.

Despite a series of devastating fires last century, the narrow cobbled lanes contain some charming old buildings and inns which are a delight to explore.

THE OLD BAKEHOUSE is a Grade II listed 16th century wool merchant's house situated in this charming town, perched on a hilltop above the leafy valley of the Little Dart River. Bypassed by turnpike roads and the railway, the town retains an olde worlde feel with many original thatched cob cottages nestling around the beautiful 15th century Church.

The property is arranged around a picturesque courtyard which is filled with flowering shrubs and roses throughout the summer.

Owned by Holly and Colin Burls, there is a tearoom and restaurant, and accommodation is provided in a pretty wing which has been rebuilt with local materials.

The interior of the restaurant has certain Grade I listed features, in particular, an oak screen and winder staircase and Colin is always happy to show those interested the original 450 year old roof beams.

The twin bedded rooms and double room are all luxuriously furnished and have their own en suite facilities.

All the food is home cooked from fresh ingredients and contains several local specialities. This really is an excellent place to stay and make your base whilst exploring the delights of the area.

The Old Bakehouse, South Molton Street, Chulmleigh Tel: 01769 580074

COBBATON. On the return journey to Barnstaple, it's worth making a detour north off the A377 to visit the home of the intriguing **Cobbaton Combat Vehicle Museum**. This unique exhibition is the brainchild of Preston Isaac, an enthusiast who began collecting World War II tanks, armoured cars and mobile weaponry as a hobby in the early 1960s.

The museum also contains a number of evocative room settings fitted out in the style of the period to create a vivid impression of domestic life in Britain during the dark days of the Second World War. (Open daily between April and October, other times by appointment.)

CHITTLEHAMPTON. The 115ft tower on the church here is generally considered to be the finest of its kind in Devon. Built in graceful Somerset style around 1520, it dominates a three-sided square of attractive thatched and slate-roofed cottages (the dwellings on the fourth side were demolished to create an open vista of the church). The church is dedicated to St Hieritha (or *Urith*), a young Celtic woman from nearby East Stowford who, in the early 8th-century, was set upon and murdered by a mob of scythe-wielding Chittlehampton inhabitants.

A well at the eastern end of the village stands at the spot she was martyred, and a shrine incorporated into the north chancel of the church marks her burial place; both were important places of pilgrimage in the Middle Ages.

According to the locals, **WESTACOTT GUEST HOUSE** in this pretty village is about 300 years old. The house served for many years as the village store and bakery before being converted to a comfortable family home. Lyn and David, who are both qualified athletics coaches, welcome guests as family, and offer bed and a 'healthy' breakfast, though the traditional English breakfast is also on offer.

The lounge has colour television and log fire while the comfortable bedrooms have tea/coffee making facilities. Bikes are available for local use and an interesting four mile loop starts at the house and is suitable for walking, cycling or running. Self-catering is also available. Local pubs provide good food. No smoking policy.

Westacott Guest House, Townsend, Chittlehampton, Umberleigh,. Tel: 01769 540463.

SWIMBRIDGE. This attractive village lies five miles east of Barnstaple on the A361 South Molton road. For 46 years from 1833, this was the home of John 'Jack' Russell, the celebrated hunting parson and breeder of the first Jack Russell terriers. A larger-than-life character who was known throughout the district, hundreds of people attended his funeral when he died in 1880 at the age of 87. Russell's grave can be seen in the churchyard of St James' parish church, an exceptional 15th-century building with an early 14th-century tower and spire.

The unusual lead-lined font is encased in an oak cupboard, complete with hinged doors, and is crowned by an elaborate carved cover and canopy. Elsewhere in Swimbridge, there are some handsome Georgian buildings and a pleasant village pub which in 1962 was renamed the Jack Russell.

FILLEIGH. Three miles further east, the village is dominated by **Castle Hill**, one of the most outstanding Palladian mansions in the West Country. Built in the late 17th-century for the Fortescue family, the magnificent sprawling building stands within a beautiful landscaped park designed by William Kent.

Ilfracombe and the North Coast

ILFRACOMBE. With a population of around 10,000, is the largest seaside resort on the North Devon coast.

Prior to 1800, however, it was a small fishing and market town which totally relied on the sea, not only for its living, but as its principal means of communication.

The boundaries of the old town are marked by a sheltered natural harbour to the north and a part-Norman parish church half-a-mile away to the south. The entrance to the harbour is guarded by Lantern Hill, a steep-sided conical rock which is crowned by the restored medieval chapel of St Nicholas.

For centuries, this highly-conspicuous former fishermen's chapel doubled as a lighthouse, the light being placed in a lantern at the west end of the building. Today, Lantern Hill provides a spectacular view of Ilfracombe's old street plan, boat-filled harbour and craggy coastline.

The town first expanded with the arrival of the new fashion for sea-bathing in the first few decades of the 19th-century. **The Tunnel Baths** with their extravagant Doric façade were opened in Bath Place in 1836, by which time a number of elegant residential terraces had been built on the hillside to the south of the old town.

Situated in an elevated position in Chambercombe Park and overlooking Hillsborough Nature Reserve is **VARLEY HOUSE.**

Originally built as a nursing home for wounded officers returning from the Boer War, this extensive late Victorian building has been home to Barbara and Roy Gable since 1982.

Now a hotel, Varley House prides itself on the high standard of personal service all guest receive as well as the excellent food that really is a treat.

This is a wonderful and relaxing place to stay. All the nine bedrooms are tastefully decorated and furnished, have en suite bathrooms and have glorious sea or country views.

The public rooms are equally comfortable and relaxing. The clean Devon air develops a good appetite and everyone enjoys the superb, imaginative, well-presented dinners complemented by an excellent wine list. Roy is happy to entertain the guests after dinner.

A former member of the Magic Circle his sleight of hand is sure to amaze and intrigue even the most sceptical of guests.

All in all, this is a wonderful place to stay. 'Highly Commended' by the English Tourist Board, Varley House has the feel of a country house rather than a hotel.

Varley House, Chambercombe Park, Ilfracombe Tel: 01271 863927

However, it wasn't until later in the century that Ilfracombe became popular with holidaymakers of all backgrounds; the railway arrived in 1874 and the harbour was significantly enlarged to take the paddle steamers which ferried trippers from Bristol and South Wales.

Much of the town's architecture, which could best be described as decorated Victorian vernacular, dates from this period, the new streets spreading inland in steeply undulating rows.

Like many British seaside resorts, Ilfracombe is a place of contrasts. The part-Norman parish church of the Holy Trinity, whose unique wagon roof braces are guarded by a series of unusual carved angels and gargoyles, lies within a half-mile radius of the Pavilion theatre, Winter Gardens, discos, bars and a modern pleasure park.

For those who prefer to expend their energy exploring the coastal path, there is some spectacular walking along the cliffs to Capstone Point to the west and Hillsborough Hill to the east. In summer, the M S *Oldenburg* sails from Ilfracombe to Lundy island, details of which appear in chapter three.

THE GEORGE AND DRAGON pub is the oldest inn in Ilfracombe; it was established in 1361. Over the years there has been some modernisation and in 1641 inglenook fireplaces were installed.

This cosy and friendly pub, owned and run by Brian and Christine

Faulkner, is popular with locals and visitors alike and it is renowned as the first winner of the Ilfracombe Civic Pride Award for clean and attractive premises.

Even the resident ghost, Celia, is friendly and Brian and Christine will happily show you her photograph.

As well as enjoying a quiet pint there is also a range of homecooked dishes available including true char-grilled steaks. For extra winter warmth, Christine serves hot roast beef muffins right up to closing time - a treat not to be missed!

George and Dragon, Fore Street, Ilfracombe Tel: 01271 863851

THE TRAFALGAR HOTEL, is situated at the end of a substantial Victorian terrace on the way into Ilfracombe from Combe Martin.

In a superb, elevated position, possibly the best in Ilfracombe, enjoying magnificent views of the harbour, Hillsborough nature reserve and across Bristol Channel to South Wales.

Trafalgar Hotel, Larkstone Terrace, Hillsborough Road, Ilfracombe .
Tel: 01271 862145

Owned and personally run by June and Tony White, this is a wonderful hotel with a nautical theme. The spacious and comfortable

Lounge and bar are decorated with prints and pictures of boats and ships with conjure up the image of the days of the 'Queen Mary' and other great ocean liners, an ideal place to relax and take a drink before dinner.

Guests can relax and enjoy the excellent meals in the spacious Victory Restaurant with its beautiful oak-panelling.

The Trafalgar has 25 bedrooms, all with private facilities, and many with panoramic views of the sea. The residents lounge is an ideal place to relax after a busy day. For special occasions such as anniversaries, birthdays or honeymoons, there is the Hamilton Suite, with its magnificent four poster bed and luxury bathroom. There are lots of good walks in the area, and a day's walk along the coastline is an ideal way to explore the area.

THE WOODLANDS HOTEL is situated in Torrs Park, a quiet protected area of Victorian mansions adjacent to the famous coastal Torrs Walk yet within a few minutes walk of the Tunnels Beaches, harbour and the centre of Ilfracombe.

This friendly, long established family hotel is owned and run by Doreen and Alan Wilkinson and prides itself on personal service and good food with a choice of menu for the four course dinner.

The fifteen bedrooms, most with en suite, are all well appointed, decorated and equipped to a high standard.

As well as receiving a warm friendly welcome, all guests can expect to have a relaxing, comfortable stay in a tranquil setting.

The extensive and mature wooded garden extends to one and a half acres and gently slopes to a stream at the bottom. While the children make use of the play area a pre-dinner drink can be enjoyed on the south facing terrace overlooking the grounds with magnificent views of the Wilder Valley beyond.

The Woodlands Hotel, Torrs Park, Ilfracombe Tel: 01271 863098

COMBE LODGE HOTEL, is a small, licensed non-smoking, Victorian establishment, built as the schoolmaster's house for the historic Chambercombe estate, just on the outskirts of Ilfracombe and overlooking the picturesque harbour and sea. Owned and personally run by Janet and Bryan Cath, this is a wonderful place to come where you can be sure of a welcoming, quiet and enjoyable holiday.

Most of the eight bedrooms have full en - suite, with two having shower only. There is a cosy Bar where guests can try their hand at a game of Bar Skittles or Shove Halfpenny or they can relax in the comfy lounge. The food is both delicious and plentiful and is served in their licensed dining room.

Bryan is an enthusiastic walker and nature lover and has written 29 self-guided walks around the North Devon coastal area and Exmoor.

He also hosts guided walks for the local Tourist Information Centre. Guests at Combe Lodge are encouraged to take to the countryside, either by foot or by cycle.

A range of routes and itineraries, for both walkers and cyclists, has been devised by Janet and Bryan so that guests can see the best of the local scenery, varying from coastal, to moorland, to pastoral and to places where time has stood still. Bryan uses his minibus to take his walkers and cyclists to and from the start and finish points as well as picking guests up from the nearest station.

Combe Lodge Hotel, Chambercombe Park Road, Ilfracombe
Tel: 01271 864518

Around Ilfracombe

The strip of coastline between Ilfracombe and Braunton, much of which is owned by the National Trust, is sometimes referred to as *Devonia*.

The area is also popular for those with either touring caravans or who like the idea of staying in a static caravan. Ideally located for a break spent exploring the Heritage Coast,

THE MULLACOTT CROSS HOLIDAY PARK at Mullacott Cross on the **A361** between Ilfracombe and Woolacombe offers the latest top quality self-catering static caravans for hire.

The Park is spacious and has a bar, restaurant, take away, launderette and shop. There is also a children's play area and riding stables nearby.

Mullacott Cross Holiday Park, Mullacott Cross, Ilfracombe.
Tel: 01271 862212

LEE BAY. Two-and-a-half miles to the west of Ilfracombe, is a rocky combe dominated by a large hotel which was formerly the manor house.

In Lee village, there is an unusual early-Victorian church filled with dark Jacobean carved woodwork, and a medieval farmhouse which at times serves teas in the garden.

The fourth turning on the left on the road to **Lee** will bring you to **LOWER CAMPSCOTT FARM** at the head of **Fuscia Valley**.

The farm offers some delighfully picturesque self catering cottages, spacious and well equipped. B & B accommodation in the farm house is also available. With plenty for the children to do, including a pets corner, this would be a beautiful place to base your holiday.

Lower Campscott Farm, Lee, Ilfracombe. Tel: 01271 863479

WOOLACOMBE Was at one time a hamlet which developed as small resort during the Edwardian era thanks to its position beside Morte Bay; this two-mile-long stretch of pale golden sand can justifiably call itself the finest beach in North Devon.

At either end lie two National Trust-owned headlands: to the north, the jagged slate crags of Morte Point protrude into the sea, and to the south, the softer shale and sandstone cliffs of Baggy Point have been worn into a giant cave known as Baggy Hole.

MORTEHOE A mile-long cul-de-sac to the north of Woolacombe leads to this ancient village with an exceptional part-Norman church and a good inn. The former is a small cruciform building with a 15th-century open-timbered wagon roof, an interesting early-14th-century table tomb, and a wonderful series of grotesquely-carved Tudor bench ends.

If the village prompts you to stay then there is a good choice in Mortehoe in the form of **THE CLEEVE HOUSE HOTEL**, which nestles in the hillside overlooking the dramatic coastline of North Devon.

This small hotel, owned and run by Marian and Richard Ashford, offers first class accommodation in a relaxing and friendly atmosphere with wonderful countryside on the doorstep.

The clean, fresh Devon air develops hearty appetites and The Cleeve House has just the answer. Full English breakfasts are served in the elegantly furnished restaurant where you can relax with the morning paper and plan out your day.

The restaurant's evening menu offers a wide variety of local cuisine served in interesting and imaginative combinations and, after your meal, why not retire to the comfortable, well stocked bar and be regaled with tales of local shipwrecking and smuggling.

Richard's family have lived in Mortehoe for over 200 years and as the local historian he can tell you a thing or two about the village!

The Cleeve House, North Morte Road, Mortehoe, Woolacombe
Tel: 01271 870719

The rugged section of coastline to the north of Mortehoe was a notorious hazard to 19th-century shipping (five ships came to grief around the aptly-named Morte Point in the winter of 1852 alone), prompting the construction of a lighthouse at Bull Point in 1879.

THE OLD VICARAGE lies in the heart of the village, on the road which leads to Bull Point Lighthouse.

The Old Vicarage, Mortehoe. Tel: 01271 870598

Rebuilt in 1746, at about the time that the vicar moved from what is now Easewell Farm near the Parish Church, the ' modernised Vicarage is home to Jean and Stuart Wood.

This charming building, in a picturesque setting, and within 10 minutes walk from the coast and National trust lands, also provides accommodation in two self - catering cottages.

Mailscot Cottage, the West Wing of the Vicarage, was added around the turn of the last century, whilst Wykeham Cottage The North Wing is much older. Both cottages provide comfortable accommodation for up to 4 people and have been furnished and equipped to a high standard.

With easy access to all the local amenities and beaches, they make a perfect location for a family holiday, though the owners regret that pets are not allowed.

Chambercombe Manor

A number of worthwhile attractions can be found on the eastern side of Ilfracombe. The part-15th-century **Chambercombe Manor** lies in a sheltered wooded combe approximately one mile to the southeast of the town centre.

An atmospheric old manor house, its irregular buildings are arranged around a series of flower-filled courtyards.

The house contains some fine Elizabethan furnishings, and there is also a huge kitchen with a 800-year-old cider press, a secret chamber, and a private prayer room with a medieval stained-glass window.

The grounds contain a delightful water garden, and there are also some fine walks through nearby Chambercombe Woods. (Open Sundays to Fridays, 10.30am (2pm on Sundays) to 5pm between Easter and end-September.)

Hele Mill, on the eastern edge of Ilfracombe, is an imaginatively-restored mill which is open to visitors.

Continuing eastwards, the A399 passes close by **Watermouth Castle**, a castellated neo-Gothic pile which was built in the 1820s and now serves as a museum and centrepiece for a fun park.

BERRYNARBOR .Lying in a steep-sided combe one mile inland, the medieval settlement of has an altogether different atmosphere. The surprisingly unspoilt village centre is set around the church of St Peter, a largely 15th-century structure with a 96ft tower, one of the grandest in North Devon.

Inside, there is an interesting collection of monuments, many to the Berry family, the former owners of the nearby 15th-century manor house which later became the village school.

Unusually for this part of Devon, the arcade in the church nave is constructed of Beer stone which would have been shipped from the south coast by sea.

Elsewhere in the village, there are some fine period cottages and a lovely old pub, **Ye Olde Globe Inn.**

COMBE MARTIN. Although it is difficult to imagine it today, this was once an important mining centre, with silver and lead being extracted here at intervals from the 13th-century right up until 1875; indeed, several of the old mine workings still run under the main road.

Fertile and protected, the combe has also long been associated with the market gardening industry. Traces of a medieval field system can still be made out on either side of the valley, a good view of which can be had from the path leading to the summit of the 1000ft Great Hangman cliff to the east of the village.

Present-day Combe Martin stretches down to a fine sandy cove which would be even more delightful than it is were it not for some over development.

The village contains two buildings of note: the parish church of St Peter ad Vincula in old Combe Martin, one mile inland, and the **Pack O' Cards Inn,** a highly-eccentric building with 52 windows and a series of thin, angled roofs built by a gambler to resemble a towering house of cards.

The pale-red sandstone church has a soaring tower, an exceptional 15th-century rood screen, and some unusual monuments and bench-ends, one featuring a now-headless dragon.

A number of modern attractions can be found in and around Combe Martin. **The Motor Cycle Museum** in Cross Street contains a unique collection of historic motorbikes and associated memorabilia. (Open daily, 10am to 6pm between end-May and end-September.) Two miles inland, shire horses can be seen tilling the land at **Bodestone Barton Farm World**, a working farm with Shetland ponies and a collection of rare farm animals. (Open daily, 10.30am to 6pm between Easter and end-October.)

Just off the A399 three miles to the southeast of Combe Martin, the twenty-acre **Combe Martin Wildlife and Leisure Park** at Higher Leigh Manor is principally a monkey sanctuary; however, there is also a miniature railway, a model village and an interesting assortment of rare animals and birds, including falcons. (Open daily, 10am to 5pm between Easter and early-November.)

One mile further east, the A399 enters the Exmoor National Park before joining the A39 Lynton Road at Blackmoor Gate. This was once the midpoint of the **Lynton to Barnstaple narrow-gauge railway**, a line which ran through some of the loveliest countryside in North Devon. The undulating landscape of the western fringes of Exmoor posed some serious problems for the engineers; however, by the spring of 1898 these had been overcome and the line was opened, though it only remained so for 37 years.

Today, the former Barnstaple Town station has been converted into a restaurant, Lynton's is a private house, and Blackmoor Gate's has been transformed into a hotel, leaving the museum in Barnstaple's old signal box as the only tribute to this once-celebrated branch line.

Also in the area which has many attractions for the visitor is **Exmoor Animal and Bird Gardens** which is at South Stowford.

Set in 12 acres of landscaped gardens it has opportunities for feeding the animals as well as having an adventure playground. family tickets available . For details phone (01598) 763352.

PARRACOMBE. The A39 to the northeast of Blackmoor Gate contours around the village; an ancient settlement which contains the earthwork remains of a Norman motte and bailey fortification still known as Holwell Castle. However, Parracombe's most exceptional feature, its part-13th-century **Church of St Petrock**, lies high above the village beside the main road.

The building fell into disrepair during the last century and indeed, it only just escaped demolition in 1878 thanks to a campaign led by John Ruskin. As a consequence, it escaped the attention of the Victorian 'restorers' and so still retains its exquisite Georgian interior complete with 18th-century box pews, musicians' gallery and three-storey pulpit.

Further above the village, the high moor is littered with prehistoric remains, including those of a Bronze Age cemetery known locally as Chapman's Barrows.

More evidence of prehistoric settlement can be found along the rugged stretch of coastline between Combe Martin and Lynmouth.

Here, the coast is characterised by a series of great hog's back cliffs which dip spectacularly into the sea; between them, remote rocky coves, such as Woody Bay and Heddon's Mouth, add to the stark beauty of the landscape.

The two tiny hamlets of Trentishoe and Martinhoe can be reached along narrow lanes from the A39; the latter has a small part-Norman church whose interior was badly vandalised in a clumsy Victorian restoration.

The dramatic wooded cliffs above Martinhoe are mainly National Trust-owned and need to be explored on foot. A path to the north of the village leads to the 800ft Beacon, site of the earthwork remains of a Roman signal station dating from the 1st-century AD. This was used to look out for Celtic raiders crossing the Bristol Channel during the short period prior to the Roman conquest of South Wales.

LYNTON AND LYNMOUTH. The A39 follows a tortuous route

from Blackmoor Gate, finally descending through to the sea at Lynmouth.

These two small resorts, although often mentioned in the same breath, are very different in character. The older settlement, Lynmouth, is a former herring-fishing village whose decline was halted when visitors began arriving to sample the delights of 'Little Switzerland' at the time of the Napoleonic wars.

Coleridge and Wordsworth were among its early visitors, arriving here on foot in the 1790s, and Shelley wrote fondly of the place when he visited in 1812.

As its name suggests, the town stands at the point where the steep-sided valleys of the Rivers East and West Lyn reach the Bristol Channel, a dramatic location whose rugged beauty conceals a dormant threat.

During the night of 15 August 1952, nine inches of rain fell onto an already rain-saturated Exmoor; as a result, an immense surge of surface rainwater cascaded into the Lyn valleys, bursting the riverbanks and sweeping away everything in its path on its journey to the sea.

Several upstream communities were devastated; however, it was in Lynmouth that the damage was most acute. Power lines were severed, and in the thundering darkness, dozens of houses were destroyed, the harbour was damaged, cars were swept out to sea, and 31 people lost their lives.

The town was soon repaired, thankfully with much improved flood control measures, but the memory of the disaster lives on to this day.

On a happier note **THE SUNNY LYN HOLIDAY PARK** lies on the edge of the beautiful Exmoor National Park and just half a mile from picturesque Lynmouth Harbour.

Sunny Lyn Holiday Park, Lynbridge, Lynton Tel: 01598 753384

Owned by Brian and Carol Selwood, this family run holiday park is delightfully quiet and is situated in the wooded valley of the River West Lyn. Many footpaths lead directly from the Park into Exmoor and the Heritage Coastal Walk is close at hand.

The holiday park offers accommodation in de luxe static caravans and attractive log cabins. Both are superbly equipped, have central heating and are furnished and decorated to a high standard.

The Park also provides many amenities that help to ensure that your holiday runs smoothly; these include a licensed restaurant, a site shop and full launderette facilities. Sunny Lyn Holiday Park also has space for touring caravans and tents.Among the structures to be rebuilt after the flood was the **Rhenish Tower**, a 19th-century affectation which was originally constructed to store seawater for the medical baths of its eccentric owner, General Rawdon.

Lynmouth is connected to its more recent sister-town by an ingenious cliff railway, the first of its kind in Britain when it was opened on Easter Monday, 1890.

With a vertical height of 450ft a gradient of 1:1.75, the railway is powered by gravitational force: twin cars are connected to each other by a looped cable; each has a 700-gallon water tank which when full, weighs around three tons; when the tank at the top is filled and the one on the bottom emptied, the brakes are released and the cars change places.

Passengers alighting at the top find themselves in Lynton, a small resort which expanded around the Lynton to Barnstaple railway terminus. With its magnificent setting, it is well worth a visit, and there is a well-established local museum containing some worthwhile background information on Exmoor and the Lyn valleys.

Situated just above Lynton, on Hollerday Hill, and standing in its own elevated, south facing grounds is **ROCKVALE HOTEL.**

This spacious and comfortable Victorian gentleman's residence retains many of its original architectural features and also commands glorious panoramic views over the town, Watersmeet Valley, Countisbury and Summerhouse Hill.

Rockvale Hotel, Lee Road, Lynton Tel: 01598 752279/753343

Your hosts, Judith and David Woodland, offer a warm and friendly welcome and the hotel provides tranquillity and peace of mind that is not always available elsewhere. They are also the proud holders of the Les Routiers award for 'outstanding quality, warm hospitality and good value'.

The eight pretty bedrooms are all either en suite or have their own private bathrooms nearby. Judith is the cook and the five course candlelit dinner is a leisurely affair with varied and imaginative delicious home cooking. For the comfort of all the guests, Rockvale is a non-smoking hotel and, regrettably, pets cannot be accommodated.

Situated in a magnificent position, overlooking the West Lyn River valley and with splendid views of the wooded slopes of Summerhouse Hill and the Bristol Channel is **THE VALLEY HOUSE HOTEL.**

This small, stone, Victorian country house, built in 1840, is the ideal place to stay for a relaxing and peaceful holiday. Joan and Russell Herbert, your hosts, have taken great care in ensuring that all visitors receive a warm and friendly welcome.

This is a small hotel and this is where the charm lies.

All the six comfortable bedrooms are en suite and offer glorious views. The two balcony rooms have the added attraction of allowing guests to idle away the hours from a superb sheltered vantage point.

Joan and Russell also take great pride in the food and wine served in the hotel. Each day's freshly prepared menu is discussed with, and adapted to reflect the wishes of the guests. Whatever your taste or need, there will be a mouth watering dinner awaiting you in the dining room.

Being situated on a steep hillside, the driveway to the hotel is correspondingly steep. A sloping pathway through the wooded grounds leads from the private car park to the terrace upon which the hotel is built. Though the car park is some thirty yards from the hotel, this walk is on the level. Valley House Hotel is a non-smoking establishment.

Valley House Hotel, Lynbridge Road, Lynton Tel: 01598 752285

One of the most popular beauty spots in the area lies at the confluence of the East Lyn and Hoar Oak Water, one mile to the east of Lynton. The wooded gorge at **Watersmeet** is now under the ownershiof the National Trust, and a restored 19th-century Gothic fishing lodge on the site has been made into a visitor centre and tea garden.

(Open daily, 10.30am to 6pm between early-April and end-October; admission free.)

A toll road to the west of Lynton leads to the spectacular **Valley of the Rocks**, a dry scarified valley which may once have been the ancient course of the West Lyn.

THE SANDROCK HOTEL is situated at the head of the magnificent Valley of the Rocks, in this unspoilt village. Behind the hotel lies Hollerday Hill with its commanding views of the coast, from Countisbury Foreland and Lynmouth Bay to the East, to Lee and Woody Bays to the West.

Originally two large Victorian houses, the owners, Maria and John Harrison, have expertly converted them to create a spacious nine bedroomed hotel.

As well as offering all their guests individual, personal attention, Maria and John pride themselves of the excellent food served in their restaurant, which is also open to non residents.

In an area where you are likely to spend a great deal of your holiday out of doors, quality of the dishes is much appreciated as is the fine selection of table wines, good service and the large and pleasant dining room. A wonderful hotel that is a great credit to Maria and John.

The Sandrock Hotel, Longhead, Lynton Tel: 01598 753307

The great rocky outcrops have been given such names as Chimney Rock, Rugged Jack, the White Lady and the Devil's Cheese Ring, and occasionally the valley's resident population of wild goats can be seen frolicking amongst them.

Enjoying panoramic views across Lynmouth Bay towards Countisbury headland, and within 5 minutes walk of 'The Valley of the Rocks', **CHOUGH's NEST HOTEL** is a good choice to base a relaxing holiday in this part of North Devon.

This elegant English country house was built one hundred years ago for a Dutch millionaire, the co-founder of Lynton Electric Company.

Interestingly, Lynton was the first town to be fitted with electric street lighting.

Today the hotel has an informal country atmosphere and offers a choice of 12 rooms, all well equipped and tastefully decorated.

All have en-suite bathroom facilities, full heating, colour television, tea and coffee making facilities and hair dryer. Some rooms have a four-poster bed.

The restaurant is superb and is popular with residents, non-residents and locals, so be sure to book well in advance. In the elegant, yet informal dining room you can enjoy a wonderful selection of beautifully prepared dishes from the extensive menu.

The host, Andrew, is a keen game fisherman and chef, so be sure to try the delightful freshly caught Rainbow Trout Fillet served with Orange and Tarragon Sauce, caught and prepared by him. Alternatively he will be more than happy to prepare a meal to your individual taste.

Whether this is your honeymoon, annual holiday or long weekend, the personal attention you will receive at Chough's Nest will help to make it a memorable one.

The hotel is situated down a quiet cul-de-sac by the side of Lynton Parish Church.

Chough's Nest Hotel, North Walk, Lynton, Nth Devon. Tel: 01598 753315

A little further on, **Lee Abbey** is now a conference and study centre run by the Anglican church; never actually a monastic house, it was built in the mid-19th-century on the site of an ancient manor farm referred to in *Lorna Doone*.

To the east of Lynmouth, the A39 rises dramatically (1000ft in two miles) to the summit of **Countisbury Hill**. One night in the winter of 1899, the crew of the Lynmouth lifeboat were unable to put to sea in a particularly severe storm. Instead, they hauled their lifeboat a distance of over ten miles up Countisbury Hill, across the moor, and down to Porlock Weir, where they successfully launched and went to the aid of a ship in distress. **Foreland Point** is the most northerly point in Devon and at 900ft, is also one of the highest sea cliffs in England. A nearby Iron Age hill fort is thought to the site of a famous victory by King Alfred's Saxons over the invading forces of Hubba the Dane. To the south lies the scenic 'Doone Valley', a long steep-sided combe of green pasture and woodland immortalised by R D Blackmore in his classic romantic novel.

The now-demolished medieval farm known as Hoccombe Combe lies just across the Somerset border; this is thought to have been the home of a wild and unruly Exmoor family whose real-life deeds provided the inspiration for the story.

CHAPTER THREE

NORTH DEVON

Hartland Abbey

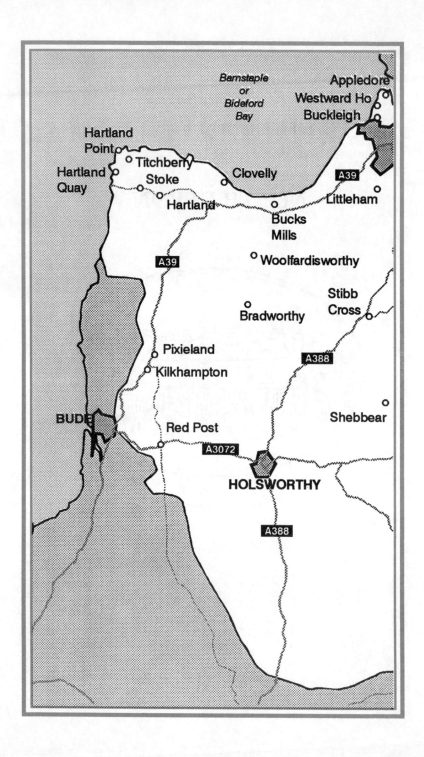

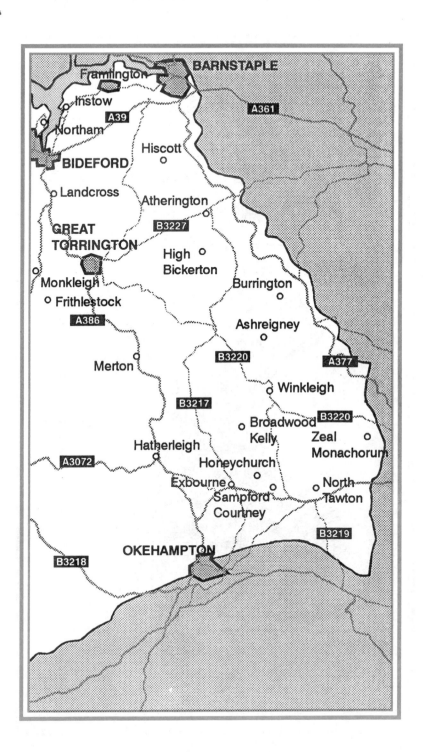

Okehampton Castle

CHAPTER THREE

NORTH DEVON - BIDEFORD TO OKEHAMPTON

Okehampton and the Northern Fringes of Dartmoor

OKEHAMPTON. The ancient market town of Okehampton stands at the foot of the soaring north Dartmoor ridge, on the main east-west route through mid-Devon.

The Saxons were the first to found a settlement here, on a hill half-a-mile west of the current town centre.

The parish church of All Saints still occupies this site; however, the present building is largely Victorian thanks to a fire in 1842 which totally destroyed the previous structure except for its 15th-century granite tower. The 19th-century church windows were designed by William Morris, the founder of the Arts and Crafts movement.

The Normans were soon to recognise Okehampton's strategic importance and built a sizable double keep on the raised strip of land between the east and west Okement rivers, a mile to the southwest of the present town centre.

The castle was extended by Hugh Courtenay, Earl of Devon, in the 14th-century, but was partially dismantled two centuries later after one of his heirs was tried and convicted of treason.

The remains are nevertheless impressive, standing as they do on top of a substantial earthwork mound (or *motte*) which dominates the surrounding valley. **Okehampton Castle** is now under the ownership of English Heritage. (Open daily, 10am to 6pm between 1 April and 30 September; also Tuesdays to Thursdays in winter.)

Now often referred to as 'the town with moor', gone are the days of the traffic bottleneck with the bypass taking hordes of screaming children down to the Cornish beaches.

Present-day Okehampton is a quiet old-fashioned town which offers visitors the opportunity to relax and enjoy the 365 square miles of Dartmoor which towers above it to the south.

Walking on the fringes of the moor is a joy, or for those who would rather see the scenery from the back of a horse, there are some excellent riding stables nearby. The locality boasts several golf courses, the one in the town itself having been reclaimed from the moor making it both a very rewarding course to play and an extremely scenic one.

For swimmers, there is a very good indoor pool in the town park, a beautiful spot with the moorland river running through it.

Okehampton is one of the last rural towns to have its own cinema, and there is also a wonderful Victorian arcade within the shopping centre which is reminiscent of London's Burlington Arcade.

Also worthy of note are the 15th-century **Chapel of Ease**, and the **Town Hall**, a striking three-storey structure which was built in 1685 as a residential house and converted to its current use in the 1820s. Another good place to visit is the **Museum of Dartmoor Life** which is open from April to October.

It is known that a licence was granted to the **WHITE HART** hostelry in Okehampton in 1623. The White Hart, as the principal Post Inn of the town was the centre of all major events in the 18th century.

Today, it still retains its popularity as a stopping place for travellers, whether seeking refreshment or comfortable accommodation.

The White Hart Hotel, Fore Street, Okehampton.
Tel. Nos : 01837 54514 or 01837 52730 Fax: 01837 53979

Set some 800 feet above sea level on the outskirts of Okehampton and situated on the very edge of Dartmoor, is an excellent home from home - **HEATHFIELD HOUSE**

Originally the Stationmaster's house but for the past eleven years it has been the home of Jane Seigal whose close affection with Dartmoor is very evident. One of the attractions of making this your base is Jane's walking tours taken at your own comfortable pace to discover the wonders of the moors, with many interesting places and wildlife pointed out as you go.

Heathfield House has spacious accommodation with bedrooms fitted out to a very high standard, all with en-suite baths or showers and other luxury facilities.

A superb new Conservatory has recently been added and is ideal for conferences and other larger gatherings. Jane does all the cooking and provides wonderful dinners and huge breakfasts using fresh produce whenever possible.. You will need some good walks to keep in shape!

A very comfortable house with a real welcome and you very quickly feel at home.

For next season, there will be a wonderful new large heated outdoor pool which is currently under construction. Special rates for children. No smoking please. 3-Crown Commended by ETB.

To find Heathfield House take the left fork at the fountain on Station road, then under the railway bridge and continue up a steep hill where you will see the gates to the house .

Heathfield House, Klondyke Road, Okehampton..
Tel: 01837 54211

Around Okehampton

MELDON. Beside the new A30, two-and-a-half miles southwest of Okehampton, limestone from the once-great Meldon quarries was used to build the striking 160ft-high **Meldon Railway Viaduct**. The dramatic surrounding heathland was once part of the hunting estate owned by the medieval Courtenay family.

BELSTONE lies three miles to the east.

A path from village leads up to the ancient standing stone circle known as the **Nine Stones** (in fact, there are well over a dozen of them). According to local legend, the group of stones under Belstone Tor was formed when a group of maidens were discovered dancing on the Sabbath and turned to stone. (This explanation conveniently chooses to ignore the fact that the circle was in place long before the arrival of Christianity.)

It is also claimed that the mysterious stones change position when the clock strikes noon. Whatever their true attributes, the view across mid-Devon from the site is breathtaking.

The village of Belstone has an attractive three-sided green, with a variety of late-Victorian and Edwardian buildings.

STICKLEPATH, one mile to the east is a peaceful community which was once bisected by the A30. It contains one of the most interesting museums of industrial archeology in Devon. Once a corn mill, then a textile mill, the **Finch Brothers' Foundry** was acquired by Robert Finch in 1814 and converted into a foundry making special tools for the region's agricultural and China clay industries.

The foundry's machinery, including its unique pair of tilt hammers, was driven by an artificial channel, or *leat*, drawn from the River Taw by way of an ingenious timber aqueduct. After the foundry closed in 1960, the old water wheel fell into disrepair until a group of local enthusiasts rescued and restored it to its former working glory.

For those seeking to escape the bustle of the foundry, a beautifully-situated Quaker graveyard lies a short distance away.

SOUTH ZEAL. THE OXENHAM ARMS at South Zeal was built in the early 16th-century as a manor house.

A lovely old granite building with mullioned windows and an impressive porch, perhaps its most distinctive feature is an ancient standing stone which has been incorporated into one of its rear walls.

Although built by the Burgoyne family, the inn takes its name from another prominent local family, the Oxenhams, a name which is linked to a mysterious white-breasted bird said only to appear when a member of the family was to die.

Three centuries after the feathered harbinger of doom was first seen, both the bird and local branch of the family are extinct.

The chapel of St Mary stands in the middle of South Zeal's broad main street; although medieval in appearance, it was rebuilt in 1713 and restored by the Victorians. More genuinely medieval is the nearby market cross which stands as a reminder of the livestock markets which once took place on this now manure-free thoroughfare.

SOUTH TAWTON. Half-a-mile to the north, the village of South Tawton has a delightful centre. Among the fine period buildings clustered in front of the church is the 15th-century church house, one of the finest examples of its kind in the county. An imposing two-storey thatched building, its unusual double external staircase forms a porch over the ground-floor door.

The adjacent church of St Andrew was built around the same time and of the same material, Dartmoor granite.

Among its noteworthy internal features are a wagon roof with carved roof bosses, a series of Beer stone columns in the nave, and an 18th-century oak pulpit inlaid with images of three of the four Evangelists (the absentee is St John).

There are also two exceptional memorials: one a reclining effigy of John Wykes which shows his feet resting, not on some mythical creature, not on a luxurious pillow, but on a trusty duck; the other is to Robert Burgoyne and his wife which shows the couple kneeling in effigy above a great slate tablet etched with the outlines of their ten children, one of which is clothed in a burial shroud.

SPREYTON. The lanes to the northeast of South Tawton lead to Spreyton, an isolated community on the northern foothills of Dartmoor which has been immortalised in the song, *Widecombe Fair*. It was from here that Uncle Tom Cobley and his companions set out on the old grey mare to make the fifteen-mile trek to Widecombe, a journey from which the horse was never to return.

Uncle Tom was a celebrated local figure who died in 1794 and was buried in an unmarked grave in the churchyard of **St Michael's parish church.** The headstone in the churchyard to 'Thomas Cobley, gent' marks the resting place of Uncle Tom's nephew to whom he left his entire estate after he had disinherited his own son for philandering.

St Michael's is approached by way of an avenue of massive lime trees, most of which were planted in 1802.

The building itself is constructed of granite and has a prominent tower and a massive oak door which has to be heaved open. Inside, there is a fine wagon roof in the chancel which is inscribed with a long rambling message in Latin from the church's 15th-century priest, Henry le Maygne, 'a native of Normandy who caused me to be built in 1451 and who wrote all this with his own hand.'

The church also contains two ancient fonts, one a model of Saxon simplicity and the other a more elaborate Norman affair whose eight sides are carved with expressive religious scenes. Spreyton's broad main street contains some pretty thatched cottages, and there is also a fine inn, not surprisingly called the Tom Cobley.

The village is also famous for its ghosts: as well as the ones of Tom and his old grey mare, spirits have been seen of a kneeling monk, a woman in black looking for gold, another woman searching for her son, and a boy who appears beside the bed while its occupants are asleep.

TEDBURN ST MARY. The village of Tedburn St Mary, seven miles further east, can either be reached via the A30 or through the network of narrow lanes which traverse the valleys of the river Troney and its tributaries.

The part 15th-century church of St Mary was altered in the 17th-century, and again in 19th. However, a number of interesting period features remain, including the brass on the chancel wall to Jane Gee, dated 1613, and the capital on the first column of the north aisle, which is carved with comical naked figures.

The newer part of the village is set around the school, pub and Methodist chapel, some distance away to the south.

Those interested in traditional Devon cider should make the detour to nearby **Lower Uppacott Farm** where it is still made in several different varieties and strengths.

Visitors are given the opportunity to taste and mix the prize-winning brews before buying.

The country lanes to the west and north of Tedburn St Mary pass through some of the most attractive rolling farmland in Devon.

BOW and NYMET TRACEY. Eight miles to the northwest of Tedburn St Mary, on the A3072 Crediton to Okehampton road, lies the long straggling village of Bow.

This was once a small market town where an annual three-day fair was held on the feast of St Martin. Before the main road drew its economy northwards, the focus of the parish lay three-quarters-of-a-mile away at Nymet Tracey, still the location of the parish church.

NORTH TAWTON. Four miles to the west, is a scattered rustic community which, like Bow, has seen better days as a small market town and wool centre. In medieval times, it was an important borough governed by a *portreeve*, an official who was elected each year until the end of the 19th-century.

As the local textile industry declined in the second half of the 18th-century, North Tawton declined with it, although a single mill at Taw

Bridge hung on into the 20th.

North Tawton also suffered badly from the ravages of fire which wiped out most the older and more interesting buildings in the town.

However, a few survivors can still be found around the Square, most notably Broad Hall, a small former manor house dating from the 1400s.

Situated on the A3072 halfway between Crediton and Oakhampton, Jane and David Pyle and family invite guests to their home -

LOWER NICHOLS NYMET FARM a working Dairy farm where you can see the cows come in for milking.

A safe area for children, old walks used by the Monks in bygone days are marked out for safe walking and exploring around the farm. There is great food to be enjoyed here, where you can waken to the early morning chorus of birds and soak up the country feeling.

Lower Nichols Nymet Farm, North Tawton, Devon. Tel: 01363 82510

SAMPFORD COURTENAY. St Andrew's parish church at Sampford Courtenay, two miles further west, contains a remarkable wood-carving of the mysterious Green Man.

Complete with characteristic disembodied head and leaves sprouting from his mouth, he can be found in the chancel above the altar. Originally a mischievous Celtic god of fertility, the Green Man was later Christianised and renamed 'Jack' or 'Robin Goodfellow', a name borrowed by Shakespeare in *A Midsummer Night's Dream*.

St Andrew's church has another unique claim to fame as the origin of the short-lived Prayer Book Rebellion. On Whit Sunday 1549, an angry group of worshippers met to protest against the abolition of the Latin Mass.

In the disturbance which followed, one of their number, William Hellyons, was killed on the steps of the nearby church house. This unusually long building has a handsome external staircase and dates from the early 16th-century, although it has since been virtually rebuilt. The nearby parish church is light and airy, despite being largely constructed of granite; it also has some fine internal features, including a Norman font and a wagon roof with some striking carved roof bosses.

HONEYCHURCH. Sampford Courtenay's long main street runs northwards for over a mile from the A3072 to the village of Honeychurch, a remote community with a tiny, almost unaltered 12th-century church which is just over 40ft long. Inside, there is an unusual tapering font dating from the 12th-century, a series of simple 15th- and 17th-century pews, and a plain Elizabethan pulpit which was sympathetically restored in the 1950s.

EXBOURNE. In the heart of Devon farming country and midway between the villages of Exbourne and Monkokehampton lies **EASTERBROOK FARM**.

The farm, owned and run by Julie and Mick Pryce, consists of 70 acres, half of which is used to produce hay and silage and as grazing for horses, the rest has been planted as woodland.

As well as numerous horses, there are goats, dogs (Irish setters bred by the owners), cats, ducks, geese and chickens around the farm.

The couple have three beautifully converted cottages which they hire out throughout the year. All the cottages are family sized, with the latest fittings, but decorated in a style that compliments their ages which range from 150 to 250 years old.

Guests are encouraged to wander around the farm during their stay and there are always tasks in which they can participate. Pets are welcome, by prior arrangement, and stabling and grass keep is also available for visiting horses. This is an ideal base for a family holiday though a car is necessary to take full advantage of the surrounding area; the nearest local pub to the farm is not within walking distance unless you are very fit!

Easterbrook Farm, Exbourne, Okehampton, Devon Tel: 01837 851674

HATHERLEIGH. Six miles to the north of Okehampton on the A386 Bideford road, the small market town of Hatherleigh lies in the heart of rural mid-Devon. Like many such inland centres, it has ancient origins, but has suffered a relative decline over the last two centuries.

The abbots of Tavistock owned a manor here from the late 10th-century until the Dissolution of the Monasteries in 1539. Indeed, the wonderful thatched George Hotel, which dates from around 1450, is believed to have been built as the abbot's court house.

The London Inn also dates from around this time, and the Old Church House is thought to be even older. Hatherleigh would have had an even richer vein of early buildings were it not for the devastating fire of 1840 which destroyed much of the old centre. Fortunately, the 15th-century church of St John the Baptist escaped the flames, although the town hall was not so lucky and had to be rebuilt later that year. The church is set high above the Lew valley, its red sandstone walls and sturdy tower forming a striking focus to this pleasant rural community. The tower had a spire until the storms of January 1990 when high winds sent it crashing through the roof of the nave.

The church interior is filled with memorials carrying the names of the families who have farmed the surrounding land for centuries. There is also a pulpit and lectern made from the remains of the old rood screen, a collection of early carved bench ends, and two ancient fonts, the most recent of which is Norman.

Hatherleigh's busy livestock market is still held in the square every Tuesday, and on the Saturday closest to November 5, the famous Hatherleigh Carnival features a torchlight procession, with colourful floats and barrels of flaming tar being dragged through the streets.

On the main road through this ancient market town towards Okehampton lies the **TALLY HO COUNTRY INN AND BREWERY.** Dating from the 15th century, the inn provides wholesome home-cooked food, real ales and a warm welcome to all travellers.

Owned and run by Megan Tidy, the inn has seen many changes over the years but retains an olde worlde charm and character.

Both the menu in the bar and the one in the á la carte restaurant are extensive, all serving a range of delicious and enticing dishes, many using beer from the adjacent brewery. The real ales are a perfect accompaniment to any meal and can also be enjoyed in the only real beer garden in the town which is also home to a wonderful collection of exotic song birds.

The brewery was started in 1990, though its history goes back some 200 years. Known then as the New Inn Brewery records show that it was producing ales in 1790.

Destroyed by fire in 1806 it recovered in 1824 only to close at the turn of the century. Situated at the back of the inn, in what was the town bakery, it can be seen through large picture windows from the inn.

Brewing takes place each week using traditional methods and the owners are delighted to show round interested guests. Four ales are produced as well as a mild and, especially for Christmas, a winter warmer.

Tally Ho Country Inn and Brewery, 14 Market Street, Hatherleigh,
North Devon Tel: 01837 810306

The narrow road from Hatherleigh to Monkokehampton runs along the northern edge of **Hatherleigh Common**, a 400-acre area of rugged heathland which was granted to the poor of the district by the abbots of Tavistock (a local rhyme falsely names John of Gaunt as the benefactor). The commoners who graze their livestock here are still known as 'Hatherleigh potboilers', and at one time, holy water taken from St John's Well on the common was used for baptisms.

BROADWOOD KELLY. This small, attractive village is ideally situated as a base for exploring the 'hidden places' which are described in this chapter.

WOODCROFT, is a family run working farm at Broadwoodkelly, Winkleigh. In the farmhouse, Jean Skinner provides warm, friendly hospitality in homely surroundings.

Cooking is her speciality and much of her food comes from the farm itself. There's always delicious sweets at dinner and a breakfast you won't believe. A holiday at Woodcroft should prove and enjoyable and relaxing experience. Children are very welcome. Ask for exact directions when phoning. 1-Crown ETB.

Woodcroft, Broadwood Kelly, Winkleigh, Devon. Tel: 01837 83405

June Weston has been involved with bed and breakfast for thirty years and has given good food and accommodation to hundreds of families. So, if you are in the area, make for **MIDDLECOTT FARM** off the A386 at Hatherleigh and on to Broadwood Kelly and ask in the village.

Middlecott Farm, Broadwood Kelly, Winkleigh, Devon.
Tel: 01837 83381

Despite lying within a few dozen miles of Exeter and the more bustling areas of South Devon, the wide expanse of agricultural land between Hatherleigh and the River Tamar gives the impression of the being one of the remotest areas in Britain.

Not that it is unpopulated; the A3072 Hatherleigh to Bude road runs through, or close by, some attractive rural settlements, including SHEEPWASH, with its delightful square and fishing inn, the Half Moon, HIGHAMPTON, with its part-Norman church, and HOLLACOMBE, with its rare saddleback church tower. It is just that here, the incursions of the 20th-century seem to have been countermanded by some greater sense of rural continuity.

HOLSWORTHY. Four miles from the Cornish border, is a larger community which, like others set back from the coast, has seen a more illustrious past. One reason for its gradual decline is that it is set within yellow clay country, a soil which rarely yields an easy or bountiful harvest.

The best day to visit Holsworthy is Wednesday when it throws off its duvet and plays host to one of the most charming rural markets in Devon. Here, visitors have the opportunity to buy locally-produced cream, butter, cheese and horticultural produce, as well as being able to savour the atmosphere of a traditional street market.

The lively St Peter's fair is also held here on 9-11 July. An interesting feature of the town is its old Victorian railway viaduct which strikes out across the valley and can be walked with the permission of British Rail.

The organ in Holsworthy church was made in the 17th-century by Renatus Hunt for All Saints church, Chelsea. After having been officially described as worn out, it was sold to Bideford in 1723 where it remained for 140 years before being written off once again and removed to Holsworthy. Its intricately-carved casing is especially worth seeing.

Although the church has been much altered and disfigured, a couple of early features have survived, including a carved Norman panel in the south porch depicting a lamb caving in under the load of a huge cross.

Before the arrival of the railway (now long since closed), a branch of the Bude canal was built to within a mile of Holsworthy. In order to cut down on expense, the engineer, James Green, constructed a series of inclined planes where four-ton barges fitted with wheels were hauled uphill using giant water-filled barrels as counterweights. Although **Blagdon Moor Wharf** is now silted up, a few of the old buildings remain. A line of mature willow trees marks the course of the old waterway which was originally built to bring fertiliser and sand to the struggling farmers of West Devon. The canal can be followed westwards to **Pancrasweek**, a loose collection of farms set around the lonely church of St. Pancras; this largely 15th-century structure has a pinnacled west tower and a fine Jacobean pulpit.

ASHWATER. The picturesque hamlet of Ashwater lies in the lanes to the east of the A388, five miles south of Holsworthy. The older buildings, mostly late-Victorian farm workers' cottages, are set around a triangular green which is overlooked by the church of St Peter in Chains.

The church contains some striking internal features, including an unusually wide wagon roof, a collection of early bench ends, a delicate-looking plasterwork coat of arms of Charles I, and a vast 15th-century chest tomb which incorporates the reclining figures of Thomas Carminow and his wife. Perhaps most exceptional, however, is the massive Norman font, one of the largest in Devon, which stands on four semicircular stone panels and is carved with lions, dragons, salamanders and other exotic creatures. The return journey to Okehampton passes close to **Roadford Reservoir**, a pleasant stretch of water surrounded by isolated villages, many of which have spectacular views of northwest Dartmoor.

Great Torrington and the Torridge Valley

GREAT TORRINGTON. The tranquil old market town of Great Torrington is one of the most dramatically-situated towns in North Devon.

It stands on an unusually exposed hilltop site several hundred feet above a steep ravine with the River Torridge at the bottom. The settlement grew up around a castle which was built in the early 13th-century to defend the important north-south route along the valley floor. Nothing of the original structure remains today, although it is still worth making the climb to the top of Castle Hill for a spectacular view of the surrounding farmland, the pattern of which has hardly changed since medieval times.

Two long, narrow strip fields can be seen from here which once belonged to a former lepers' hospital at Taddiport. An inscription in chapel there laments how ownership of the fields was unjustly taken away.

The church of **St Michael in Torrington** was the site of one of the most infamous deeds of the English Civil War. During the siege of 1646, the defending Royalists had been using the building as a gunpowder store; when they finally surrendered to the Parliamentarians, General Fairfax's troops rounded up the remaining Royalists, herded them into the church and ignited the gunpowder, causing an explosion which blew off the roof and resulted in the deaths of over 200 people. The church was rebuilt later that century, but has since been poorly restored by the Victorians.

Palmer House in New Street is an elegant redbrick residence with neoclassical pilasters which was built in the 18th-century for John Palmer, a local man whose wife, Mary, was the sister of the painter, Sir Joshua Reynolds. Both Sir Joshua and Dr Johnstone are believed to have stayed here.

THE BLACK HORSE INN is situated across the road from the town hall in the Square. It has been here so long that the precise age of the building is unknown, but it is generally accepted to be the oldest pub in Devon.

The Black Horse Inn, High Street, Torrington, Devon
Tel: 01805 622121

It certainly dates back before the 16th century, as it is known that General Fairfax used the Inn as his headquarters during the Civil War. This is a very popular and busy pub, a fact attested to by its inclusion in the 'Good Pub Guide - 1992'. The Black Horse is renowned for the fine ales it serves, and the food available ranges from bar snacks in the cosy bar to a full a la carte meal in the 36 cover restaurant. Proprietors David and Val Sawyer also offer comfortable bed and breakfast accommodation for weary travellers, with a choice of double and single rooms.

All rooms are en-suite with colour television and tea making facilities, and reduced rates are offered for children. With its sense of history and convivial atmosphere, the Black Horse would certainly make an ideal base from which to explore both Exmoor and Dartmoor and the coastline of North Devon and Cornwall. There is plenty to see locally too, and you may like to try one of the Inn's special Weekend Breaks which are available at a very reasonable rate.

THE NEWMARKET INN, just off the square, used to be a small country town ale house which backed onto the Blacksmith's shop. Today, it is a bustling town inn serving a selection of real ales and beers and has a menu which has to be tried for it's unbeatable quality and value.

At weekends, live bands and disco's take place in the function suite which is separated from the inn allowing customers to enjoy a meal or a drink in the comfortable bars, but by stepping across the car park, customers can find themselves in a modern club setting.

The Newmarket Inn, South Street, Great Torrington, North Devon.
Tel: 01805 622289

Other noteworthy buildings in the town include **No. 28 South Street,** dated 1701, and the **Baptist chapel,** off New Street. Elsewhere the architecture is mostly Georgian and Victorian.

Like many inland towns whose economy was based on wool and agriculture, Great Torrington declined from the early 19th-century. In recent years, however, the arrival of new light industry has helped turn the situation around. Perhaps the best-known newcomer is **Dartington Glass** (now **Dartington Crystal**) in Town Park, a company which was established in the early 1970s as part of Dartington Hall Trust's rural development programme. Factory tours can made from Monday to Friday, and there is also a shop, restaurant and visitor centre which open seven days a week. Those interested in cultural events should pick up a programme from **the Plough Arts Centre** in Fore Street, a branch of the Beaford Centre.

The river Torridge around Great Torrington is crossed by a number of interesting old bridges. To the northwest, Rothern Bridge dates from the 15th-century and has been much-widened since; to the south, New Bridge was constructed in the 1840s to replace Taddiport Bridge of 150 years earlier.

The curious collection of buildings known as Town Mills can been seen nearby. They were built in the mid 19th-century by Lord Rolle, a local entrepreneur who was also responsible for constructing the five-mile-long canal which once connected Torrington to the navigable section of the Torridge above Bideford bridge.

At one point, a great stone aqueduct had to be built to carry the canal across the valley. This can still be seen today, although the waterway itself has long since disappeared (in a smart move, Lord Rolle sold it to a railway company in 1871).

If you have a soft spot for small steam trains, and who doesn't, you should not miss the **GREAT TORRINGTON RAILWAY** at Town Mills, next to Rosemoor RHS Garden on the southern outskirts of Torrington. Owned and run by Roy Roster, the miniature stream train takes passengers of all ages on a delightful trip up a beautiful little wooded valley boasting a rocky stream, wild flowers and many species of butterflies and birds. After the ride simply sit and enjoy the valley with a cup of tea or whatever.

Great Torrington Railway, Mill Lodge, Town Mills, Torrington,
Devon Tel: 01805 623328

On the A386, travelling out of Torrington towards Bideford, is the town's old railway station which has been converted into the **PUFFING BILLY** family pub and restaurant. Owned and run by Roger and Cheryl Grimshaw the pub reflects its railway past and many of the buildings' original features remain.

The Puffing Billy, Torrington Railway Station, Torrington, Devon
Tel: 01805 623050
There is also a large beer garden with amusements for the children.

This unusual pub also has an interesting and well thought out menu of typical and unusual bar food; the steaks and grills are well known local specialities of the house. As this is Devon there is also plenty of local cider on tap and for those wanting tea the traditional Devonshire version with lashings of clotted cream.

In the old station carpark on the Bideford Road in Torrington is **TORRINGTON CYCLE HIRE**. Right on the famous Tarka Trail, cycles for all shapes and sizes can be hired by the hour, day or week so the whole family can enjoy a leisurely ride through beautiful countryside.

Torrington Cycle Hire, Station Yard, Great Torrington, Devon
Tel: 01805 622633

On the road out of Torrington towards Taddiport is the **RIVER VIEW GUEST HOUSE**. Jessie Barnes' home is her pride and joy and she has worked hard to produce a real gem of a guest house where you can be sure of a warm welcome and a very happy stay.

Jessie's breakfasts are famous, she is a farmer's daughter after all, and evening meals are available by arrangement. This well travelled lady is also an expert on the Solomon Islands so you will also have a very interesting visit.

River View Guest House, 132 Mill Street, Great Torrington, North
Devon Tel: 01805 623195

On the outskirts of Great Torrington, in the heart of some wonderful scenic countryside and within easy reach of a wide range of good, secluded beaches, lies **GREENWAYS VALLEY**.

This delightful holiday park, owned and personally run by Margaret and Tony Woodman, offers self-catering holidays in a range of fully-equipped chalets and fixed, modern caravans. Touring caravans are also welcome, though the numbers are limited, on a level, grassy, well sheltered sun trap.

Apart from the delights of the surrounding area, Greenways has much to offer itself. There is an outdoor heated swimming pool, a tennis courts, valley shop with off-licence, children's playground and fully-equipped laundry. This is a beautiful spot in which to make your holiday base, the only building that can be seen from the site is the church steeple four miles away at Little Torrington.

Greenways Valley, Torrington, Devon Tel: 01805 622153

AROUND GREAT TORRINGTON

MONKLEIGH. Off the main road between Bideford and Torrington, near the village of Monkleigh, is the beautiful **DOWNES**, a Grade II listed late Georgian building. It is owned by Mr and Mrs Stanley-Baker who offer self-catering accommodation in one wing of the stone built house.

The couple are very keen gardeners and their 15 acre garden is a real picture with landscaped lawns, magnificent views and a wide variety of unusual trees and shrubs.

Little Downes, The Downes, Monkleigh, Near Bideford, Devon
Tel: 01805 622244

WEARE GIFFARD. Two miles downstream, the course of the old canal passes close to Weare Giffard (pronounced *Jiffard*), an attractive village focussed around a fine manor house built in the 15th-century by the Fortescue family. Although its outer walls were partially demolished during the English Civil War, the gatehouse, with its double diamond-braced doors, has survived. (Perhaps this is due to the presence of the fierce-looking lions which stand guard at the entrance.)

The main hall has a magnificent hammer-beam roof, and several of the other rooms are lined with Tudor and Jacobean oak panelling. The nearby parish church of the Holy Trinity has an impressive 14th-century west tower, the rest of the building having been completed in the 15th- and 16th-centuries.

The splendid roof in the nave is thought to have been constructed by the same team of craftspeople who were responsible for the hall. There are also some fine monuments to the Fortescue family, a series of bench ends carved with heraldic beasts, and a medieval mural depicting the martyrdom of St Edmund.

LANDCROSS, a little further downstream, lays claim to being the smallest parish in Devon. Its little squat church dates from the 15th-century, although the distinctive carved font is an early-Norman survivor. General Monck, one of Cromwell's most effective military commanders, was baptised here as an infant in 1608.

In the village lies the charming Victorian gentleman's country house, **BEACONSIDE COUNTRY HOUSE HOTEL** This is truly a family run hotel, the owners, John and Stella Tucker run the business with the help of their four daughters Lynette, Elaine, Celestine and Lucy.

Set amid 25 acres of natural broad leaf woodlands with nature trail and with a large formal garden this really is a secluded and peaceful spot for a holiday.

The hotel features many fine public rooms and includes a sheltered veranda on the two sides from which the gardens can be enjoyed whilst taking morning coffee or a traditional afternoon cream tea.

The hotel boasts nine comfortably furnished bedrooms which turn the house into a home rather than a hotel and also three self-catering cottage apartments, all with the latest in modern comforts. The extensive grounds were once part of a larger estate and, at the turn of the century, a Japanese Garden, with bamboo and other ornamental plants, was planted. These unusual gardens are being restored to their former glory and the Beaconside Nature Trail, beautifully laid out in the grounds, makes an interesting walk.

Beaconside Country House Hotel, Landcross, Near Bideford, Devon
Tel: 01237 477205

ATHERINGTON. The B3227 to the east of Great Torrington leads across some sharply-undulating countryside to Atherington, a striking hilltop village whose church, **St Mary's**, is a landmark for miles around. On a clear day, the churchyard offers a marvellous view across the surrounding countryside to Exmoor and the Bristol Channel.

The church interior contains a feature which is unique in Devon - a rood loft - the only one of hundreds in the county to survive. This alarmingly top-heavy gallery is believed to have been made by two Chittlehampton carvers in the 1530s and is an exceptional example of their art. Other features to look out for are the window in the north aisle which is entirely made of medieval glass, the carved and crocketed bench ends, and the imposing 14th-century effigies of Sir Ralph Willington and his wife, Lady Eleanor. The tomb of Sir John Basset of Umberleigh on the north side of the chancel shows the knight's twelve children arranged in groups beneath his two wives.

HIGH BICKINGTON, two miles to the south on the B3217, is another good example of the ancient hilltop settlements which characterise this remote and little-visited part of Devon. Standing at almost 600ft above sea level, the village commands excellent views in all directions. It also has a fine 16th-century inn, THE GEORGE which is set amongst a delightful group of thatched cottages.

The parish church dates from the 12th-century and is renowned for its exceptional collection of carved bench (or pew) ends, around seventy of them in all, most of which are either Gothic (characterised by fine tracery) or Renaissance (characterised by rounded figures) in origin. The more recent carving on the choir stalls depicts an appealing collection of animals and birds.

ROBOROUGH. The B3217 to the south of High Bickington connects a series of interesting villages. Roborough is a scattered community of old thatched cottages which stands in the lanes to the west of the main road.

DOLTON and DOWLAND, further south, are the unlikely hosts of an international arts festival. Each year in May and June, performers, artists and visitors come to the area from all over the world, a remarkable accomplishment for such a remote and sparsely-populated place. St Edmund's church in Dolton has an extraordinary font which is thought to have been fashioned from two large sections of a carved Saxon cross.

In the wall of the south aisle there is also a series of three memorial tablets by Laurence Whistler to the sculptor J H M Furse and his two wives, the first of which died in 1887 after only one year of marriage.

The arched arcade in the church of St Peter at Dowland was constructed of oak around 1500 and is one of only two such examples in the county. The nearby church house is an impressive thatched building with massive stone chimney stacks and unusual arched window frames.

BURRINGTON. Travel along the A377 and turn off at the Portsmouth Arms Sawmill, to lead you to BOUCHLAND FARM. Offering unusual facilities for this type of accommodation, it is a good touring base for several days stay. The menu of carefully prepared fresh food is nearer to restaurant standard. You are invited to roam around the farm and see the animals, there is a games room, lounge with television and late night drinks are available.

John and Eileen Chapple have created an ideal family holiday spot within their 140 acre working farm and guests can be assured of a safe, away from it all, carefree holiday in a happy family atmosphere.

Bouchland Farmhouse, Burrington, Umberleigh, Devon.
Tel: High Bickington 01769 560394

IDDESLEIGH, a mile-and-a-half further south, is a charming village of cob and thatch cottages which stands on a prominent position above the River Torridge. Its unspoiled 15th-century church contains some fine Jacobean wood-carving and a reclining effigy of a 13th-century knight. Jack Russell, the hunting parson of terrier fame, was rector here for seven years before moving on to Swimbridge, near Barnstaple.

BEAFORD. The return route to Great Torrington passes through Beaford, a pretty but unexceptional village were it not for the presence of **the Beaford Centre**. This imaginative institution was opened in the 1960s with the assistance of the Dartington Hall Trust and others, and provides a focus for arts and cultural activities throughout the whole of rural north Devon. The Centre is also the home of **the Beaford Archive**, a collection of over 4000 historic photographs chronicling the rural history of the area.

MERTON. Situated it this tiny hamlet near Okehampton is **BAROMETER WORLD**, the long established specialist centre for the restoration and manufacture of barometers run by Philip Collins.

In March 1995 the Banfield Family Collection of English Barometers was opened. This is the first barometer museum in the United Kingdom and the largest of its kind in the world. The permanent exhibition charts the history and progress of the domestic barometer from the late 1600s to the present day and includes traditional mercury and aneroid barometers, barographs and pocket barometers. This is no stuffy museum for eccentric enthusiasts. The displays are entertaining and informative. Children are particularly catered for with an activity sheet, colouring competition, children's books for sale, and hands-on pressure tester.

Barometer World, Quicksilver Barn, Merton, Okehampton, Devon
Tel: 01805 603443

ST GILES-IN-THE-WOOD. Three miles northwest of Beaford, and a mile to the north of the B3220, lies this charmingly-named village (sadly, now somewhat devoid of trees).

The nearby Stevenstone estate is the family seat of the Rolles, one of Devon's wealthiest and most influential old families, who built a succession of mansions on the site, the first Tudor brick, the second elegant 18th-century (some contemporary outbuildings remain), and the third Victorian mock-Gothic. The last-named was built in the 1870s by the Hon. Mark Rolle, an act which was described by the historian W G Hoskins as, 'the richest man in Devon building himself the ugliest house.'

The once-handsome village church suffered a similar fate at the hands of the Hon. Mark, having been designed, like the house, by Sir Charles Barry, architect of the Houses of Parliament.

A few early monumental brasses survived this Victorian mauling, including those of Alyanora Pollard, a proud 15th-century lady in a broad hat and free-flowing gown, and Johanna Risdon. The Risdons lived a mile away to the east at Winscott Barton, a handsome manor house with an 18th-century exterior and a charming dovecote in the grounds. Another member of the family, Tristram, lies buried in the church chancel; he is remembered for his epic *Survey of Devon*, a work which took him 25 years to complete, but sadly wasn't published in full until 171 years after his death. Between St Giles-in-the-Wood and Great Torrington lies the beautiful Royal Horticultural Society-owned garden, **Rosemoor**, home of the national collections of cornus and ilex. (Open daily, all year round.)

FRITHLESTOCK. A fine pub can be found just to the west of Torrington in the village of Frithlestock. **THE CLINTON ARMS** is well situated on the green and owner Robert Andrews runs a very friendly and comfortable establishment.

The Clinton Arms, Frithlestock, Torrington, Devon Tel: 01805 623279

His calm exterior belies the amount of work that goes into the smooth running of this traditional Devon inn. The fine old building provides excellent accommodation, outstanding food and fine ales, and all are welcome, including children.

You can relax in the pleasant walled orchard garden, an absolutely wonderful spot to let the cares of the day slip away. There is private fishing available on the River Torridge, which not only provides great sport for guests but also wonderful dishes to be enjoyed in the delightful dining room. **The Simon Gawesworth School of Fly Fishing** is run from the inn and Robert arranges fly fishing holidays from here. The menu is a delight to read with many exotic dishes including frogs legs, African desert locusts, wild boar, kangaroo and alligator. For the less adventurous more traditional, though no less mouthwatering, dishes also feature. Opposite the pub is the Church and the old Priory ruin, interesting features of the village and well worth a look.

To the west of Great Torrington, the valley of the upper Torridge forms a broad expanse of wood- and farmland which is seldom visited by the casual visitor.

Those with an inclination to explore this maze of narrow lanes will find themselves in one of the most unspoilt parts of rural England. This is a quiet upland area of cob and thatch cottages, picturesque greens, restored medieval churches and atmospheric inns.

SHEBBEAR, one of the more exceptional villages, lies seven miles southwest of Torrington in the centre of the triangle formed by the A386, A3072 and A388. The village is set around a square laid out in the Saxon manner with a church on one side and an 18th-century inn, **the Devil's Stone Hotel**, on another. The inn takes its name from the large and mysterious lump of rock which lies in a hollow just outside St Michael's churchyard.

This is of a type identical to the great 'blue' megaliths which were transported all the way from the Preseli Hills in Pembrokeshire to Stonehenge in Wiltshire during the late Neolithic Age. (It is likely that the church was built on a site whose religious significance predates Christianity.) According to local folklore, the boulder was placed here by the Devil who challenged the villagers to move it, promising that disaster would strike if they were unable to do so. Each year since then, a ceremony has taken place on November 5, a date which was established long before the Gunpowder Plot of 1605: after sounding a peal of bells, the bell-ringers come out of the church and set about the boulder with sticks and crowbars; then once they have successfully turned it over, they return in triumph to the bell tower to sound a second peal.

The present church is largely 14th-century, although it has a Norman south doorway carved with a row of weird and wonderful heads; it also has an elaborately carved Jacobean pulpit and some noteworthy tombs.

BRADWORTHY. A number of isolated settlements lie in the remote area to the west of the A388 Holsworthy to Bideford road. These include Bradworthy, an attractive village centred around a delightful open square which again is laid out to a Saxon plan. Although its origins date back to around 700 AD, the earliest buildings on the square are now no older than 18th-century.

The church of St John the Baptist is also thought to have Saxon foundations; a largely 16th-century building, it has a handsome Norman font, a collection of medieval Barnstaple tiles in distinctive floral designs, and an elaborately-carved Jacobean pulpit. Straddling the Cornish border three miles to the southwest lie the **Tamar Lakes**, a pair of artificial lakes which were constructed in the 1820s to supply water to the Bude canal. They now provide some excellent recreational facilities for those keen on watersports, fishing, bird-watching or walking.

An unusual visitor attraction lies to the east of Bradworthy on the West Putford road. **THE GNOME RESERVE AND WILD FLOWER GARDEN** is an eccentric collection of over 1000 hand-painted garden gnomes and pottery pixies which are set in an attractive woodland setting.

The gnomes demonstrate a variety of human occupations, including miners, musicians and carpenters, and the grounds also incorporate an area with over 250 labelled species of wild flowers, ferns, grasses and herbs. (Open daily, 10am to 6pm between mid-March and end-October.)

The Gnome Reserve and Wildflower Garden, W.Putford, Nr Bradworthy.
Tel/Fax: 01409 241435

WEST PUTFORD, two-and-a-half miles to the northeast of Bradworthy, was perhaps too remote to attract the attention of the Victorian church restorers. As a result, the cruciform **church of St Stephen** is an unspoilt gem which has hardly changed since the 14th-century. It has a whitewashed plasterwork interior, and the chancel floor is almost entirely covered in late-medieval Barnstaple tiles; there is also a simple Norman font and some fine 18th-century carved woodwork.

Near West Putford's tranquil tree-filled churchyard stands Churston House, a plain late-Elizabethan manor house with a distinctive weather vane perched precariously on top of a stone pinnacle.

Bideford and the Hartland Heritage Coast

BIDEFORD. This attractive coastal town lies at the northwestern end of an ancient track which once linked the north Devon coast to Crediton, at the time the most important religious centre in Devon until the see moved to Exeter in 1050.

The first bridge across the shallow neck of the Torridge estuary was constructed in the last quarter of the 13th-century to connect Bideford with its aptly-named suburb, East-the-Water. This impressive 650ft-long structure was built of massive oak lintels of varying length, creating a series of irregular arches of between 12 and 25 feet in width. The wooden bridge lasted for almost two centuries before it was replaced by one of stone around 1460; however, since the original bridge was used as scaffolding during the construction of its replacement (indeed, fragments of the original timbers were found lodged between the stone pillars when the medieval bridge was widened in the 1920s), the irregular pattern of arches has persisted to this day.

Bideford bridge is managed by an ancient corporation of trustees, or *feoffees*, whose income, derived from property in the town, not only pays for the upkeep of the bridge but also supports local good works.

A good place to stay if you wish to explore this town can be found near to the old bridge. The breakfasts served at **BURSCOTT HOUSE** are so impressive that we heard of them long before we met the lady who prepares them! Sheila Turner obviously believes that the first meal of the day is the most important one and her guests would no doubt agree.

Located in Buttgarden Street immediately behind the church tower near the old bridge, Burscott House is an elegant listed Georgian town house that dates back to 1729 when it was built for Sir John Gower. The house is superbly appointed and the view from the second floor sitting room is simply breathtaking. From this vantage point on a level with the top of the church tower, you can see Bideford's famous bridges, the splendid quayside and the whole of the lower town below you, all framed by the rolling hills of North Devon.

Burscott House, 3, Buttgarden Street, Bideford, N. Devon.
Tel: 01237 478262

This is a very special bed and breakfast establishment which can be best summed up by taking a glance at the comments in the Visitor's Book. 'Most elegant house, lovely landlady and splendid breakfasts' - succinctly put, and in our opinion, totally justified.

Despite its early origins, the medieval development of Bideford was overshadowed by Barnstaple, its rival seaport along the coast. With the coming of the Elizabethan era, however, an important trade in wool and raw materials began to develop, especially with the newly-established colonies of North America. Tobacco was imported in large quantities from Virginia and the Carolinas, and Bideford entered an era of prosperity which lasted for over two centuries until the combined effects of American Independence and the collapse of the domestic woollen industry brought about a decline.

Evidence of this golden age can still be seen in the opulent merchants' residences in Bridgeland Street, and most particularly in the Royal Hotel in East-the-Water, a former merchant's house with a pair of little-seen plasterwork ceilings which are perhaps the finest and most extravagant examples of their kind in Devon.

Many of the townsfolk busying themselves with their day to day life in Bideford, will many times have passed by or entered **THE ROYAL HOTEL** without any idea or knowledge of the long history of this fine building. Standing by the Quay in this historic port, the Royal Hotel combines four hundred years of history with every modern comfort.

When Bideford opened up new and thriving trade with North America in the seventeenth century, the town's new wealth was reflected in the fine buildings erected at that time. The Colonial House, as the Royal Hotel was then known, was built in 1688 with a plain exterior, whilst the inside was ornate with plaster ceilings constructed by Italian Artists, pine-panelled rooms, and featured a fine oak staircase.

After Bideford's overseas trade decreased in the eighteenth century, Colonial House was in decline and reached a low period. It passed through several ownership's; the house being used successively as Workhouse, Gaol and ordinary hotel. In 1889 after many mortgages and much restoration, the building re-opened as the Royal Hotel and gained the title of 'the most modern hotel in the West of England'. It had stabling with room for modern four-in-hand coaches and provided such luxuries as hot and cold baths. With the coming of the railways, the hotel enjoyed further success, and, having its own platform became the pride of the town.

The hotel suffered as the railways declined and from that period had a succession of owners and achieved little of note until the second world war when it was used as headquarters by distinguished officers of His Majesty's Forces in preparation for the attack on the Normandy Beaches in 1944. The hotel was purchased in 1968 by Mr. & Mrs. Brend, local business people, and became the first of the ten luxury hotels now owned by the Brend family. Nowadays, this fine family hotel, whose most famous guest Charles Kingsley penned most of Westward Ho!

here, has 30 spacious bedrooms all with en-suite bathroom and shower and a variety of accommodation. All have satellite television, phone, and expected luxuries, and are furnished in lovely matching Sanderson fabrics. A twenty-four hour room service provides for your every need including any meal brought directly to your room.

The hotel has an excellent reputation for firstclass cuisine offering a wide choice from bar lunch to a banquet. You can meet and relax in the lounge where coffee and afternoon tea is served, take an evening aperitif in the main bar, and dine in the elegant and luxurious restaurant. Whatever your need, the hotel management will take care to ensure your satisfaction, and if you ask, will provide a tour of the old 'cells' which remain in their original state and will show other historic items of interest.

Royal Hotel, Barnstaple Street, Bideford, Nth. Devon.
Tel: 01237 472005
Central information & reservations Tel: 01271 44496

Bideford Quay is another pleasing reminder of the town's maritime past; broad and tree-lined, it stands at the foot of the narrow maze of lanes which once formed the nucleus of the old seaport.

The rest of the town rises up on either side of the Torridge to reasonably pleasant effect, the dominant architecture being a mellow Victorian yellow brick.

The **RIVERSFORD HOTEL** is a family concern owned and managed by the Jarrad family for the last twenty five years.

The lovely Victorian house with its preserved features is set around three acres of gardens with magnificent views of the River Torridge. Arrangements can be made locally for water sports, fishing or golfing.

All of the thirteen bedrooms have full en-suite bath or shower rooms along with colour television, telephone and tea and coffee facilities. There are rooms to suit different occasions; for a touch of romance and old fashioned comfort select one of the four-poster suites.

In the restaurant, which overlooks the gardens and waterfront, you can enjoy English and Continental cuisine of a high standard together with speciality local seafood dishes. This peaceful and secluded setting is ideal for a relaxing and comfortable stay for all the family.

Riversford Hotel, Limers Lane, Bideford.
Tel: 01237 474239 & 470381

The parish church of St Mary was rebuilt in the 1860s on the site of its 14th-century predecessor. Fortunately, the tower and some of its finer internal features have survived, including the plain late-Norman font, the ornately-carved 16th-century screen in the tower arch, and the canopied tomb of Sir Thomas Grenville, a member of the great Bideford family who owned much of the town until the 18th-century.

A later Grenville, Sir Robert, was a great Elizabethan sea captain whose daring exploits on board *The Revenge* were the subject of Tennyson's poem of the same name. Bideford's most notable literary connection, however, is with Charles Kingsley whose swashbuckling heroes set out from here in *Westward Ho!*. 250,000 words long, the novel is claimed to have been written at various addresses in the town in only seven months. Kingsley's statue, looking suitably academic, can be seen on the Quay.

AROUND BIDEFORD

LITTLEHAM. THE CREALOCK ARMS in the village of Littleham, near Bideford, is named after a local family whose tombs can be seen in the parish church.

The Crealock Arms, Littleham, Bideford, Devon Tel: 01237 477065
Originally an old manor house, the inn is owned and run by George

and Margaret Honey and is very popular with the local inhabitants.

A lively place with fabulous views from well kept gardens, this is a lovely place to stop and enjoy a meal and a glass of real ale. Margaret, the cook of the couple, is famous for her excellent dishes, all freshly prepared.

The menu is interesting and daily specials are chalked up on a blackboard which offer the best of the season. George's brother, Donald, is the local butcher, so you can be sure that the meat is tip top quality as well.

BUCKLEIGH. From the A39 at the T junction past Bideford roundabout, take the B3236 signposted to Westwood Ho! Reaching the village of Buckleigh you can find the charming home of Nan and Clive Hunt known as **UPPER LODGE**. This stone built, former lodge and gatehouse, has been substantially extended to three times its original size and can be identified by its distinctive spire.

From the sun lounge and terrace there is a remarkable vista of the coastline of Bideford Bay and the Torridge Estuary taking in the Royal North Devon Golf Links and Northam Burrows Country Park.

Five minutes walk will take you to Kipling Tor and the North Devon Coastal Path whilst 50yds away is the school which Rudyard Kipling attended.

Inside the house, the original character has been retained, the oldest part being the staircase built from timbers and brass rails salvaged from shipwrecks on this notorious coast. With a maximum of just six guests, Clive and Nan will look after you very well, providing traditional English breakfast or special diets. No request is too much trouble and you may well decide to extend your stay here.

Upper Lodge, Bay View Road, Buckleigh, Near Bideford, N. Devon.
Tel: 01237 478239

WESTWARD HO! To mark the great success of the famous story, the Victorians renamed the site on the coast to the northwest of Bideford, 'Westward Ho!' Now a fine seaside resort of the classic British variety, it stands at one end of the only significant stretch of sandy beach between Bideford and the Cornish border.

This is a good place for a holiday, plenty of activities are available to participate in. If golfing is your game or walking is your aim, head for the **CULLODEN HOUSE HOTEL** where you will be rewarded with a choice of eight local golf courses and wonderful Coastal path or inland walks, also nature trails and the famous 'Tarka' Trail are close by.

Ian and Angela will welcome you to their lovely Victorian home in a most friendly manner where the spacious rooms and superb views overlooking Bideford Bay will be sure to impress. The four- course dinners and substantial breakfasts will keep you fortified during your stay and the well stocked bar will help you relax before retiring to your comfortable room.

Children are catered for and pets accommodated too. The hotel has AA and RAC two star category.

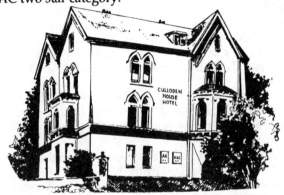

Culloden House Hotel, Fosketh Hill, Westward Ho! Devon.
Tel: 01237 479421

Relief from the bustle of the town can be found on the headland which projects into the mouth of the Taw-Torridge estuary to the north. An important natural habitat for several rare species of flora and fauna, **Northam Burrows** lies sheltered from the sea by an extraordinary naturally-occurring pebble ridge, 20ft high, 50ft wide and nearly two miles long.

Once an area of common grazing land, the local people using it were known as *potwallopers*. (The annual tradition of *potwalloping*, a task which involves returning stones from the pasture to the pebble ridge, still takes place on Whit Monday.) The headland is now an attractive country park with its own visitor centre which is set around a celebrated 18-hole golf course.

Known locally as the *Skern*, the area of salt marsh to the east is an important feeding ground for a wide variety of wading birds.

LUNDY. Throughout the year, the M S *Oldenburg* provides a regular boat service from Bideford Quay to the small island of Lundy, 25 miles away to the northwest.

A high granite plateau roughly three miles long and half-a-mile wide, the island rises sharply to a height of over 400ft and provides a safe haven for an abundance of bird, animal and plantlife. The island marks the entrance to the Bristol Channel and was given its name (which means *puffin island* in early Nordic) by Viking sailors who spotted large numbers of these comical sea birds nesting on the cliffs.

Lundy is still a breeding ground for great colonies of puffins, razorbills and guillemots, and it also provides a welcome stopping-off point for land-based birds migrating between northern and southern Europe.

For centuries Lundy was used as a base by pirates and smugglers who made a living attacking passing ships or raiding towns along the Devon and South Wales coasts.

Perhaps the most notorious of these was Sir William de Marisco, a buccaneer knight who terrorised the surrounding coastline before being caught and hanged in 1242. The castle at the southern end of the island still carries his family name; now ruined, it was built in the time of Henry III in an attempt to reassert the King's authority. The remains of an ancient chapel can also be made out near Beacon Hill, at 471ft, the highest point on the island.

This was also the site of the island's first lighthouse of 1819; however, because its light was often obscured by low cloud, two lower structures had to be built at the northern and southern ends of the island in 1897.

Lundy has changed hands many times throughout the centuries; however, in 1969 it was acquired by the National Trust is now administered and maintained on its behalf by the Landmark Trust. Present-day visitors landing in the shelter of Rat Island (so-called because it's thought to be one of the last refuges of the indigenous black rat) make a steep climb into a surprising little village containing a pub, a small hotel, a Victorian church and a handful of residential buildings. However, the true delight of the island lies beyond, in its wildlife, its views, its spectacular rugged coastline, and its splendid isolation.

WESTLEIGH. Back on the mainland, the area between Bideford and Barnstaple to the south of the Taw estuary contains a number of interesting settlements.

At Westleigh, two miles to the northeast of East-the-Water, the part-13th-century church of St Peter has a ceiled wagon roof with some fine gilt roof bosses, an excellent set of carved pew ends, and several memorials to the Clevland family, the former owners of nearby **TAPELEY PARK**.

This exceptional part-Queen Anne mansion occupies the site of a former Domesday manor house and was acquired and remodelled at the turn of the 20th-century by the Christie family, founders of the Glyndebourne Opera in Sussex. The house and its beautiful Italianate

Puffins at Lundy

gardens stand overlooking the confluence of the Taw and Torridge estuaries in one of the finest settings in the West Country. The grounds incorporate a superb terraced formal garden, extensive lawns, a walled kitchen garden, and a number of unusual romantic features, including an 18th-century shell house, ice house, ilex tunnel, and shepherd's shed. There is also a woodland walk leading to a series of lakes, and a number of more up-to-date attractions, including a pets' corner, tearoom and family of Berkshire pigs which are kept in the old kennels. (Gardens open daily except non-Bank Holiday Mondays, 10am to 5pm between Easter and 30 September.)

Tapeley Park, Westleigh Tel: 01271 42371

INSTOW Two miles to the north, this small resort sprawls northwards along the east bank of the Torridge estuary. The original part of the village lies half-a-mile inland from the quay and stares across at Appledore on the other side of the water.

Sit in the window of **THE QUAY INN** eating freshly caught fish from the village trawlers whilst you look at the many little boats bobbing about in the harbour, and you might almost feel yourself in a Mediterranean scene, but this is the harbour of Instow.

The Quay Inn, 1 Marine Parade, Instow, Nth. Devon. Tel: 01271 860665

The Quay Inn has a most delightful appearance with is attractive windows, arched entrance, white walls and terrace. Paul and Jacki extend a welcome to all and can happily accommodate the disabled, children and pets. A vast array of food is available daytime and evening, seven days a week, though fresh fish is the speciality of this traditional English pub. Have time to spend here.

Back at the foot of the hill, there are some fine early-Victorian villas on the seaward side of the old Bideford to Barnstaple railway, now part of the coastal footpath. Instow's parish church of St John the Baptist is a much-altered part-Norman structure which contains some interesting memorials and a rare set of medieval Barnstaple floor tiles.

Tapeley Park

Instow really is a charming little sea-side village and it is here you will find a hotel with more to offer than the norm. -THE ANCHORAGE HOTEL has an excellent location on the Quay overlooking the Estuary.

It has an instant appeal with its white frontage outlined in black and attractive Victorian verandas. The sixteen bedrooms are extremely well appointed, all are generous in size with facilities for all requirements, included in these are the often neglected disabled.

In addition there is a first class annexe immediately opposite the hotel for those seeking a little more privacy. Food - plenty of it, well prepared and beautifully presented must come high on most peoples requirements when considering a holiday.

Here all three are provided in abundance by Margaret Cann who is a fully qualified Cordon Bleu chef. The local fisherman present the best of their catch fresh each morning to the hotel, and fresh game is obtained from Dartmoor to meet Margaret's very high standards. Because of this no menu is printed, the extensive choices for each meal being decided according to the days fresh produce. Jon presents the evening menu with a prodigious feat of memory at each table showing the care and attention that both Margaret and Jon take over the food, to earn the high reputation the cuisine enjoys locally, as the Dining Room, where guests are requested not to smoke, is open to non- residents as well as hotel guests.

Both Margaret and her husband Jon are internationally known golfers and can offer specially packaged holidays for both the individual player and for larger parties. Eight top standard golf clubs are within easy distance of the hotel including the Royal North Devon Golf Club. The hotel will arrange for their guests to play at any of these clubs. Shooting is also available on a nearby estate, all arrangements can be made through the hotel.

Children are provided for, pets are acceptable by arrangement and there's plenty of off-street parking. Enjoy a sporting and gastronomic holiday here.

The Anchorage Hotel, The Quay, Instow, Nr. Bideford, Devon.
Tel: 01271 860655/860475. Fax: 01271 860767

TAWSTOCK , two miles upstream from Barnstaple, is a beautiful village which was once part of the estate belonging to the Earls of Bath.

Their original family mansion, Tawstock Court, was built in Tudor times, although sadly it burnt to the ground in 1787; only the Elizabethan gatehouse, dated 1574, remains.

By all accounts, its present-day namesake is a poor replacement, having been designed and built by Sir Bourchier Wrey, a family descendent, in curious neo-Gothic style at the turn of the 19th-century.

Much more impressive is Tawstock's church of St Peter: a delightful building, in a superb position, with an exceptional collection of internal features. It can be found to the east of the village on a gently-sloping hillside which falls away to the River Taw.

The Anchorage Hotel, Instow

The Tarka Trail

The novelist Henry Williamson wrote the enchanting tale of
' TARKA THE OTTER '

over 60 years ago . This ever popular book was set in a place called " The
Land Of Two Rivers ", inspired by the landscape of the Taw and Torridge
valleys and the adjoining coastline..

Today the Tarka Trail takes the traveller on a figure of eight route ,180
miles long, which passes through some spectacular scenery as it traces the
routes and places mentioned in the story.
There are many ways of exploring the trail, be it on foot by rail, by bike,
by car or by bus.

The railway covers some of the route , and the trail attracts people
time and time again as they explore different parts of it.
The trail is centred on Barnstaple where you will find a permanent
exhibition at the North Devon Museum. It is also here that the train runs
along the river to Exeter, a memorable day out in itself.

Alternatively you can enjoy the trail by bike and at West Yelland
Nr Barnstaple , **Yelland Cycle hire** has cycles for all the family and
your pet too!
For a modest charge you can have a fun day out. You can start directly
at the beginning of the trail just off the B3233. Open from Easter to October,
or by arrangement. Secure car parking.

Yelland Cycle Hire can be contacted on 01271 861424.

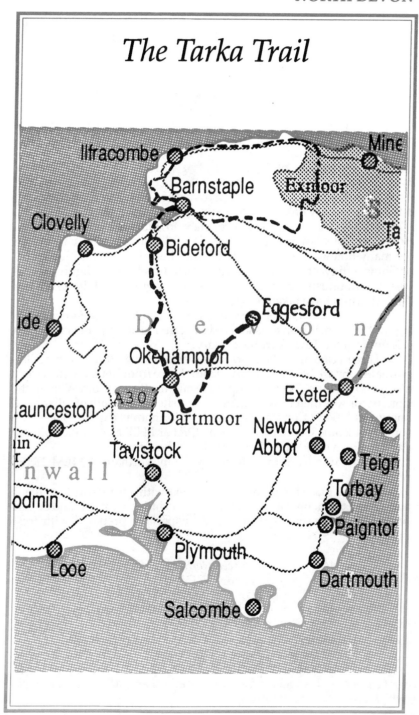

The Tarka Trail

This must be one of the finest minor ecclesiastical buildings in Devon; built to a cruciform plan around 1340, it has a rare central spire, a part-medieval stained-glass window, an open wagon roof in the south chancel, and some fine plaster ceilings in the transepts. The ornate sundial on the wall above the south door carries the sobering inscription, 'Watch and pray, Time slips away'; it was erected in 1757 by John Berry, the maker of the famous sundial at Marwood.

The church's finest feature, however, is its spectacular array of monuments. Widely considered to be one of the most outstanding collections in England, the building is literally crammed with ostentatious tombs to generations of Bourchiers, Fitzwarrens, Wreys and Earls of Bath. Too many to list here (Nikolaus Pevsner devotes several pages to them in *The Buildings Of England*), perhaps the oldest and most charming is the 14th-century oak effigy to an unknown lady of the parish.

HORWOOD. The return journey to Bideford passes close to Horwood, a pleasant village with a delightfully-situated church. Among the many noteworthy features to be found inside are the 15th-century reclining effigy of Emma Pollard; a striking alabaster figure, she is wearing an unusual mitred headdress and a great cloak in which her three children have taken refuge.

NORTHAM. On the opposite, western, side of Bideford, the village of Northam lies on the sheltered eastern side of the peninsula which juts out into the Taw-Torridge estuary.

Three years after the Norman invasion, King Harold's three illegitimate sons are believed to have landed here from Ireland with a force of over sixty ships. Their attempt to regain the throne from William the Conqueror was mercilessly put down at a site to the south of village still known as Bloody Corner. Present day Northam is a quiet, place with some handsome Georgian houses on Orchard Hill and a much-altered church which stands on a low cliff above the estuary.

Fifty yards from the village square in Northam is **MEMORIES** restaurant.

Just the place for an intimate evening with a truly excellent menu and where the main course price always includes a 'starter' and superb home- made dessert. (All to order as specially prepared with fresh produce.)

Memories, 8 Fore Street, Northam, Bideford, Nth. Devon.
Tel: 01237 473419

For centuries, the church tower in Northam has been a welcome landmark for mariners returning to their home ports; the churchyard below provides the resting place for generations of their kind.

Although the view from here is the outstanding, the church interior is disappointing, the only features of note being a 13th-century wagon roof carved with angels and a rare example of an early cello, or *bass viol*, which has sadly lost its strings.

APPLEDORE. One mile to the north, this delightful old seafaring community overlooks the treacherous bar at the mouth of the Taw estuary.

A surprisingly unspoilt village of narrow winding lanes and solid 18th- and 19th-century fisherman's cottages, this was the first place ships could tie up in safety and escape the storms of the open sea.

The streets of the old quarter are too narrow for cars, although not is seems for the occasional small fishing boat which is pulled up from the harbour and parked between the buildings. Appledore's nautical tradition has not been preserved merely for the benefit of the tourist: it is also the location of one the largest boat-building yards in the region. The yard is capable of constructing and refitting quite sizable ships, and has managed to survive in the face of harsh economic conditions.

It seems appropriate that the **NORTH DEVON MARITIME MUSEUM** should also be situated in this truly nautical setting.

Winner of the Museum of the Year Small Museum Award in 1994, this fascinating oasis in Odun Road is the place to visit for an insight into the history of North Devon's seafaring people.

Besides the wealth of nautical memorabilia, the museum also houses a unique collection of historical records and maps; visitors can also learn about the Great Panjandrum. (Open daily, 2pm to 5pm between Easter and 31 October; also Mondays to Fridays, 11am to 1pm between 1 May and 30 September.)

At the mouth of the River Taw lies **THE ROYAL GEORGE.** This historic inn and restaurant is dramatically positioned right on the sea wall and the high tide level is literally two feet from the dining tables!

The establishment is under the personal supervision of Barry Lewis, the owner, who himself has been a chef in Bermuda and Switzerland. As you might imagine, fresh fish, straight off the local boats, features prominently on the interesting menu and there are mouth-watering game dishes when in season. Accommodation is also available and like the restaurant this is very popular so pre-booking is necessary.

The Royal George, Irsha Street, Appledore, Devon Tel: 01237 474335

Close to the George is a real 'hidden gem'. Step through the unpretentious black door in Irsha Street, one of Appledore's quaintest narrow streets, and enter into the secret garden and surprising **WEST FARM**. Not for a moment would you expect such a find; here you have grace, elegance and peace. The 17th century farmhouse originally formed part of the hamlet of Irsha which was absorbed by Appledore about 200 years ago.

West Farm is the truly luxurious home of Gail Sparkes who is pleased to share it with a maximum of six guests.

Each of the three guest rooms has an elegant full bathroom en-suite, and all rooms are furnished to exceptionally high standards with antiques and choice pieces of furniture; flowers and plants providing the finishing touches.

The same high level of comfort is provided in the elegant lounge and the dining room. Traditional breakfasts are a delight, prepared with local specialities. Given a little notice, Gail will prepare a superb five course evening meal, home cooked and professionally presented. Highly commended by the Tourist Board, it is hard to imagine more idyllic surroundings.

West Farm, Irsha Street, Appledore, Bideford, Devon. Tel: 01237 425269

This beautiful unspoilt village is also renowned as a haven for artists and provides an appropriate environment for leading craftsmen to display their work. founded in 1991, **THE APPLEDORE CRAFTS COMPANY** is an exciting venture by a group of North Devon craftsmen.

It is co-operatively run, and offers an unusual range of high quality crafts - from dolls houses and ceramics to textiles and glass. It is also one of he very few galleries to feature an extensive collection of contemporary furniture, with four cabinetmakers represented.

The gallery stocks a wide range of work produced in the members' own studios and workshops, which are nearly all within a few miles of the gallery. Commissions are welcomed, whether inspired by something in the gallery or a customer's particular needs, and meetings with the craftsmen can easily be arranged.

It also stages a series of special exhibitions by other craftsmen from around the South West region throughout the year.

Open from 10am until 6pm seven days a week (Easter to October) and from 10am until 4pm Wednesday to Sunday through the winter, the shop is staffed by the craftsmen themselves.

The Appledore Crafts Company, 5 Bude Street, Appledore, Nth Devon Tel: 01237 423547

Appledore has a 'Hidden Place' that certainly shouldn't be missed if you are looking for a holiday base.

In 1993 Barbara Potter returned to the village of her childhood, Appledore, and fell in love with its special charm all over again. This tranquil and unspoilt fishing village, founded by Cistercian monks in the 14th century, with narrow streets and cobbled courtyards is now mostly a conservation area and an ideal place to spend a holiday. With this in mind, Barbara set up **POTTER ABOUT IN APPLEDORE**, a group of fisherman's cottages that she has lovingly restored and turned into holiday homes.

Of varying size the cottages are all furnished to a high standard and fitted with all the necessities to make them a real home from home. What makes the cottages special, however, is the attention to detail; a welcome basket containing amongst other things milk, bread, eggs, tea and coffee awaits each family and a first night cooked meal can also be ready and waiting for you. Self-catering has never been so easy!

Potter About in Appledore, 1 Retreat Place, Appledore, Devon Tel: 01237 474628

Also located in Appledore is a wonderful centre called **SKERN LODGE** which has been providing activity holidays since 1976.

Primarily aimed at school children providing enjoyment and learning through adventure, the centre also offers activity weekends (which are not training courses) for adults, which are either company based, or just for a group of friends out for fun.

Its an opportunity to do something completely different. Throughout the season open courses are planned for individual adults, children and families under close supervision and with a high standard of instruction. There is so much to enjoy at the centre for all age groups; Surfskiing, Windsurfing, Climbing, Cliff Rescue, Sailing, Abseiling, Off-road Cycling, Canoeing and Horse Riding to name just a few. Skern Lodge has a real commitment to providing a safe, happy learning environment, with staff trained to the highest level and using the best equipment. So if you or your family want adventure and enjoyment - look further into the activities of Skern Lodge.

Skern Lodge, Appledore, Bideford, Nth. Devon. Tel: 01237 475992

To the west of Bideford, the A39 passes close by a number of pleasant, but unexceptional, settlements, some of which are noted for their fine part-Norman churches; these include ABBOTSHAM and PARKHAM.

WOOLFADISWORTHY is correctly pronounced *Woolsery*, and it too has a fine part-Norman church.

Here, **LANE MILL FARM** offers bed and breakfast with a difference - a heated swimming pool, kept at 80 deg. The lovely white farmhouse and large garden is three quarters of a mile outside the village of Woolfardisworthy. . Leave the village with the school on your right and take the left fork outside the village.

The farmhouse has family and double bedrooms with en-suite shower facilities. Television can be enjoyed in the lounge/dining room, where, in the morning, you can enjoy a hearty breakfast.

Guests can visit the smaller farm animals and will doubtless enjoy the peacocks and golden pheasants to be seen strutting about the grounds. Additional accommodation is offered in two self-contained self-catering cottages converted from the village mill, in use until forty years ago.

The owner, Mrs Chris Leonard, assures you of a restful holiday in this beautiful countryside with its nearby coastal walks. In the village is the Manor House dating from 1122.

At one time it was an hotel but has recently undergone

refurbishment and now has a restaurant which has been created from the oldest part of the building.

Lane Mill Farm, Woolfardisworthy, Nr. Bideford, Nth. Devon.
Tel: 01237 431254

BUCK'S MILLS is a relatively unspoilt fishing village which lies at the bottom of a steep-sided combe on the coast near Woolfardisworthy. The remains of a substantial lime kiln can be seen near the seashore; this was used to convert limestone brought in by sea from South Wales into a fertiliser which would temper the acidity of the local soil.

CLOVELLY, three miles along the coast path to the west, has not escaped the attentions of the outside world. In fact, this acknowledged beauty spot has been extremely popular with visitors since Victorian times, thanks in part to Charles Dickens' mention of it in his story, *Message From The Sea*. As at Buck's Mills, the village is set in a deep combe which once carried a fast-flowing stream to the sea.

The cobbled main street is too narrow for cars and is so steeply-sloping that in places it has had to be stepped; on either side, it is lined with picturesque cottages which seem almost to be sitting on top of each another. Visitors have to leave their vehicles by the visitor centre at the top of the hill and walk down through the village to the delightful little fishing harbour at the bottom. (A four-wheel-drive vehicle is usually available for those requiring a lift back to the top, or for the more traditionally-minded, a donkey.)

Clovelly's stone pier was built in Elizabethan times by George Cary, a London lawyer and sheriff of Devon whose family owned the local manor for over 250 years. By so doing, he created the only safe mooring on the coast between Appledore and Boscastle in Cornwall.

When the last Cary died childless in 1724, Clovelly Court was acquired by Zachary Hamlyn who remodelled the building in a style which has since been described as 'Cockney Gothic'. Subsequent Hamlyns were responsible for building Hobby Drive, a scenic three-mile toll road which runs from the A39 near Buck's Cross to the main Clovelly car park, and for refurbishing many of the cottages in the village in romantic rustic style (The initials of Christine Hamlyn can be seen on many exterior walls).

The church of All Saints stands well above the cramped confines of the village, just below Clovelly Court. Although the building is largely 15th- and 16th-century, the south porch and font are Norman. Charles Kingsley's father was rector here in the early 19th-century, and it is believed the author of *Westward Ho!* based one of his main characters on William Carey, the Jacobean lord-of-the-manor whose initials are carved on the pulpit he donated to the parish; nearby stands a 18th-century hourglass.

Elsewhere in the church there are a number of interesting monuments, including ones to the Carys, the Hamlyns, and the First World War commander, General Asquith.

Given the reliability of British weather **THE MILKY WAY,** largely undercover, is one of the most enjoyable of Devon's attractions, offering a full day of entertainment for the whole family.

Conceived by the Stanbury family in 1984, The Milky Way has moved a long way from its' origins as one of the country's first farm parks and whilst it's informal, hands on approach and country roots have been maintained, the appeal has been widened with a range of activities and professional shows. Recent additions include a Sports Centre featuring archery tuition from two of the worlds top archers and Time Warp the south west's largest indoor adventure zone including a 25ft death slide the Black Hole.

The Milky Way, Downland Farm, Clovelly, Nth. Devon. Tel: 01237 431255
Fax: 01237 431735

THE NORTH DEVON BIRD OF PREY CENTRE run by dedicated enthusiast and entertainer Jonathan Marshall provides truly spectacular flying displays daily (except Saturdays), while the adjacent bird hospital gives an insight into Jonathan's work rescuing injured birds of prey.

All the animals are still there for the kids to cuddle and feed, whilst another recent addition, the dairy experience, tells the history of milk production with the help of life size animatronic farmer Joe and his cows.

The North Devon Sheepdog Training and Breeding Centre, The Countryside Collection, The Lynbarn ride-on Railway, laser target shooting, the list is endless. This is a great countryside experience where the Stanbury family will give you a warm Devon Welcome. Open: Daily. 1st. April to 31st. October 10.30am to 6pm. Please note - No Birds of prey flying displays on Saturdays and no Sheepdog demonstrations on Sundays.

Close to the junction of the B3237 and the A39, one mile to the south, can be seen the extensive series of concentric earthworks known as **Clovelly Dykes**. This massive Iron Age hill fortification covered almost 23 acres and once stood at the point where three ancient trackways converged.

As well as being used for defence, it is thought to have served as an early livestock enclosure and cattle market.

HARTLAND POINT. To the west of Clovelly, the North Devon coast path undulates sharply on its way to Hartland Point, the *Hercules Promontory* of ancient Roman geography which marks the place where the Bristol Channel becomes the Atlantic.

Here, the sea is characterised by a savage tidal race which rips along the coastline in all weathers. High above the waterline, a grim cliff rises untidily to nearly 350ft, and about half way up, a lighthouse built in 1874 warns vessels to stay clear. Lundy is only twelve miles away at this point, and a traditional folk rhyme uses the island as a means of forecasting the weather:

> Lundy high, sign of dry,
> Lundy plain, sign of rain,
> *Lundy low, sign of snow.*

To the east of Hartland Point, the shingle beach at Shipload Bay can be reached by descending over 250 steps, and to the west, the coastline turns sharply southwards and turns into the stark, yet spectacular, stretch known as the 'iron coast'.

Here, centuries of Atlantic storms have created one of the finest rocky seascapes in the West Country; infant coastal streams cascade abruptly to the shoreline, and strata of more resilient rock jut out into the sea like rows of jagged teeth.

Good views in all directions can be had from Damehole Point, and at Hartland Quay, the remains of a small harbour can be made out, the rest having long succumbed to the fury of the waves; further south, a series of attractive little waterfalls can be seen at Speke's Mill Mouth.

STOKE. One mile inland from Hartland Quay lies the hamlet of Stoke, the location of Hartland's unexpectedly grand parish church.

At 128ft, the 15th-century tower of St Nectan's is the tallest in North Devon; it can be seen from miles out at sea, and is the vestige of a collegiate church which was founded around 1050 by Gytha, the Saxon noblewoman and mother of King Harold, after her husband had been delivered safely from a shipwreck. Often referred to the 'cathedral of

North Devon', this massive buttressed structure is adorned with gargoyles, battlements and pinnacles, and can be climbed by arrangement with the vicar. Inside, St Nectan's, Stoke is equally impressive; its superb rood screen extends 48ft across the nave and is a wondrous example of the 15th-century wood-carver's art.

There is also an elegantly-carved Norman font, a pair of richly-painted wagon roofs, and a set of well-preserved 16th-century pew ends.

A good place to base a stay in the area can be found by taking the A39, aiming for Hartland and continuing through the village to Stoke. Turn left immediately on entering Stoke and continue on this road for a mile and a half following the Bude signs. Take the 4th turning right after leaving Stoke and you arrive at **GREENLAKE FARM** where Mrs Ann Herd has been providing bed and breakfast accommodation for many years. Greenlake is a 200 acre mixed farm set in unspoiled countryside where guests are welcome to watch the farm work in progress.

The two letting rooms are comfortably furnished and have tea and coffee making facilities. There is a television lounge and separate dining room. You are assured of a friendly welcome at Greenlake.

Within two miles of the farm are cliff top walks and secluded beaches to discover. Ideal for the children.

Greenlake Farm, Hartland, Nr. Bideford, Nth. Devon. Tel: 01237 441251

HARTLAND ABBEY is a 'must' to visit. It has been a family house since the 16th century though the Abbey was originally founded in 1157. It descended to the present day through a series of marriages and has never been sold and remains a lived-in home.

The house has fine architecture and is set amongst Shrub gardens of rhododendron, azalea and camellia. Peacocks and donkeys can be seen in the surrounding parkland. The Abbey retains a unique collection of documents dating from A.D. 1160; a Victorian and Edwardian photographic exhibition, pictures, furniture and porcelain.

A short distance on from Hartland you reach Devon's rugged coast and Hartland Quay, the site of an ancient and historic port. The old customs houses and warehouses have long since been converted into a family hotel. - The **HARTLAND QUAY HOTEL** is reached by a spectacular drive from the cliff-top and overlooks the Atlantic with its spectacular coastal scenery; a view seen from a number of the hotel's sixteen bedrooms.

Lunches and evening meals can be provided as can packed lunches. Children are welcome and can be served with High Tea in the early evening. The hotel also houses the **Hartland Quay and Coastal Museum**. The Quay beach is safe for bathing and a number of coves are within walking distance. Free parking for resident's cars.

Hartland Abbey, Nr. Bideford, North Devon. Tel: 01237 441264

Hartland Quay Hotel, Hartland, Nr. Bideford. North Devon. Tel: 01237 441218

Three miles from the village of Hartland and a mile from Hartland Point and Lighthouse is **WEST TITCHBERRY FARM**, a traditional stock farm of over 160 acres.

West Titchberry Farm, Hartland, Near Bideford, Devon
Tel: 01237 441287

Yvonne Heard, carrying on a family tradition of over 50 years, offers excellent bed and breakfast accommodation at the farmhouse with the addition of evening meal, if required.

This charming old Devonshire farmhouse is tastefully decorated

Hartland Abbey

and retains its original oak beams. The original open fireplaces have now been fitted with wood burning stoves. Yvonne, a trained cook, enjoys having guests around and from the selection of cereals in the dining room people staying a fortnight can have a different one each day.

As much home produced meat and fresh vegetables as possible are used in the evening meals and special diets can be catered for. A cottage on the farm has been renovated to offer self-catering accommodation all year round. This is a wonderful place to stay in the peace of the countryside. The Heritage Coastal Path crosses the farm.

HARTLAND. In the centre of the Hartland peninsula one-and-a-half miles to the west, the old market town of Hartland bravely resists the elements. An agricultural centre with a history dating back to the time of King Alfred, its market died away in the 1780s and today, its population is little more than half what it was in the mid-19th-century.

The town's former importance is reflected in the handsome shops and residential buildings which line the main street, and despite its decline, it remains a pleasant place to stop and take on provisions.

Situated on the main street of the old village of Hartland is the 16th century **ANCHOR INN.**

There has been a pub on this site since the 13th century and the inn was used as a billet for Royalist Cavalier soldiers during the Civil War.

Much of the pub's ancient character has been maintained by the owner Andrew Hodges; there is a warm and lively atmosphere and in winter roaring log fires. As well as running the pub, Andrew also runs the adjacent Plozevet restaurant, which is named after the village's twin town in France. The restaurant is very popular not only for its range and quality of food but also for its excellent value. This is a superb country inn, offering accommodation, with fine ale, food and glorious views over the Hartland Vale from its beer garden.

The Anchor Inn, Fore Street, Hartland, Devon Tel: 01237 441414

Situated close to the village of Hartland, **GOLDEN PARK FARM,** lies in a designated area of outstanding natural beauty with magnificent cliff scenery. This secluded farmhouse is owned by Lynda and Stephen

Yeomans and they offer excellent bed and breakfast accommodation in the farmhouse or there are two self-catering cottages on the farm.

The farmhouse really is a picture. Lynda has worked hard at furnishing the guest rooms in superb Victorian style including the fabulous patchwork quilts which she, herself, has made.

In the heart of some fantastic countryside and on the Hartland Path; Stephen can fill you in on all the local places of interest and will return walkers to the path after their stay.

A charming couple, who will make you feel one of the family, this is a delightful hidden place to stay.

Golden Park, Hartland, Near Bideford. Tel: 01237 441254

WELCOMBE. Four miles to the southwest, the parish church at Welcombe is also dedicated to St Nectan, the 6th-century Irish missionary who visited these remote shores in the 6th-century. An isolated community of low windswept buildings, this is also the location of a holy well from which the village takes its name. Welcombe lies within a mile of the Cornish border and seems to have more in common with its neighbours to the south and west, than those to the east.

The village inn has been converted from a former blacksmith's forge and the tiny church has a squat west tower; inside, however, it contains some exceptional features, including a plainly-carved Norman font, a restored Tudor pulpit, a Jacobean lectern, and an early-14th-century rood screen which, with the exception of its cornice, is considered to be oldest surviving example of its kind in Devon.

There are also a number of interesting memorial slabs which provide an insight into the social history of the parish. To the west, the road descends through the combe to **Welcombe Mouth**, an exposed bay with a small wave-cut beach and tall cliffs on either side. Like much of the 'iron coast', the rows of jagged rocks which project into the sea make this a treacherous place for bathers and mariners alike.

On that rather sombre note we must take our leave of this beautiful part of the country and make our way to the equally brooding atmosphere of Dartmoors

Clovelly

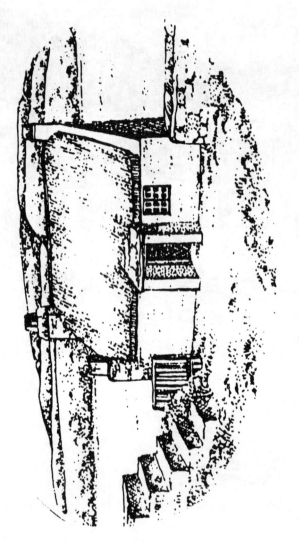

Cottage, Newton Abbot

CHAPTER FOUR

DARTMOOR

Postbridge

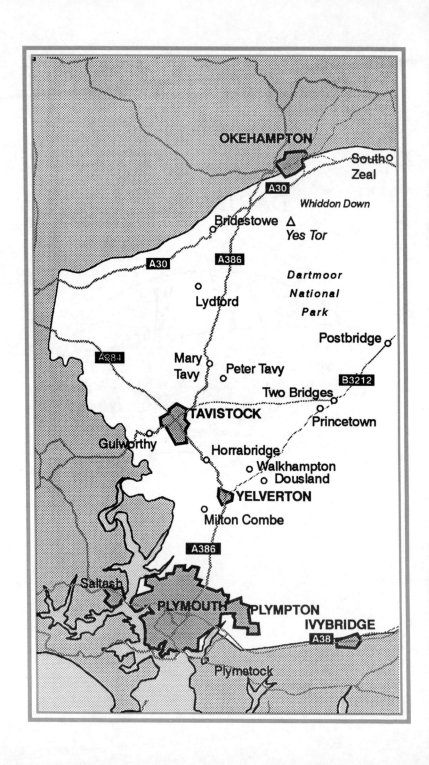

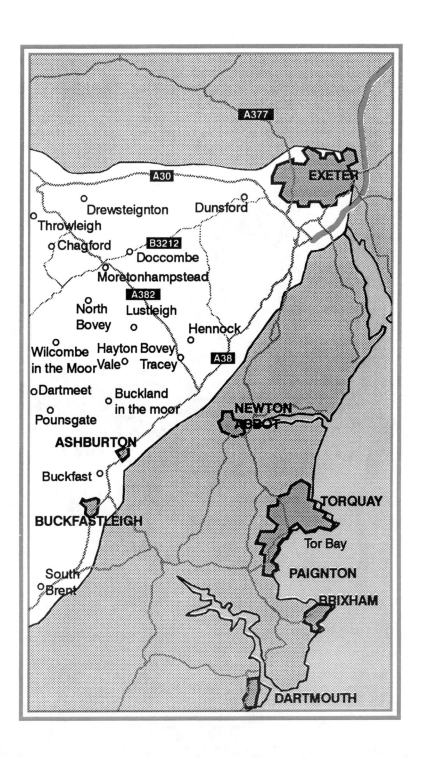

Bowerman's Nose, Manaton.

CHAPTER FOUR

DARTMOOR

Introduction to Dartmoor

DARTMOOR. Roughly 21 miles long and 15 miles wide, Dartmoor is a 300 square mile area of fissured volcanic tableland which was formed under immense pressure around 400 million years ago.

Geologists believe that at one time, the surface of the region may have stood at an altitude of 15,000ft above the Devonian Sea; however, countless centuries of erosion have reduced it to a plateau of whale-backed granite ridges with an average height of only 1200ft. The highest and most dramatic area of the moor lies to northwest on Okehampton Common where the connected summits of High Willhays and Yes Tor rise to a height 2038ft and 2029ft respectively.

Dartmoor's most characteristic topographical features are its *tors*, the great chunks of fragmented granite which have stood up to the centuries of ice, rain and wind better than the less-resistant rock which once surrounded them. There are around 200 of these distinctive outcrops on the moor, almost all of them in the northern two-thirds. Some of the most spectacular, and consequently most often visited, are Hay Tor and Hound Tor near Ilsington to the east, and Great Mis Tor and Vixen Tor near Merrivale to the west.

Perhaps the one with the most colourful history is Crocken Tor which stands in the centre of the moor just to the north of Two Bridges; for over 400 years, this was the meeting place of the ancient Stannary parliament, a body which existed until the 18th-century to regulate the affairs of, and settle disputes between, rival Dartmoor tinners.

After several million years, the moor has become littered with fragments of surface granite, or *moorstone*, which has been used for centuries by man as a building material, uncut since the Bronze Age and cut since Saxon times. Between Dartmoor's tors lie great tracts of deep blanket bog which are hazardous to humans and livestock alike.

Walkers should take great care to avoid the mires, and in particular the *featherbeds*, the deep pools of saturated moss which heave up and down when disturbed.

At the turn of the 20th-century, a network of safe pathways were negotiated between one area of firm ground and another, and many of the original granite marking posts, complete with their distinctive weathered brass plaques, can still still be seen today.

Thanks to a much milder climate than today, Dartmoor was relatively densely-populated during the late-Neolithic and Bronze Age periods. As the result, the moor is now strewn with an abundance of prehistoric remains.

Dozens of Bronze Age burial mounds have been identified, many of which have been found to contain stone caskets, or *keasts*, where the ashes or crouched bodies of ancient tribal leaders were placed.

The approaches to some of the more impressive burial cairns are marked by single, double or even triple rows of ancient standing stones; a single row of over 150 stones stretches to the east of Down Tor above Burrator reservoir, and there are triple rows on Holne Moor and at Yar Tor. On the northeastern side of the moor, good double rows can be seen above Chagford on Shovel Down, and one mile further north, the mysterious Scorhill Stone Circle is another indication of Bronze Age habitation.

Most impressive of all, however, is Grimspound, a complex settlement of around 25 dwellings dating from around 1000 BC which can be found on Hamel Down to the north Widecombe-in-the-Moor.

The desolate areas of blanket bog which lie in the middle of northern and southern Dartmoor give rise to dozens of small rivers, most of which run south to the English Channel, the Taw and the Okement being the only exceptions.

As Dartmoor's granite core gradually wore down, the action of these streams washed significant amounts of alluvial minerals into the valleys, and during the Middle Ages, these became a focus for large-scale open-cast tin-mining. (Although it's hard to imagine today, Dartmoor was once one of the largest tin-producing regions in the world.) Evidence of this early industrial activity can still be seen in the overgrown spoil heaps and ruined smelting, or *blowing*, houses which litter the valleys running off the high moor.

The medieval tinners were responsible for building Dartmoor's famous *clapper* bridges, a design where vertical stone pillars were linked together by great unmorticed slabs of granite.

The bridges were built to enable packhorses loaded with smelted tin to make their way in all weathers down to the four Stannary towns of Ashburton, Chagford, Tavistock and Plympton where the tin could be weighed and stamped. The most complete clapper bridge can be seen beside the B3212 at Postbridge, and there are also less-intact examples at Dartmeet and Bellever.

Mining activity on Dartmoor reached its peak in the 16th-century, by which time shaft mining had replaced open-cast working. The industry then began a long period of decline, interspersed with shorter spells of revival, until the last mine closed in the 1930s.

Today, the moor is dotted with disused mine workings, pump houses, smelting houses and other relics of its mining heritage, and there are also some impressive remains of the early mineral railways which were used to transport ore and other materials towards the coast. Perhaps the most interesting of these is the early-19th-century tramway on Haytor Down whose carriages ran along grooves cut into large granite blocks instead of along raised metal rails.

The only mineral extraction still to be carried out on Dartmoor is granite quarrying at Merrivale and china clay extraction at Lee Moor, just outside the National Park boundary to the southwest; here, centuries of excavation have created a strange bleached landscape of cone-shaped spoil heaps and murky water-filled settling tanks.

A number of artificial channels, or *leats*, were built to provide Dartmoor's mills and mine workings with a regular supply of water. The most spectacular of these is the thirty-mile-long Devonport leat which was built in the 1790s by French prisoners-of-war to supply the new naval dockyard at the mouth of the Tamar.

Although it now terminates after fifteen miles, the stretch from the weir on the West Dart above Two Bridges to Burrator reservoir near Yelverton provides some wonderful easy walking as the 6ft-wide channel contours through some of the loneliest areas of south Dartmoor.

(Because of the way the leat maintains its elevation in relation to the rivers in the valleys, it sometimes gives the uncanny impression of flowing uphill.) Although it can be followed for most of its length, the stretches where it flows through the grounds of Dartmoor prison and where it disappears into an underground tunnel for quarter-of-a-mile between the catchment areas of the West Dart and Meavy rivers, are out of bounds.

One of Dartmoor's distinctive medieval crosses can be seen approximately midway between the two tunnel entrances near the derelict farmhouse which takes its name.

Nun's Cross stands over seven feet high and is one of many such stone crosses which were erected to mark the ancient ecclesiastical trackways across the moor.

This one stands on the path from Buckfast Abbey on the Dart to Buckland Abbey on the Tavy and is believed to have been erected in the 12th- or 13th-century. The words 'Boc Lond' (Buckland) and 'Siward' can just be made out on either side, indicating that the cross also marked the boundary between the lands belonging to Buckland Abbey and the royal hunting forest belonging to the crown.

Dartmoor Forest subsequently passed to the Duchy of Cornwall whose current incumbent, Prince Charles, continues to own large tracts of the moor. Perhaps the most accessible medieval stone cross is Bennet's Cross which stands beside the old pilgrims' route from Moretonhampstead to Tavistock (now the B3212), two miles northeast of Postbridge.

Most of Dartmoor is contained within one immense parish and at one time, the only graveyard for the local inhabitants was located at Lydford on the northwestern edge of the moor. This meant that each time a parishioner died, the body had to be carried a distance of up to twelve miles to Lydford church along an ancient trackway known as the Lych Way, or 'Path of the Dead'. (The name is taken from the Old English word, *lich*, meaning corpse, as in *lychgate*, the covered gateway to a churchyard where coffins are placed prior to burial.)

Now an excellent way to see some of the remoter parts of west Dartmoor, the Lych Way begins at the old clapper bridge over the East Dart at Bellever and takes a route past Bellever youth hostel, Powder Mills Farm, Wistman's Wood, and a number of interesting prehistoric sites (sadly, certain sections can be waterlogged at times).

Powder Mills Farm takes its name from the old gunpowder works which was sited here during the 19th-century. A scattered collection of industrial buildings, it is said that the walls were built several feet thick in order to contain the blast should there ever be an explosion. Recently restored and opened to the public, the old Powder Mills are well worth visiting for anyone interested in industrial archeology.

The mysterious Wistman's Wood is an ancient copse of English oaks which is one of only three on the largely treeless Dartmoor. (It can also be reached along a muddy track from Two Bridges.)

The oaks have survived in this severe environment thanks to their sheltered position at the bottom of the steep-sided West Dart valley and to the fact that the seedlings have been able to take root in the scree, or *clitter*, which has spilled down from the surrounding tors.

They nevertheless have a strangely bedraggled and stunted appearance caused by the combined effects of high altitude, harsh climate and the invasion of moss and lichen.

Those interested in more demanding hikes across the moor might like the idea of hunting for one of Dartmoor's many 'letterboxes', small weatherproof boxes containing a rubber stamp and ink pad which are concealed at selected sites throughout the moor.

The idea began around 1850 when walkers reaching remote Cranmere Pool on the northern moor got into the habit of leaving a visiting card in a proscribed place.

Later, a visitors' book was left for walkers to sign, and it also became the practice to leave a self-addressed postcard which the next walker would take and post in their home town. It took over eighty years for a second letterbox to appear at Duck's Pool on the southern moor; however, in the last thirty years the practice has snowballed, and there are now estimated to be between three and four hundred of them scattered throughout the moor.

Those requiring further information should contact the Dartmoor Tourist Office at Princetown (0822) 890414.

Bovey Tracey and East Dartmoor

BOVEY TRACEY. A pleasant old market town with a population of around 4000, **Bovey Tracey** is a good base to explore the eastern fringes of Dartmoor. A settlement was founded at this ancient crossing point on the River Bovey in pre-Norman times, and by the 13th-century, it had grown sufficiently to be granted its own weekly market and an annual three-day festival.

The parish church of **St Thomas of Canterbury** stands high above the north bank of the river. An imposing building with a 14th-century tower, it contains a number of impressive internal features, most notably its eleven-bay rood screen of 1427 which was sympathetically restored by the Victorians.

Among the many striking roof bosses in the church, the central boss in the south porch showing the heads of the King, Queen, Bishop and Mayor is perhaps the finest. Other noteworthy features include a brass eagle lectern dating from the 15th-century, a set of three *misericords*, one depicting a fox making off with a duck, and a number of interesting monuments and tombs.

Several of the church's finest treasures were hidden away by the vicar following the execution of Charles I in 1649. He didn't return them until the Restoration, when he put up notices voicing his disapproval at the events of the previous eleven years (these in turn have become treasures in their own right).

For those preferring a central location for Bed and Breakfast accommodation, **'CLARENDON '**, on Newton Road in Bovey Tracey is a good choice. Many fabulous walks can be taken, literally from the front door of this gracious Victorian family home.

Newly redecorated throughout to a high standard, all bedrooms are large, comfortable and tastefully furnished having central heating, en-suite facilities, television and hot drink making facilities.

Full traditional English breakfast is served in the Victorian dining room which has an ornate ceiling and handsome marble fireplace. Special diets can be catered for with advance notice. No smoking please.

Clarendon, Newton Road, Bovey Tracey, Newton Abbot, Devon.
Tel: 01626 833357

At the foot of the town, the present-day bridge over the Bovey was built in 1643 and widened two centuries later. The water wheel on the nearby 'mill' was originally used to raise water to a tank in the little tower above. (This building has never in fact been a mill, rather it was the stables and domestics' quarters of nearby Riverside House.)

Across the river, St John's church near the old station was built in high Victorian mock-Gothic style in the 1850s; the striking mosaic reredos behind the altar is believed to be by Salviati.

Apart from the church house and one or two Tudor residences in Fore Street, the buildings in the centre of Bovey Tracey are largely Georgian and Victorian.

As its name suggests, **THE EDGEMOOR HOTEL** nestles comfortably on the Eastern boundary of Dartmoor, one of England's greatest National Parks.

Built in 1870, the Edgemoor has a romantic architectural style and is set in two acres of delightful gardens and mature trees. Only minutes from the A38 Exeter to Plymouth road, the hotel is located by following the sign to Hay Tor through Bovey Tracey.

Owned and managed by Rod and Pat Day, the hotel has recently been refurbished to a level compatible with the 1990's. Throughout the hotel, careful choice of fabrics and furnishings have created a feeling of elegance and charm in keeping with this Country House hotel; nowhere more so than in the en-suite bedrooms where luxury and comfort is provided in good measure with all possible comforts.

The restaurant offers sophisticated table d'hôte menus with English and French dishes in a candlelit atmosphere whilst the bar and lounge offer comfortable surroundings for lighter meals.

Children are catered for and can enjoy their own high tea menu. Guests with disabilities should discuss their needs in advance. Dogs respecting their surroundings are welcome too. A splendid hotel with every facility. 4-Crown ETB. Three Star AA & RAC.

The Edgemoor Hotel, Lowerdown Cross, Bovey Tracey, Devon
Tel: 01626 832466 Fax: 01626 834760

The headquarters of Dartmoor National Park are located at **Parke**, a handsome late-Georgian house standing beside the B3387 Widecombe road on the western edge of Bovey Tracey.

The house stands within beautiful 200-acre grounds which also contain an interesting privately-run rare breeds farm and a delightful nature trail which descends through the woods to the river.

Two miles to the west, the National Nature Reserve at **Yarner Wood** is a protected breeding ground for several uncommon species of birds. The road then continues northwestwards past the prominent viewpoint on Trendlebere Down before dropping down to the impressive, if well-visited, beauty spot of **Becka Falls**.

HENNOCK. To the northeast of Bovey Tracey is the village of **Hennock** where there is a lovely B & B.

Pretty as a picture with pink washed walls and part thatched roof, **FROST FARM** has lots of character, a lovely country garden to sit in and a relaxing homely atmosphere.

To find Frost farm, take the B3344 (from A38) in a southerly direction for 3/4 mile. Turn right towards **Chudleigh Knighton** and turn right in the centre of the village towards Bovey Tracey.

After 1/2 mile turn right at the crossroads and continue for one mile and you'll see the sign to the farm.

Ramble and amble around the farm and see the old cider orchards, woodlands and wildlife.

The three bedrooms are tastefully decorated with comfy chairs, TV. central heating, hot drink making facilities and wash basin if not en-suite. The less-abled will appreciate the ground floor bedroom with walk-in shower.

A three course evening meal is specially cooked to order and a hearty country breakfast awaits you in the morning.

Frost Farmhouse, Hennock, Nr. Bovey Tracey, Sth. Devon.
Tel: 01626 833266 Fax: 01626 835758

ILSINGTON. The lanes to the southwest of Bovey Tracey lead up to the ancient Dartmoor village of **Ilsington**.

Like so many rural communities in Devon, this was once an important centre of the wool industry.

The village is focused around a characteristic trio of late medieval buildings: church and church house and inn. **St Michael's church** is a part-14th-century cruciform building which was enlarged and re-roofed a century later.

Perhaps its most impressive feature is the mindboggling arrangement of arched beams and roof timbers which seem almost to hang in midair above the nave.

Other notable internal features include a set of medieval pew ends which are thought to be the only in Devon to be carved the distinctive 'poppy head' design, a mid-14th-century effigy of a woman in the north transept which sadly is now damaged, and an elaborately-carved 16th-century rood screen.

Entry to the churchyard is through an unusual lychgate with an upper storey; its single first-floor room once served as the village schoolroom. The present structure is relatively modern and was built to replace a medieval predecessor of similar design which is said to have collapsed when the gate below was slammed too enthusiastically.

The nearby church house was built in the 16th-century and has since been subdivided into residential dwellings known as St Michael's Cottages.

The sizable parish of Ilsington reaches up onto an area of eastern Dartmoor which incorporates the three well-known tors of Rippon, Saddle and Haytor Rocks. The last-named is perhaps most dramatic, especially when approached from the west along the B3387.

A twin granite mass 1491ft in height, Haytor's western side forms a near vertical face which provides a popular challenge for rock climbers. The spectacular view from the summit, which can also be approached from the more accessible eastern side, extends over Dartmoor to the west and across the Teign Valley to English Channel to the east.

In the early 19th-century, the shallow valley to the north of Haytor Rocks was the location of an important group of quarries which supplied the granite used to build London Bridge, the British Museum and several other prominent buildings.

Quarried stone was removed from the site along a unique tramway whose carriages ran along parallel grooves cut into large granite sleepers (most remarkable were the junction blocks with their primitive system of points). The original line ran for seven miles into the Teign valley and operated until the quarries were abandoned in the 1850s.

Powered by gravity on the way down, the carriages were pulled back to the top by teams of horses. The remains of this extraordinary track, now a protected monument, can be seen among the bracken on Haytor Down.

The B3387 to the west of Haytor Rocks passes to the north of Rippon

Buckland in the Moor

Tor before descending to

WIDECOMBE-IN-THE-MOOR. One of the most popular tourist destinations on Dartmoor. The village owes its huge popularity to two main things: its location in the lovely valley of the East Webburn river, and its connection with the old Devon folk song, *Widecombe Fair*.

The famous Fair continues to be held here on the second Tuesday in September and still retains something of its time-honoured atmosphere, despite the encroachment of modern tourist. In summer, coaches converge on the village from far and wide to spill their eager cargoes into the gift shops and tearooms that have grown up to satisfy their desire for a taste of 'genuine' Dartmoor.

Despite this regular saturation, Widecombe has managed to retain a measure of its original charm. At its centre is an attractive square with some exceptional old buildings, including **Glebe House**, a handsome 16th-century residence which has since been converted to a retail unit, and the **Church House**, an exceptional colonnaded building which has been a brewery and a schoolhouse in its time and is now under the ownership of the National Trust. (Open Tuesdays and Thursdays, 2pm to 5pm between June and mid-September; admission by donation).

Widecombe's **St Pancras church** is sometimes referred as 'the cathedral of the moor'. Its massive 100ft granite tower stands as a tribute to the 14th-century tinners who were responsible for its construction.

The rest of the building was enlarged in the 15th- and 16th-centuries and contains some fine internal features, including a rood screen, which has been reduced in height but still boasts over thirty paintings.

The homely verse on the panelling in the north aisle describes the disastrous events which befell the church on the afternoon of 21 October 1638 when a terrible bolt of lightning struck the tower and caused huge blocks of masonry to fall onto the church, killing four and injuring over sixty. (Local legend has it that Satan had been spotted earlier that day spitting fire and riding an ebony stallion across the moor from the adjoining parish.)

The network of lanes to the south of Widecombe lead to a number of interesting settlements.

BUCKLAND IN THE MOOR. Is a delightful village which stands in a romantic setting high above the river Dart.

The church of St Peter stands by a crossroads and is one of many on Dartmoor to be built of surface granite, or *moorstone*. Instead of numerals, the clock on the tower has twelve gilt letters which, when read from the 'nine', spell out the sentimental message, 'My Dear Mother'. Inside, there is a richly-carved Norman font, an impressive rood screen with a remarkable primitive painting on the reverse, and a rare timber staircase leading to the rood loft above.

The road to the south of the church drops dramatically to the Dart, and half-a-mile further on, there is a pleasant grassy meadow with a good natural bathing pool at **Spitchwick**.

A stiff climb from the road to the east of Buckland village leads up onto **Buckland Beacon**, another magnificent viewpoint and location of the famous Ten Commandments Stone, a lump of granite which was inscribed with the Ten Commandments during the 1920s. An inscription at the summit commemorates the chain of beacons which were lit to celebrate King George V's silver jubilee in 1935.

To the south of Buckland-in-the-Moor, the river Dart flows around a high wooded peninsula known as **Holne Chase**, at the tip of which stands a circular earthwork believed to date from the late Iron Age period.

The road from Ashburton to Dartmeet crosses the base of this peninsula, and at either side, an early 15th-century bridge crosses the river Dart: Holne Bridge to the east and New Bridge to the west.

The entrance to the popular **River Dart Country Park** lies a short distance downstream from Holne Bridge, and upstream, there are some delightful riverside walks through the National Trust-owned **Holne Woods.**

HOLNE. This village lies at the junction of half-a-dozen lanes and is a superb example of a moorland fringe settlement.

A pleasant mixture of cob and thatch and more recent residential buildings, the village has the quiet, genteel atmosphere of an English rural community whose modern function is part-agricultural, part-dormitory and part-haven for the retired.

The old church house is an attractive 16th-century building which has long functioned as the village pub; it is fittingly named the **Church House Inn.** Charles Kingsley, the author of the Victorian swashbuckler, *Westward Ho!*, was born in the vicarage when his father was curate here in 1819, although the family moved on only six weeks later.

The nearby church is a handsome early-14th-century building with a sturdy west tower which stands in a pleasant leafy churchyard; inside, there is a richly-carved 16th-century pulpit and a truncated rood screen of a similar age which incorporates some unusual primitive paintings.

BUCKFAST. The lane winding southeastwards from Holne passes close to the site of **Hembury Castle** before dropping steeply towards the ancient ecclesiastical centre of **Buckfast.**

An abbey was founded here around 1020 by the Saxon King Canute, then 130 years later, the monastic lands passed to the Cistercians whose sheep and cattle farms yielded great wealth.

After the Dissolution of the Monasteries in 1539, the abbey was completely demolished save for the great tithe barn and a section of the abbot's residence, and it wasn't until 1882 that the Benedictine order purchased the site and began a programme of rebuilding which culminated in 1938 with the completion of the church tower.

A curious, but not unpleasant, combination of mock-Norman and Early English styles, the abbey church was built by the monks themselves on the foundations of the 12th-century original, a truly remarkable achievement for such a small community.

Buckfast Abbey

The Chapel of the Blessed Sacrament was added in 1966 and today, **Buckfast Abbey** stands as a testimony to the devotion and enterprise of its resident brotherhood, whose activities now include the production of honey, mead and tonic wine.

Much of the rest of Buckfast is geared up to serving the thousands of visitors who come each year to visit the abbey and its subsidiaries; even the striking late-18th-century woollen mill by the river is now devoted to retailing rather than manufacture.

BUCKFASTLEIGH. Buckfast's more recent sister-village to the south originally lay in a clearing, or *lea*, in the dense woodland of the Dart valley. developed in late medieval times as a small market, wool and industrial centre, although its growth was impeded by its proximity to the more important Stannary town of Ashburton, three miles to the northeast.

The part-13th-century parish church of the **Holy Trinity** is set away from the centre in an impressive position on a limestone rock overlooking the Dart valley. Inside, there is an unusual red sandstone font demonstrating the cable carving which is so characteristic of the Norman period.

The ruins in the churchyard are of a chantry chapel dating from the 13th-century. Buckfastleigh once stood on the Totnes-Ashburton railway line, a branch which ran alongside the beautiful river Dart for most of its length. Although the line was closed in the 1960s, it was given a new lease of life in 1969 when the Dart Valley Railway Company purchased the track and began operating a steam train service between Buckfastleigh and Totnes.

The line has since changed its name to the South Devon Railway and operates regular services throughout the summer. With its carefully-chosen advertisements and railway memorabilia, Buckfastleigh station is now a delightful reminder of the heyday of the Great Western Railway. An interesting butterfly farm is also located on the same site. (Open daily between late-March and October.)

ASHBURTON. From Buckfastleigh, the route of the old A38 runs north to , an ancient market, wool and Stannary town which lies approximately midway between Exeter and Plymouth.

The town grew in importance during the second half of the 12th-century when local tin mining began on a serious scale; smelted tin was carried by packhorse from the blowing houses of Dartmoor to be weighed and stamped, before being transported on to the metalworkers of England and beyond.

Not long after, the expansion in demand for woollen cloth led to a further upturn in Ashburton's fortunes as a number of water-powered fulling mills were established beside the river Ashburn, the tributary of the Dart from which the town takes its name. (The *fulling* process increased the volume of woven cloth by a process of washing, beating and rolling.) Despite the eventual downturn in both these industries, Ashburton continued to prosper in the 18th-century thanks to its position on the busy northeast-southwest coaching route.

Many of its handsome inns, shops and residential buildings date from this period, a typical Ashburton town house being tall, narrow and hung with vertical slates.

Among the noteworthy buildings in the town is the **Old Grammar School** of 1314 which stands on a site behind the ruins of St Lawrence chapel. The parish church of **St Andrew** is an imposing part-14th-century structure with a pinnacled granite tower which is set back from the street on the western edge of the town centre.

The building has a beamed roof with some fine carved bosses. Restoration work on the chancel in 1840 revealed a number of small pottery urns which were found to contain the desiccated hearts of local men who had been killed while fighting on foreign soil.

From Ashburton, a number of attractive lanes lead northwards onto the moor.

To the south of Ashburton is the now very busy A38 and just across the main road are the signs to WOODLAND and DENBURY.

Situated between Dartmoor and the sea, **HIGHER MEAD FARM** offers truly outstanding holiday facilities for all the family.

Accommodation is available in a selection of recently built fully equipped two, three and four bedroom cottages, or superbly equipped static caravans. Once settled in, the youngsters will be eager to explore this working farm and its many animals.

This well organised farm offers evening farm walks during the main holiday season to feed the animals together. Take a stroll through the wood and look for wildlife or climb the nearby hill and admire the view over miles of countryside.

Pets are very welcome and have fields for exercise; they must otherwise be under control and on a lead. All can enjoy the games room and family bar. There is also a touring site with electric hook-ups and all facilities. RAC. AA. Tourist Board ////

Parkers Farm Holidays, Higher Mead Farm, Ashburton, Newton Abbot, South Devon.   Tel: 01364 652598   Fax: 01364 654004

EASTERN DARTMOOR.

Further north, the area of Dartmoor to the north of the B3387 Bovey Tracey to Widecombe road contains some exceptional natural features.

MANATON. Two of the most remarkable of these lie alongside the road approaching the village from the south.

Hound Tor is an impressive granite mass from which there is a spectacular view across the Teign valley to the sea. The remains of a medieval village which was first occupied during the Bronze Age lie below the rocks, 400 yards to the southeast.

Evidence of four Dartmoor longhouses can be made out here, along with a number of barns, outbuildings and field boundaries.

A deteriorating climate finally forced the villagers to abandon the settlement in the 14th-century. The mysterious rocky outcrop known as **Bowerman's Nose** stands on Hayne Down, three-quarters-of-a-mile to the north. This tall column of fragmented granite is said to resemble the head and upper body of a giant and has been compared to the sculptures on Easter Island.

According to folklore, Bowerman was a local huntsman who was warned against hunting on the Sabbath; one Sunday, he was out with his hounds as usual when the hare he was chasing changed into a witch and turned them all to stone (his petrified pack are said to lie scattered around the base of Hound Tor).

Manaton stands on a rise above the river Bovey, one mile to the northeast of Bowerman's Nose. An attractive collection of thatched stone cottages, the nucleus of the village lies to the north of the main road around an unusual wedge-shaped green.

One of the finest buildings is the church house, a substantial thatched granite structure which lies half inside the churchyard. The church itself is approached through a lychgate and features a curious two-storey porch and a wagon roof with some striking carved bosses. Perhaps its finest feature is an immense eleven-bay rood screen spanning the nave and both aisles which was painstakingly restored in the 1980s. The parish of Manaton also includes Grimspound, the enormous Bronze Age farming settlement on Hamel Down which is mentioned in the introduction to Dartmoor.

NORTH BOVEY. One of the most charming country pubs in Devon can be found in the village of **North Bovey**, a mile-and-a-half to the northwest of Manaton. **THE RING - O BELLS- INN** is one of many delightful old thatched buildings which stand on the gently-sloping village green.

A rare feature in this undulating part of the county, the green is lined with commemorative oaks and features a medieval cross, mounting block and village pump. The parish church of St John the Baptist contains some exceptional chancel roof bosses and a 15th-century rood screen which has undergone a number of unfortunate modifications. Half-a-mile to the northwest, **the Manor House** is a striking mock-Jacobean pile built in 1907 for the Viscount Hambleden.

This is undoubtedly one of the loveliest of Devon villages and it is here you will find the
BLACKALLER HOTEL AND RESTAURANT.
Surrounded by woods and moor, this delightful house is a sanctuary from modern day pressures.

On the banks of the Bovey river, this house was a woollen mill in the 17th century. The Blackaller prides itself on excellent home cooking using local produce whenever possible; fish from the rivers Teign and Dart, Devon lamb, and there are some interesting West Country local cheeses. The dining room and well stocked bar is open to non-residents.

The bedrooms are en-suite and have central heating. television and tea/coffee making facilities. Breakfast offers home produced honey, yoghurt and muesli. The hotel also has an attractive self-catering two bedroomed ground floor flat.

Blackaller Hotel & Restaurant, North Bovey, Devon. Tel: 01647 440322

LUSTLEIGH. A mile downstream from North Bovey lie the remains of an old clapper bridge, below which there is a delightful walk through **Lustleigh Cleave**, a wooded section of the steep-sided Bovey valley. At the far end, the village of **Lustleigh** stands on a small tributary between the Bovey and the A382 Bovey Tracey to Moretonhampstead road.

An established and well-visited beauty spot, the village contains some fine old thatched granite buildings, notably the Parsonage whose charm does much to offset the encroachment of gift shops and cafés. The part-13th-century church of St John the Baptist contains some early effigies and a richly-carved rood screen which is believed to date from the time of Mary Tudor.

Midway between Bovey Tracy and Moretonhampstead on the A382 is **EASTWREY BARTON HOTEL** owned and run by Victor and Susan Carn. Firm believers in maintaining creature comforts when away from home, they put good food high on the agenda.

The emphasis is on traditional English cooking with fresh local produce when in season, and there's a good selection of excellent wines to accompany the meal.

The hotel has six spacious, individually designed bedrooms with full en-suite bathrooms, colour television and hot drink facilities. Many outstanding beauty spots are within easy reach and the area is particularly suitable for keen walkers and birdwatchers. Dogs are allowed but not in public rooms and guests should note the no smoking request.

Eastwrey Barton Hotel, Lustleigh, South Devon. Tel: 01647 277338

MORETONHAMPSTEAD. From Lustleigh it is only a short distance to, **Moretonhampstead**, three-and-a-half miles to the northwest.

This pleasant former market town grew up around a busy road junction and has long been seen as a gateway to northeastern Dartmoor. The most noteworthy building in the town is the row of 17th-century almshouses which stand on the Exeter road; a striking arcade of sturdy granite columns, it is now owned by the National Trust, but is not open to visitors.

A giant elm known as the Dancing Tree once stood nearby; it was so-called because it supported a platform which served as the town's bandstand. The part-15th-century parish church of **St Andrew** has a massive granite tower but a disappointing interior. Perhaps most interesting are the tombstones in the south porch which commemorate a pair of French officers who died here while being held prisoner during the Napoleonic wars.

DOCCOMBE. Continuing through the Dartmoor National Park, two miles east of Moretonhampstead on the B3212 to Exeter, you arrive at the pretty hamlet of Doccombe where David and Gill Oakey provide bed and breakfast accommodation in their lovely granite farmhouse.

GREAT DOCCOMBE FARM is a 16th century Grade 11 listed Longhouse set in eight acres and is ideally situated for walking, touring or a spot of fishing. You might well want to talk 'gardens', since the owners are the 1995 winners of the top '*Moretonhampstead in Bloom*' award, or browse amid the owners collection of exotic Tropical Orchids.

The farmhouse is newly decorated and has two en-suite bedrooms with shower, TV, and tea/coffee facilities; the smells of a traditional farmhouse breakfast, cooking, will draw you from your comfortable slumbers.

Great Doccombe Farm, Doccombe, Moretonhampstead, Devon.
Tel: 01647 440694

CHAGFORD. This former market and Stannary town lies in the lanes to the west of the A382, four miles to the northwest of Moretonhampstead. An ancient settlement centred around a pretty market square, it lies in a beautiful setting between the pleasant wooded valley of the North Teign river and stark grandeur of the high moor. Chagford reached the peak of its importance in late-medieval times when the combined activities of tin-mining and woollen cloth manufacture generated considerable wealth for the people of the parish. The long and gradual decline since then has left the town with a delightful blend of 16th- to 19th-century vernacular buildings.

One of the finest is **THE THREE CROWNS INN,** an early-Tudor granite structure which was formerly the house of the Guild of St Katherine.

The market square in front was the scene of a skirmish during the English Civil War during which Sidney Godolphin, a young Royalist officer, was killed. Chagford's parish **Church of St Michael** stands between picturesque thatched cottages and merchants' houses.

A handsome 15th-century granite building, it contains some striking monuments to local merchants and land-owning families.

Whether you are nature lovers, hikers, country sports fanatics or artists. **THORNWORTHY HOUSE** is an ideal retreat where you can succumb to the calls of Dartmoor.

Hugh and Sheila Rogers invite you to stay in their superb Devonshire home high up on Dartmoor where you can walk straight out onto the High Moor and admire the most lovely panoramic views. The house is easily accessible being just three miles from Chagford and offers many areas of interest for guests all year round.

A haven for artists and birdwatchers; nearby there is fishing at Fernworthy reservoir, riding, golf and National Trust gardens.

The two and a half acre garden includes a stream, small pond, tennis court and croquet lawn. For accommodation, a choice is offered - your stay can be in the house where you will enjoy tastefully furnished bedrooms with armchairs, double glazing and a warm and comfortable atmosphere.

Alternatively, two very well equipped and comfortable cottages offer privacy and independence for up to six people whilst enjoying the facilities of the house. You are assured of a splendid holiday with complete relaxation. House 2-Crown Commended & cottages 4 & 3 Key Commended by ETB. AA selected.

Thornworthy House, Chagford, Devon.   Telephone & Fax: 01647 433297

To the west of Chagford, an exceptionally pleasant lane leads upstream from Chagford Bridge through the wooded valley of North Teign river. (For a mile-and-a-half of its length, this lane is joined by the **Two Moors Way**, the long-distance footpath which runs all the way from Ivybridge on the southern edge of Dartmoor to the Bristol Channel coast.)

A rock beside the river known as the Holed Stone contains a large round cavity, and according to local folklore, those climbing through it without falling in the water will be cured of anything from rheumatism to infertility.

The land to the south of here rises abruptly towards Kestor Rock and Shovel Down, the sites of impressive Bronze Age settlements and field systems, and a little further on, the imposing Long Stone stands at the point where the parishes of Gidleigh and Chagford end and Duchy of Cornwall land begins.

GIDLEIGH. After crossing the North Teign to the west of Chagford, the lanes lead northwestwards to the scattered community of **Gidleigh**, a remote and beautiful spot which is the unlikely location of a ruined Norman keep. **Gidleigh Castle** was built around 1300 by the Norman lord of Okehampton on the site of a Saxon manor house belonging to Gytha, the mother of King Harold.

All that remains today is a square tower containing a single room above and a cellar below. Better preserved is the nearby parish church of the Holy Trinity, a plain granite building dating from the early 16th-century which has a low rood screen, a part-medieval stained-glass window, and an unusual chest tomb by the north door.

The area of Dartmoor lying immediately to the west of the village contains some interesting prehistoric remains, including the stone circles on Buttern Hill and Scorhill Down.

THROWLEIGH. A mile-and-a-half to the north, Gidleigh's sister village is another peaceful settlement of thatched moorstone buildings, the most notable of which are the church house and the Barton. The part-15th-century parish **Church of St Mary the Virgin** has an unusual priest's door and a pulpit made from the remains of the dismantled rood screen. Despite being dated 1663, the sundial over the south porch was only erected here in 1914 after it was discovered in a junk shop in Exeter.

Close to this picturesque and ancient village near Okehampton, lies **WELL FARM**, the home of Bryan and Sheelagh Knox. The farmhouse, a Grade II listed medieval Dartmoor longhouse with later additions dating from the 16th and 17th centuries, is set in beautiful and peaceful surroundings.

This is a working, family run dairy and outdoor pig farm, with peacocks, ornamental pheasants and free range poultry. There are two bedrooms in the main house and a ground floor annexe flat, suitable for disabled visitors, available to guests.

All visitors are treated as one of the family and, though a car is useful when exploring the surrounding area, guests can also be met at Exeter station by arrangement.

Fresh local produce and cider are served with the daily three course evening meal, taken en famille, and the hearty farmhouse breakfast sets up even the flagging holiday maker ready for another days enjoyment. This is a wonderful, relaxed and friendly establishment which makes a perfect base for any holiday in the magnificent Devonshire countryside.

Well Farm, Throwleigh, Near Okehampton, Devon Tel: 01647 231394

In the village of Whiddon Down, just off the Throwleigh road, lies **Tor View**, the delightful, modern home of Liz Knox, her husband and their young family.

This is a very pleasant establishment, offering bed and breakfast accommodation in two rooms with full English breakfast. Liz has three children of her own and all visiting children will be made most welcome and find plenty of toys and a large garden in which to play.

This well furnished, attractive home is ideally situated right on the edge of Dartmoor and there are some magnificent views of the moorland from the house. A very cheerful and friendly couple, Liz and her husband will ensure that your stay is as near perfect as possible.

Tor View, Whiddon Down, Okehampton, Devon Tel: 01647 231447

Within the Dartmoor National Park, on the edge of this pretty village is the ideal holiday location of **THROWLEIGH MANOR,** offering excellent bed and breakfast accommodation and three cosy self-catering cottages. This impressive country house was built in the 1850's and offers a wealth of oak panelling and ornate plaster ceilings.

It stands in a peaceful parkland setting of twelve acres, including extensive formal gardens with panoramic views across the rolling hills and meadows of Dartmoor.

Nature lovers can wander down the woodland walk through a

colourful mass of Springtime flowers to the picturesque lake and watch the abundant wildlife. Children will enjoy feeding the doves and ducks and can let off steam in the play area.

There is a large, well equipped games-room, croquet lawn and an outdoor solar heated swimming-pool to keep the teenagers and adults happy, with golf, riding, fishing, sailing and other amusements nearby.

Take a leisurely drive around the spectacular National Park or aim for the beaches and entertainment of the English Riviera at Torquay. The facilities of Throwleigh Manor are superb, with three attractive and comfortable en-suite rooms, whilst the cottages offer well-equipped and private accommodation. Very happy and friendly atmosphere.

Throwleigh Manor, Throwleigh, Devon. Tel: 01647 231630

SOUTH ZEAL. Just inside the National Park boundary at the foot of Cawsand Hill and on the main road between Whiddon Down and Okehampton, on Ramsley Common near the village of South Zeal, lies **THE POLTIMORE HOTEL.**

Originally built as three thatched cottages, the hotel offers the best in country hotel accommodation and dining. Owned and run by Peter Wilkens, this excellent, quiet, homely establishment also has three charming, self-catering cottages for hire.

Poltimore, Ramsley, South Zeal, Okehampton, Devon Tel: 01837 840209

FAIRHAVEN FARM. Is a traditional mixed farm situated in the village of Gooseford near Okehampton and within the Dartmoor National Park. Owned and run by April Scott this traditional farmhouse offers bed and breakfast accommodation in a choice of three rooms.

A friendly and relaxed atmosphere puts all visitors at their ease immediately and able to enjoy the fantastic views of rolling Devonshire countryside that make this a much enjoyed holiday destination.

As this is a working farm, you can expect a delicious and filling breakfast and evening meals can be arranged. There is also plenty to entertain children who are most welcome and are encouraged to play in the large farmhouse gardens. A super place to use as a base for your family holiday.

Fairhaven Farm, Gooseford, Whiddon Down, Okehampton, Devon
Tel: 01647 231261

One of the most striking Bronze Age burial tombs in Devon can be found in a field at Shilstone, two miles due east of Throwleigh (although further by road). **Spinster's Rock Burial Chamber** is megalithic dolmen consisting of three uprights and a 12ft horizontal capstone which was lifted back to its proper place in 1862.

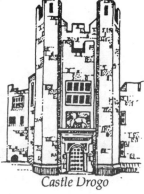

Castle Drogo

Crossing the A382 towards the next landmark at Castle Drogo the road passes through **Sandy Park** where there is a marvellous hotel called **THE GREAT TREE HOTEL**

Strictly speaking, there is no actual 'Great Tree' to which the name of the hotel applies, but perhaps you could choose your own favourite from the many beautiful examples surrounding it. With Dartmoor on its doorstep, it is conveniently situated about two miles off the A30 near Chagford.

The hotel is set amidst the splendour of the Dartmoor National Park looking out across wooded valleys and the eighteen acres of its own grounds.

The originality of this hotel owes much to it previous use as a hunting lodge, and the 'Colonial' character is evident in such features as the ornate fireplace in the entrance hall and the beautifully carved wooden stairway.

Most of the hotel bedrooms are at ground level, overlooking the gardens and very comfortably furnished. Each room is centrally heated, has private bathroom and to help you relax after your busy day, television and hot drinks facilities are provided.

The elegant restaurant will certainly tempt you with its five-course table d'hôte menu offering local lamb and game, fresh fish from Brixham, and other fine dishes carefully prepared by Luigi, with fresh vegetables grown in the hotel gardens.

Special diets will willingly be prepared given a little advance warning. Realistically priced prestigious wines encourage guests to experiment and expand their knowledge of the many fine wines available. Less-able guests will find the hotel convenient and helpful with their needs, while children and well-trained pets are made very welcome.

The hotel will assist with bookings for golf, fishing and offshore sailing and other sports. This is a wonderful walking area and a great base for those exploring the popular towns of Brixham, Dartmouth, Polperro and Salcombe.

Great Tree Hotel, Sandy Park, Nr. Chagford, Devon. Tel: 01647 432491

A short distance further east, the National Trust-owned *Castle Drogo* stands on a rocky promontory, 900ft above the gorge of the River Teign. Designed by Sir Edwin Lutyens and constructed between 1911 and 1930, this extraordinary granite-built mansion was the last great country house of its kind to be built in England.

It was made for Julius Drewe, the founder of the Home and Colonial Stores, who sold the company and retired at the age of 33.

Of particular interest are the 1930s bathroom and kitchen fittings, and the internal telephone system, one of the first to be installed in Britain. The house stands at the foot of a modest but beautifully-landscaped garden which make up part of the 600-acre estate. (Open daily except Fridays, 11am to 5.30pm between end-March and end-October.)

A delightful circular walk can be joined at Castle Drogo. It starts as the 'Hunter's Path' and traverses the northern edge of the Teign gorge before dropping down through the woods to **Fingle Bridge**, a Tudor packhorse bridge and well-known beauty spot which lies at the foot of Prestonbury Iron Age hill fort, one mile to the east.

The return route, the 'Fisherman's Path', follows the riverbank and passes a tranquil trout pool and iron footbridge before climbing back to the top.

DREWSTEIGNTON. One mile to the northeast of Castle Drogo, this charming village contains some lovely old thatched cottages, a part-15th-century church and a handsome church house, all built of granite.

However, its most legendary establishment is **THE DREWE ARMS** the village pub known locally as Aunt Mabel's, which has been run by the same landlady for over half a century.

More like a living room than a pub, Mrs Mudge goes off to a back room to fetch the orders of cider and beer (don't expect to find cocktails here). Local folk singers and musicians often congregate in the bar on Saturday evenings.

DUNSFORD. Five miles to the east, **Dunsford** stands in a delightful setting on a rise above the lower end of the Teign gorge.

The village contains some fine thatched cottages and is dominated by the castellated tower of **St Mary's Church**. This striking building dates from the 14th-century and contains some impressive Jacobean wood-carving and a number of tombs to the Fulfords, a long-established military family with a history dating back the time of Richard the Lionheart.

Their family seat, Great Fulford, is an imposing early-Tudor mansion lying two-and-a-half miles to the northwest. Built around a courtyard, it was remodelled externally at the turn of the 19th-century; it is also believed to be the last house in England to have retained a resident jester.

THE ROYAL OAK, is a traditional Victorian village inn, situated in the centre of this beautiful thatched village which is only ten minutes drive from Exeter.

The en-suite bedrooms are in a 300 year old converted granite and cob barn to the rear of the inn.

Each room has its own front door which opens onto an attractive walled courtyard.

The Royal Oak is well known for its selection of unusual and varied home-made meals which include vegetarian dishes, served seven days a week. The cosy bar offers Real ales from all over Britain, English fruit wines, and real Devon cider. Ask about special 'off peak' breaks.

The Royal Oak, Bridge Street, Dunsford, Nr. Exeter. Devon.
Tel: 01647 252256

STEPS BRIDGE. A couple of pleasant woodland walks begin at **Steps Bridge,** half-a-mile to the southwest of Dunsford.

On the south bank, a nature trail runs through the beautiful National Trust-owned Bridford Wood, and to the north, a footpath follows the river all the way to Clifford Bridge. Both are particularly rewarding in spring when wild daffodils line the woodland floor.

Set in the beautiful Teign Valley on the road between Exeter and Moretonhampstead is the delightful **STEPS BRIDGE INN.**

This bar and restaurant, with also offers bed and breakfast

accommodation, is surrounded by meadows and woods and overlooks the River Teign.

An excellent centre for exploring Dartmoor and for walking, fishing and sightseeing this is certainly not a place to be missed for a quiet get away from it all break. There are plenty of tasty home cooked dishes to choose from on the menu and Barbara Woodford, the owner, is always ready to extended a warm welcome to visitors.

Steps Bridge Inn, Dunsford, Exeter Tel: 01647 252313

To the south of Bridford Wood, the ground rises steeply towards **Heltor Rock**, a striking granite outcrop which offers a magnificent view of the Teign Gorge and the northeastern fringe of Dartmoor.

BRIDFORD. Two miles due south of Dunsford, the former mining and quarrying village of **Bridford** lies in the hills above the western bank of the Teign.

The past prosperity of the parish is reflected in its church, a gem of a building dating from the early 14th-century which has one of the finest interiors of any small church in Devon. Its crowing glory is its intricately-carved rood screen, an exceptional example of its kind which ranks alongside those at Cullompton or Chulmleigh.

Dating from around 1530, it was donated by Walter Southcote, the incumbent rector at the time, whose initials appear above the door to the rood-loft. The screen retains its unusual pale pigmentation and features several carved emblems, including the double rose of Henry VIII and the pomegranate of Katherine of Aragon.

(The church at Bridford is one four exceptional churches in this beautiful section of the Teign valley, the others being at Doddiscombsleigh, Dunchideock and Higher Ashton.)

DODDISCOMBSLEIGH. To the east of Bridford, the road falls steeply into the valley of the Teign to meet with the B3193. After crossing the river, the lanes rise eastwards towards **Doddiscombsleigh**, an attractive village with a good pub, **THE NOBODY INN** and a 15th-century church which contains one of the finest concentrations of medieval stained-glass in the region.

With the exception of Exeter Cathedral, the five 15th-century windows in the north aisle are the only such examples in Devon to remain virtually intact; the east window, with its bold depiction of the seven sacraments, is perhaps the finest.

DUNCHIDEOCK. To the east, the road rises onto the crest of Haldon ridge before falling abruptly towards **Dunchideock**, a delightfully-situated settlement which hugs the sides of a steeply-sloping combe.

At the northern end stands a farm, a converted rectory and the modest red sandstone church of St Michael.

Although heavily restored by the Victorians, the church contains an unusual number of noteworthy internal features, including a medieval font, a set of carved pew ends, and a richly-carved rood screen which at one point makes a surprising diversion around three sides of an octagonal roof column.

Among the monuments is one to Major-General Stringer Lawrence of the Indian Army who left a legacy of £50,000 to his lifelong friend, Sir Robert Palk, when he died in 1775.

Palk proceeded to build himself a mansion, Haldon House, half-a-mile to the south, along with a folly in memory of this benefactor.

Known locally as Haldon Belvedere or Lawrence Castle, this tall triangular structure stands on the summit of Haldon ridge and can be seen for miles around.

Another impressive fortification, an Iron Age hill fort known as Cotley Castle, lies further along the ridge, two-and-a-half miles to the north. According to local folklore, Dunchideock House stands above a legendary treacle mine, and once every two years, the owner agrees to take visitors on a guided tour of the cellars in return for a small fee (which presumably goes to pay for the treacle).

HIGHER ASHTON.   From Lawrence Castle, a lane drops down to **Higher Ashton**, a mile-and-a-half to the southwest. This scattered village of thatched stone cottages contains the fourth of the celebrated Teign valley churches, a charming 15th-century building which has managed to retain most of its period fittings. The church is known for the exceptional panel paintings on its rood and parclose screens, with those on the reverse of the rood screen being considered among the finest in Devon.

It also contains a number of other fine internal features, including a square-sided Jacobean pulpit with a canopy and hour-glass stand, and an unusual painted monument to two 17th-century members of the Chudleigh family. The return journey to Bovey Tracey passes close to the country park at Canonteign Falls and the pleasant Teign valley villages of Trusham and Hennock.

Tavistock and West Dartmoor

TAVISTOCK. Is a busy little town on the western edge of Dartmoor which continues to fulfil its traditional function as a market serving a large area of rural west Devon.

With a population of around 10,000, it lies far enough from Plymouth to have its own, very different character. Although there is some evidence of Celtic and Saxon occupation, the town is essentially the creation of two institutions: Tavistock Abbey, which was founded in 974 and dominated the town until the Dissolution of the Monasteries in 1539, and the Russell family, who as the dukes and earls of Bedford, owned much of the town until 1911.

Tavistock's Benedictine abbey, one of the grandest in the West Country, had its own great church, cloisters and chapter house, and was surrounded by immense castellated wall. The abbey soon gave rise to a prosperous lay community, which in 1105 was granted permission to hold a weekly market and an annual three-day fair. (The weekly market still takes place on Fridays in the pannier market, and the annual event has evolved into the Goose Fair, a wonderful traditional street fair which is held on the second Wednesday in October.) When the expansion in tin mining on Dartmoor began at the end of the 12th-century, Tavistock was established as a Stannary town.

For centuries, smelted ore was transported here by packhorse from all over the western sector of the moor to be weighed and stamped, before being sold on to merchants and metalworkers. The effects of the industry's eventual decline was tempered by the expansion of the woollen industry in the 16th-century when Tavistock became known for the manufacture of fine serge.

When this also began to decline during the 1700s, the discovery of rich deposits of copper around Mary Tavy heralded a new era of prosperity which lasted until the end of the 19th-century.

The Russell family acquired the site and estates of Tavistock abbey following the Dissolution, and after demolishing most of the abbey buildings (a few disconnected remains can still be seen between the river and the parish church), they created the town plan we see today. During the 1840s, the Dukes of Bedford, as they subsequently became, built the Guildhall and several other civic buildings, remodelled the Bedford Hotel, and constructed the model estate of artisans' cottages on the western side of town.

Indeed, one of the few public buildings in Tavistock to escape the paternalistic influence of the Bedfords was the parish church of St Eustace whose patrons were the wealthy clothiers of the 14th- and 15th-centuries.

Tavistock .The Town Hall and Abbey Gatehouse

A convenient place to stay in the town is **EKO BRAE**, a lovely grade 11 listed Georgian Villa with light colour-washed walls and striking white paintwork overlooking this historic market town.

Its lawns and gardens gently slope away from the terrace with a colourful display of flowers, giving this bed and breakfast accommodation a most welcoming appearance.

The standard continues inside where furnishings and appointments are of a high standard. Bev Rodgers and her family take good care of their guests and do their utmost to please.

Some bedrooms have en-suite bathrooms, and television and hot drink facilities are provided in all rooms. A hearty breakfast is offered so you won't leave Eko Brae hungry. Children are welcome, as are pets by prior arrangement. Good parking. ETB. 2-Crown Commended.

Eko Brae, 4 Bedford Villas, Spring Hill, Tavistock, Devon.
Tel: 01822 614028

The Bedford family's great wealth was based on their ownership of land once belonging to Tavistock abbey which was found to contain rich deposits of copper ore.

Around Tavistock.

By the early 19th-century, the output from the mines around Mary Tavy, three miles to the north, justified the building of a canal to Morwellham Quay, the highest navigable point on the Tamar for seagoing vessels.

Completed in 1817, much of the work on this ambitious project was carried out by French prisoners-of-war who were given the task of driving a mile-and-a-half-long tunnel through Morwell Down. The tunnel emerged on a hillside, 240ft above the Tamar and from here, loaded barges were attached to trolleys and sent down a perilous inclined plane to the quay.

Although it is hard to imagine it today, for over half a century, the quiet riverside settlement of **Morwellham Quay** was one of the busiest copper ports in the world. (During the mid-1850s, Devon and Cornwall were responsible for producing over 50% of the world's copper.)

Huge quantities of ore were transported to the quay, both from the mines around Mary Tavy and from the vast Devon Great Consols mine a few miles upriver at Blanchdown, to be loaded onto seagoing vessels weighing up to 300 tons. However, by the turn of the 20th-century, the copper had been mined out; the barges stopped arriving and Morwellham was simply abandoned.

For over seventy years, the inclined plane, quays, arsenic furnaces and miners' cottages were allowed to decay, until in the 1970s, a process of restoration was begun which was to turn Morwellham Quay into a flourishing outdoor museum of industrial archeology.

Visitors can now explore the old port workings, view the giant water wheel which was removed from a mine on Dartmoor, and ride along an underground tramway into a disused copper mine.

There is also an inn, a collection of workshops staffed by craftspeople in period costumes, and an indoor museum which provides a fascinating insight into life in a 19th-century industrial port.

(Open daily, all year round.)

GULWORTHY. Two miles out from Tavistock on the Gunnislake / Liskeard road, you will arrive at Gulworthy where the charming stone built **RUBBYTOWN FARM** is situated.

This splendid 17th century character farmhouse nestles in 260 acres of woodland and pasture abounding with wildlife.

It is the home of Mary and Roger Steer who provide very comfortable bed and breakfast accommodation.

The period furnishings are a delight and all the bedrooms have four-poster beds. Rooms have either en-suite or private bathrooms and tea/coffee making facilities are provided. Mary and Roger assure guests of every comfort and those requiring dinner should ask about Mary's speciality - stuffed country chicken. Lots of free brochures available on places to visit. ETB. 2-Crown Highly Commended.

Rubbytown Farm, Gulworthy, Nr. Tavistock, Devon. Tel: 01822 832493

MARY TAVY. To the north of Tavistock, the A386 Okehampton road passes through the old mining community of **Mary Tavy**.

From the end of the 18th- to the middle of the 19th-century, the village was surrounded by a group of around forty copper mines which included the Bedfords' famous Devon Friendship Mine, a vast concern which occupied a thirty-acre site to east of the main road.

The only indication of the network of shafts and tunnels which once riddled this now peaceful area of west Dartmoor is a collection of abandoned leats, ruined mine buildings and overgrown spoil heaps which are gradually returning to the landscape.

One of the most distinctive landmarks in Devon can be found in the lanes, two miles to the west of Mary Tavy.

If you are looking for a holiday base on the west side of Dartmoor or a place to break your journey close to the main A386 route, then make for **MOORLAND HALL** at Mary Tavy, a delightful Victorian country house secluded in five acres of gardens and paddocks.

The hotel is personally managed by the resident proprietors Gill and Andrew Farr.

The main lounge has a large open fireplace with roaring log fire for chilly evenings and a well stocked cocktail bar. A separate quiet lounge offers a good selection of books.

Bedrooms are comfortably furnished and thoughtfully decorated. They are well appointed with electric blankets, television, tea and coffee making facilities and all have private bathrooms.

Two of the spacious rooms have four-poster beds.

As holders of an AA rosette for cuisine, you will find a well balanced choice of menu, carefully produced using fresh local produce whenever possible. A warm welcome awaits.

3-Crown Commended by ETB. 2 Star AA.

Moorland Hall, Brentor Road, Mary Tavy, Tavistock,. Devon.
Tel: 01822 810466

St Michael's Church, Brentor.

PETER TAVY. Close by here is the village of Peter Tavy where it can be said of Julie Bellamy at **HARRAGROVE FARM**, 'if you don't feel at home here, you won't feel at home anywhere'!

Julie loves people and will really make you feel welcome when you call for bed and breakfast.

She has a very nice house in a peaceful location on the edge of Peter Tavy village, off the A386 near Tavistock.

There are no worries with children, there's plenty of open space and it's very safe with room to run.

There are three letting bedrooms and the atmosphere is very warm and friendly. Julie cooks one of those 'last all day' breakfasts. Its a good touring location for Dartmoor and surrounds.

Harragrove Farm, Peter Tavy, Nr. Tavistock, Devon. Tel: 01822 810409

The church of St Michael at **Brentor** stands on top of a 1100ft volcanic plug which rears up from the surrounding farmland in dramatic fashion.

Built around 1140 by Robert Giffard at his own expense, the church has since been added to in the 13th- and 14th-centuries; it is constructed of stone quarried from the rock beneath it and is surrounded by a steep churchyard which contains a surprising number of graves given its precarious, seemingly soil-less position.

Though sometimes lost in low cloud, on a clear day the scramble to the summit is rewarded with magnificent views of Dartmoor, Bodmin moor and the sea at Plymouth Sound.

LYDFORD. Three-and-a-half miles to the northeast, was once one of the most important towns in Saxon Devon.

It was one of only four boroughs to be established by King Alfred to defend the county against the Vikings, and for several decades it had its own mint. In the 11th-century, the Normans built a fortification and earthwork rampart here which was superseded a century later by the present **Lydford Castle**, an austere stone keep which for several hundred years served the independent tin-miners of Dartmoor as a court and prison.

The justice which was meted out by the Stannary Parliament was notoriously harsh, and there are several accounts of offenders having been hanged without a trial. (Castle open daily, all year round.) The parish of Lydford includes a vast area of central Dartmoor and for many centuries, dead bodies were brought down from the moor along the ancient Lych Way for burial in to St Petrock's churchyard.

The church itself is an unassuming building which was constructed of granite in the 15th-century and extended in the 1890s. Near the south entrance, the grave of local man, George Routleigh is inscribed with an epitaph which is liberally sprinkled with amusing puns relating to his occupation as a watchmaker.

Standing outside **THE DARTMOOR INN**, one can imagine how bleak and frightening it must have been in olden days, to be lost, or of necessity travelling this part of the moor on horseback on a cold black night; what a welcome sight and refuge this inn would be.

In the 16th century the inn served packhorse drivers and mounted travellers and was used as a halfway point for those of Drake's captains and seamen living in north Devon.

These days, Paul and Margaret extend a warm welcome to all travellers and it is certainly a great place to stop and take some welcome refreshment.

The character remains here, with open fires, low ceilings and panelled walls. Open throughout the year, Paul and Margaret serve up home-cooked traditional pub food and real ales. Well worth a visit.

The Dartmoor Inn, Lydford, Okehampton, Devon. Tel: 01822 820221

To the southwest of the village, the valley of the River Lyd narrows suddenly to form **Lydford Gorge**, one of Devon's most spectacular natural attractions.

Now under the ownership of the National Trust, visitors can descend on foot into the beautiful steep-sided ravine with its canopy of oak and broad-leaved trees.

The mile-long walk beside the rushing waters of the Lyd takes in a series of dramatic cascades, rapids and potholes, including the famous

Devil's Cauldron. At its southern end, a tributary drops 90ft into the gorge to form the spectacular White Lady Waterfall. During the 17th-century, Lydford Gorge was used as a lair by the Gubbins family, a notorious band of robbers and highwaymen who attacked travellers journeying between Okehampton, Launceston and Tavistock. (Open daily, 10am to 5.30pm between end-March and end-October; restricted opening during winter.)

BRIDESTOWE. This small settlement can be found north of Lydford between the A386 and A30. Just across the A386 is a good place for a picnic or short walk at Meldon Reservoir. This is also a good area for birdwatching.

A warm welcome awaits all visitors to **WEEK FARM**, a listed 17th century Farmhouse just off the A30 near the village.

Set in the rolling Devonshire countryside, the farmhouse has been in the Hockridge family for three generations and the present inhabitants, John and Margaret Hockridge, have been welcoming guests for nearly 30 years.

There are five en- suite bedrooms, all beautifully decorated and furnished, in the farmhouse, and self - catering units in very attractive barn conversions. The delicious, traditional farmhouse breakfast sets up the guests for a busy day exploring the many local attractions, including the wonderful scenery of the moorland, leafy lanes and hedgerows, and numerous picturesque towns and villages of the area.

After a busy day's sightseeing, relax in a heated outdoor swimming pool before the delicious homecooked four course evening meal, with mouthwatering desserts served with lashings of Devonshire clotted cream.

Though unlicensed, guests are encouraged to bring their own wine which Margaret is delighted to serve with your meal. A very comfortable and relaxing place to stay that guests return to again and again.

Week Farm, Bridestowe, Okehampton. Tel: 01837 861221

A number of interesting old houses can be found in the villages and countryside to the west of Lydford. The Tudor home of the Reverend

Sabine Baring-Gould, theologian, novelist and author of *Onward Christian Soldiers*, can be seen at **Lewtrenchard**; it is now a hotel. Half-a-mile away to the east, an attractive Tudor residence known as the Dower House stands with some farm buildings beside a menhir.

MILTON ABBOT. Overlooking the Tamar one mile to the southwest of , **Endsleigh House** is a country mansion standing within outstanding landscaped grounds which incorporate an arboretum, a rock garden and a shell house.

Referred to somewhat perversely as a 'cottage', this romantic pile was built around 1810 for the Dowager Duchess of Bedford to a design by Sir Jeffrey Wyatville; it is set in a 'natural' garden laid out by Humphry Repton which once required a staff of over thirty gardeners to maintain it. (Open Saturdays and Sundays, 12 noon to 4pm between 1 April and 30 September; admission by donation.)

PRINCETOWN. To the east of Tavistock, the B3357 rises sharply towards **Princetown**, a desolate exposed village standing 1400ft above sea level which is the location of the famous **Dartmoor Prison.**

This part of the moor is noted for its atrocious climate and receives an annual rainfall of between 80 and 100 inches, around four times the average for the South East of England.

That a settlement should be located here at all was the brainchild of one man, Sir Thomas Tyrwhitt, the owner of a local granite quarry who proposed that a special prison should be built to house the thousands of troops captured during the Napoleonic wars who were becoming too numerous and unruly for the prison ships moored in Plymouth Sound.

The work was completed in 1809 by the prisoners themselves using granite which presumably came from Sir Thomas's quarries (they also built the nearby church of St Mary, the main east-west road across the moor, and the famous Devonport leat which supplied water to the dockyard).

At one time, the prison held as many as 9000 French, and later American, inmates, but by 1816, the ending of hostilities stemmed the flow of prisoners-of-war and the building closed. Princetown virtually collapsed as a result, and it wasn't until 1823 that its granite quarries were given new life with the completion of the horse-drawn Dartmoor Railway. The prison was eventually reopened for long-serving non-military convicts in 1850, and since then, it has been considerably enlarged and updated; it continues to be used for medium-security inmates to this day. The old prison officers' club has recently been refurbished as an information centre for the Dartmoor National Park.

TWO BRIDGES.

This settlement lies at the junction of the two roads which cut through the heart of Dartmoor where the B3357 and the B3212 meet. In spite of its remote location there are places to visit and stay amongst spectacular scenery.

It would take several pages to outline the history of Prynse Hall as it was originally called, one of the ancient tenements of Dartmoor where property has stood on the site since 1443. **THE PRINCE HALL HOTEL** is a unique, intimate country house hotel retaining the atmosphere of a family home. The hotel enjoys spectacular views set in the very heart of Dartmoor National Park and offers guests comfort, hospitality and good food in tranquil and secluded surroundings. This most comfortable of hotels has welcoming log fires, lots of books and interesting pictures and paintings all complimenting the country house atmosphere.

The eight spacious bedrooms are, quite simply - lovely. All en-suite and with every amenity. If there is anything you have forgotten, then the hotel will provide it if at all possible.

The menu is changed daily and offers cuisine to suit the discerning palette supported by a choice of fine wines. Special rates apply for young children, and well behaved dogs will certainly enjoy the exercise and space. All this luxury comes at a very reasonable price so allow enough time to enjoy it all.

Prince Hall Hotel, Two Bridges, Yelverton, Devon.
Tel: 01822 890403 Fax: 01822 890676

Buckland Abbey

CHERRYBROOK is a small family run hotel, set on the high moor in the heart of Dartmoor National Park.

Originally a farm, the hotel retains three and a half acres of land and from the garden there is an open vista across the moor. Andy and Margaret Duncan are the very welcoming owners of Cherrybrook who are enthusiastic about providing every comfort for their guests. - as witness the visitor's book.

The bedrooms are comfortably furnished, centrally heated and have private facilities.

Good home-cooked food is prepared with fresh local produce and herbs from the garden; the four course evening meal can be rounded off with a selection of Devon cheeses. Children are welcome and boxes of toys are provided to keep them happy. Dogs will love it here and so will you. 3-Crown Commended by ETB. AA - QQQQ & RAC, Michelin.

Cherrybrook Hotel, Two Bridges, Yelverton, Devon.
Tel. & Fax: 01822 880260.

The Clapper bridge at Postbridge

POSTBRIDGE. Further along the B3212 towards Moretonhampstead is the small village of **Postbridge.**

In the heart of Dartmoor, in Postbridge village, lies the **LYDGATE HOUSE HOTEL.** Sheltered in a secluded valley and at the end of a private lane, this really is an idyllic setting.

The peaceful and relaxed atmosphere of the hotel makes it a delightful place to stay; with excellent, imaginative home - cooked food and charming cosy rooms, who could ask for more ?

Lydgate House Hotel, Postbridge, Yelverton. Tel : 01822 880209.

YELVERTON. The B3212 heading in the opposite direction from Princetown to Yelverton descends through a landscape of scattered tors towards one of the most pleasant areas of the Dartmoor fringe.

DOUSLAND. A small village to the south of the B3212 near to the Burrator reservoir.

Here you will find **PEEK HILL FARM** which dates back to the 16th century, although the farmhouse itself is more recent, having been constructed during the 19th century.

This B & B accommodation is ideally located in beatiful country-side to make a superb base for a family holiday. The bedrooms offer a high standard of comfort and are equipped with Television, heating and en suite facilities. A good traditional farmhouse or vegetarian breakfast is provided. 2-Crown Commended by ETB.

Peek Hill Farm, Dousland, Yelverton, Devon.   Tel: 01822 852908

WALKHAMPTON. A lane to the north of Dousland leads to **Walkhampton**, a pretty village whose remote church has a disproportionately large tower; half-a-mile further on, the medieval Huckworthy Bridge over the River Walkham is a pleasant spot for a picnic.

On the opposite side of the B3212, **Burrator Reservoir** is a picturesque artificial lake which was built in 1898 to hold Plymouth's water supply; it is held back behind a dam made of six-ton blocks of granite which were quarried locally and dressed on site.

A magnificent view of the reservoir and the surrounding country-side can be had from the top of **Sheeps Tor**, a typical Dartmoor tor which also gives its name to the hamlet lying at its base.

The church at Sheepstor is a charming little building with a low pinnacled tower and some surprising tombs, including that of Sir James Brooke, the white Rajah of Sarawak.

MEAVEY. One mile to the southwest, **Meavy** is an archetypal Dartmoor village with a part-Norman church, a huge gnarled oak tree on the village green, and a delightful white-painted inn, **the Royal Oak,** which was formerly the church house.

There's fresh country air, breathtaking views and scrumptious farmhouse food when you stay at **GREENWELL.**

This family farm welcomes you to share their piece of the countryside two miles from Yelverton roundabout on the country road leading to Ivybridge.

The farmhouse has three large bedrooms which are either en-suite or have private bathroom. Matching decor and soft furnishings are designed and made with guests' comfort in mind. The rooms are heated and have radios and hospitality trays.

The large Dining/TV lounge has an inviting wood burning stove to warm your toes by. Three course suppers using home cooked food are available with a selection of wines. Greenwell is a working farm and guests are invited to view and even participate at times. Walking is unlimited either on your own or guided, and help will be given to arrange all kinds of country pursuits. ETB 3-Crowns.

Greenwell Farm, Near Meavy, Yelverton, Devon. Tel: 01822 853563

Arriving at Yelverton, **THE MANOR HOTEL** on A386 offers a family style welcome.

Gerald and Roz Hicks are the owners and are great hosts. Roz is quite a gem with a great sense of humour and will chat with you about where to go and what to see while ensuring your stay is a comfortable one. Children are made welcome and cot can be provided.

The en-suite bedrooms are centrally heated and have television and tea making facilities. The bar is bright and roomy and there is large dining room where generous portions of good food are served.

The hotel has a large sheltered lawn and good car parking space. Modestly priced and comfortable.

The Manor Hotel, Tavistock Road, Yelverton, Devon. Tel: 01822 852099

CRAPSTONE. Around Yelverton there are a number of villages well worth exploring and all conveniently situated close to Plymouth yet in beautiful countryside.

'MIDWAY' is a large modern detached house converted into two large and very attractive self-contained holiday apartments, (sleeping six in each), in the sleepy village of Crapstone one mile from Yelverton.

The name of the house seems appropriate since this location offers easy access to many places of interest.

Five minutes walk takes you to the edge of Dartmoor, nine miles sees you in Plymouth and Tavistock is just six miles distant, while the beaches of Devon are easily accessible.

The apartments are fitted out to a luxury standard with everything you need - just like home. The ground floor apartment has a conservatory and is easily accessible for level-3 disabled. The garden is self-contained and suitable for young children, and for whom a baby sitting service is available. English Tourist Board awarded four-star Highly Commended.

Midway, (Mrs Sue Eggins), Leigh Farm, Roborough, Plymouth.
Tel: 01752 733221

HORRABRIDGE. Between Yelverton and Tavistock is the village of Horrabridge approximately one mile from the yelverton roundabout on the A386 is **THE OVERCOMBE HOTEL.** which combines two large semi-detached houses built in 1911 and converted in 1976.

The present owners, Brenda and Maurice Durnell acquired the hotel in 1989 which has a reputation for being a friendly, pleasant hotel, where guests can relax in the comfortable homely atmosphere and enjoy the personal service.

There is a lawned garden for residents to sit in and where children can play. The interior of the hotel is bright with comfortable lounge and small informal bar. Most of the eleven bedrooms are en-suite, and all have television, radio and tea/coffee makers. A ground floor bedroom has full facilities for disabled guests.

A view to high Dartmoor is seen from the dining room where in the evening an interesting menu is offered. Maurice and Brenda arrange

HORRABRIDGE. Between Yelverton and Tavistock is the village of Horrabridge approximately one mile from the yelverton roundabout on the A386 is **THE OVERCOMBE HOTEL.** which combines two large semi-detached houses built in 1911 and converted in 1976.

The present owners, Brenda and Maurice Durnell acquired the hotel in 1989 which has a reputation for being a friendly, pleasant hotel, where guests can relax in the comfortable homely atmosphere and enjoy the personal service.

There is a lawned garden for residents to sit in and where children can play. The interior of the hotel is bright with comfortable lounge and small informal bar. Most of the eleven bedrooms are en-suite, and all have television, radio and tea/coffee makers. A ground floor bedroom has full facilities for disabled guests.

A view to high Dartmoor is seen from the dining room where in the evening an interesting menu is offered. Maurice and Brenda arrange special 'walking weekends' in the winter where Dartmoor is explored and evening illustrated talks are given.

Members of the ETB. AA & RAC. recommended.

Overcombe Hotel, Horrabridge, Yelverton, Devon. Tal: 01822 853501

Between Yelverton and Plymouth, the A386 runs across Roborough Down, an area of low open moorland which is popular with picnickers and Dartmoor ponies.

BUCKLAND ABBEY, the National Trust-owned village lies mid-way between the villages of Buckland Monachorum and Milton Combe. Founded in 1278 by the Cistercians, at the Dissolution it passed to the Grenville family who converted the core of the abbey, including the church, into a country mansion.

It eventually passed to Sir Richard Grenville of the *Revenge* who sold it to Sir Francis Drake in 1581, shortly after the great mariner's return from his circumnavigation of the world on board the *Golden Hind.*

The house now contains an interesting exhibition on Drake's life and times; among the exhibits is his famous drum, an item which fortunately survived a devastating house fire in 1938.

(Open daily, except Thursday, 10.30am to 5.30pm between end-March and end-October; weekends only in winter.)

Among the other surviving monastic buildings are the old refectory, now an attractive tearoom, and the great tithe barn, a massive structure over 150ft long which was used to store one tenth of all produce grown by the abbey's tenant farmers.

MILTON COMBE. Lying in a steep-sided ravine half-a-mile to the south, the village of Milton Combe is perhaps best-known for its ancient and intriguingly-named inn, the **Who'd Have Thought It**, which hosts a regular folk club on Sunday evenings.

This is also where you will find the delightful**BLOWISCOMBE BARTON FARM GUEST HOUSE** - home of Philip and Pauline Fisk, is located just off Green Lane near Milton Combe.

Turn right at the brown tourist signs for the Garden House and Buckland Abbey; Left down Green Lane for a mile then follow the B & B signs. Blowiscombe Barton is a period farmhouse in idyllic surroundings overlooking a valley, home to many wild birds and animals.

The colourful garden has a heated swimming pool for the summer months and loungers, barbecue and garden games are provided.

Accommodation is available in the house, West Wing Cottage (sleeps 7), or the Penthouse Flat; comfort is assured whichever you choose. All amenities are provided including heating, en-suite bathrooms etc. Children are welcome and free baby sitting is provided.

From here you have the choice of country relaxation, lovely local walks and beaches within easy drive. 3-Crown Commended for the house and four and five key Commended for the self catering.

Ideal for a family holiday.

Blowiscombe Barton, Milton Combe, Yelverton,Devon.   Tel: 01822 854853

BUCKLAND MONACHORUM. A mile-and-a-half to the north, **Buckland Monachorum** is also the location of the **Garden House**, one of the most enchanting walled gardens in the West Country which has been

Buckland Abbey

lovingly and painstaking restored from the remains of a Tudor vicarage in the years since World War II. Recommended. (Open daily, 10.30am to 5pm between early-March and end-October; also plant centre and tearoom.)

A mile-long walk to the northwest of Buckland Monachorum leads to **Double Waters**, one of the loveliest places on the margins of Dartmoor where the rivers Tavy and Walkham meet in dense wooded countryside. A mile-and-a-half downstream, Denham Bridge provides one of the few approaches to the Bere peninsula, the isolated triangle of land projecting into the estuaries of the Tamar and Tavy. A rich market gardening area, the peninsula is known for its daffodils, strawberries, cherries and early potatoes.

BERE ALSTON, The largest settlement, is a dormitory town with a long mining heritage which is joined to Plymouth by the lovely Tamar valley railway.

BERE FERRERS is two miles to the south. Here the east window in the part-14th-century church of St Andrew is believed to contain some of the oldest stained glass in the county outside Exeter cathedral; it also boasts a richly carved Norman font, an impressive set of carved bench ends, and an assortment of medieval tombs.

It is here, on the banks of the River Tavy, and with the city of Plymouth in our sights, that we leave this part of the world and head for the area covered by the next chapter, South Devon.

CHAPTER FIVE

SOUTH DEVON

Totnes

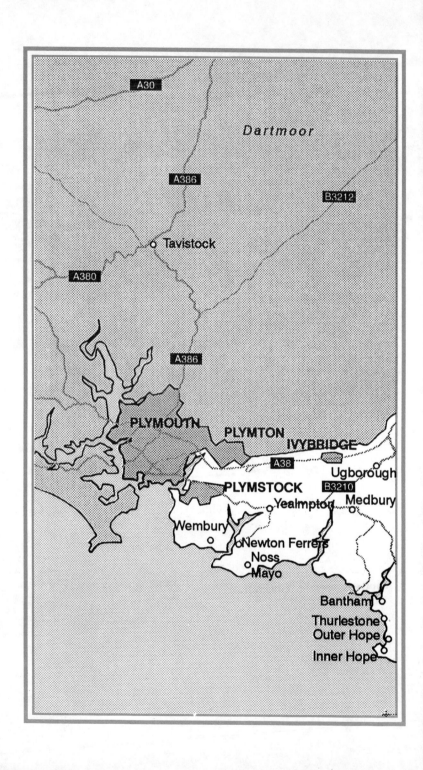

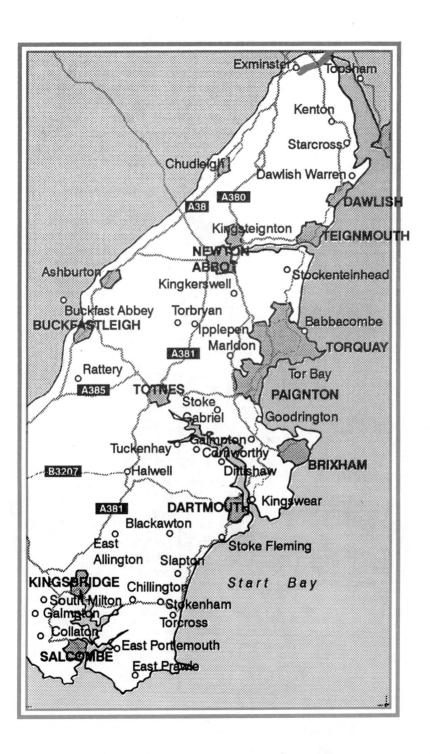

Teignmouth Promenade

CHAPTER FIVE

SOUTH DEVON

Newton Abbot to the Exe Estuary

NEWTON ABBOT. Although its origins date back to the foundation of Torre Abbey at Torquay in the 12th-century, Newton Abbot only really came of age with the arrival of the Great Western Railway in 1846. During the reign of Queen Victoria, the town's population tripled to over 12,000, and it now has over 20,000 inhabitants, more than Barnstaple, the largest town in North Devon. Newton Abbot's growth as a railway town was due to its position at the head of the Teign estuary. Because the main London-Plymouth line was forced to skirt southwards around Haldon Hill, this became the ideal place to site the junction with the branch lines to Torquay and Kingswear to the south, and Bovey Tracey and the Teign valley to the north. The town's expansion was also due to its traditional function as a market town: it stands at the centre of one of the richest areas of farmland in the West Country and still holds a regular livestock and retail market; in recent years, it has also become a centre for light industry.

For those with a fondness for post-industrial domestic architecture, there are some excellent terraces of artisans' houses on the steep hillsides to the south of East Street. The more well-to-do lived a little further to the north in the Italianate-style villas which were built around Devon Square and Courtenay Park. Evidence of pre-19th-century Newton Abbot is hard to find. All that remains of the 14th-century church of St Leonard is the tower, the rest having been demolished in 1836. Ford House to the south of the station is a handsome Jacobean manor house with some good carved woodwork and plasterwork ceilings; it is now occupied by the offices of the district council.

AROUND NEWTON ABBOT

HIGHWEEK. To the northwest of the town centre, the old parish church at Highweek stands in a magnificent position at the end of a high ridge overlooking the Teign valley.

WOLBOROUGH Although less spectacularly situated, the church of St Mary at Wolborough has a much more impressive interior; as well as an intricately-painted early-16th-century rood screen, it contains a 15th-century brass eagle lectern, a bell in the nave cast in 1390, and a richly-cared red sandstone font of the Norman type. Half-a-mile to the west, the National Trust-owned **Bradley Manor** stands in the delightful wooded valley of the River Lemon. A small 15th-century manor house built of roughcast stone, its finest features are the great hall, chapel, buttery and solar. It is still lived in by the Woolner family and is open on Wednesdays only, 2pm to 5pm between end-March and end-September.

KINGSTEIGNTON. A little further on, the road to the northeast of Newton Abbot passes the most southwesterly National Hunt racecourse in Britain. Nearby Kingsteignton is a settlement with Saxon roots which has grown into a large dormitory village. Of interest here is the 15th-century church of St Michael, a surprisingly large structure which has some delicate carving around the doorways and font, and a truncated rood screen which is painted with an assortment of saintly-looking figures. A pretty stream flows through the churchyard before disappearing underground by the west door.

BISHOPSTEIGNTON. At Bishopsteignton, two miles to the east, the south wall in the church incorporates an extraordinary Norman pediment, or *tympanum*, which portrays the three wise men arriving at the scene of the Nativity.

TEIGNMOUTH. The main railway line to the east of Newton Abbot runs along the northern edge of the muddy Teign estuary before arriving in the coastal town of Teignmouth. This pleasant seaside resort began attracting fashionable visitors as early as the 1760s, and by the time the Great Western Railway arrived in 1846, it had already established itself as a stylish place to take the bracing waters of the English Channel. Among the visiting celebrities was John Keats, who stayed at 20 Northumberland Place in the spring of 1818 (his comments about the appalling weather at the time were recorded for posterity). A number of attractive thoroughfares date from the Regency and early-Victorian periods, including Regent Street, Northumberland Place and Den Crescent; the last-named is a grandiose development set back from the seafront which incorporates the Assembly Rooms of 1826 (it has since been converted to a cinema). The offices of the district council occupy Bitton House, a small mansion of a similar age which stands within beautiful landscaped grounds overlooking the estuary; the gardens are open to the public all year round.

The part of Teignmouth facing the sea has a classic holiday atmosphere, with a pier, a wide promenade and a charming, if slightly out-of-date character. However, the town has something of a dual personality, for as well as being a holiday resort, it is also an established seaport with its own inshore fishing and boat-building industries, activities which take place some distance away from the beach in the shelter of the bar which projects across the mouth of the Teign estuary. A new quay was constructed here in 1821 for loading granite from the quarries on Haytor Down onto ships bound for the building sites of London Bridge and the British Museum. Potters' clay from the pits of the lower Teign valley is still exported from here, and boat building continues on a small scale.

SHALDON. A road bridge and passenger ferry links Teignmouth

with Shaldon, a tranquil suburb on the southern side of the Teign estuary which is noted for its handsome Georgian residential buildings.

The five-mile stretch of railway to the north of Teignmouth is one of the most beautiful in Britain. Here, the track passes through a series of short tunnels as it weaves its way along the very edge of the seashore.

DAWLISH. Here the railway stands between the town and its long sandy beach and Brunel's engineers were obliged to build the station on a low granite viaduct, a novelty executed in curious Egyptian style, which allows beach-goers pass underneath. Dawlish had been a small, yet fashionable resort for several decades before the first trains arrived in 1846. The local stream, Dawlish Water, had already been landscaped into a series of rather twee waterfalls, and John Nash had been brought in to design some of the town's most ostentatious 'cottages', including Luscombe Castle, a baronial pile with grounds by Humphry Repton lying a mile to the west of the parish church which was built for a wealthy banker in 1804; a chapel by George Gilbert Scott was added 58 years later. Among the resort's early patrons were Jane Austen and Charles Dickens, both of whom refer to it in their novels. Dawlish also contains a number of elegant early-Victorian terraces, including Brunswick Park and Barton Terrace, and today, it remains a quiet, gentile seaside resort where nothing very much happens.

Brunel intended that the stretch of track between Exeter and Totnes should be powered by a revolutionary new system dubbed the **Atmospheric Railway**: the trains were to be attached to a third rail, which in fact was as a long vacuum chamber, and the carriages were to be drawn along by the effects of air pressure. His ingenious system cost over £400,000 to install and involved the building of ten great Italianate engine houses beside the line at three mile intervals. Sadly, the idea was a total failure, largely because the leather seals were quickly eaten away by the combined forces of rain, salt and hungry rats. The engine house at Starcross was the last to survive.

POWDERHAM. To the north of Dawlish, the railway line skirts the nature reserve and golf course on Dawlish Warren before passing along the edge of the **Powderham Castle** estate. This enormous fortified mansion lies within its own tree-filled deer park on land which was reclaimed from the Exe estuary in the 18th-century. The estate has been in the hands of the Courtenay family, the Earls of Devon, since the late 14th-century and parts of the present house date from that time, although the majority of the building was added between the mid-18th and mid-19th-centuries. During the 1750s, the old great hall was converted into a reception chamber with a majestic staircase which rises the full height of the building, then in the 1790s James Wyatt was called in to design a magnificent music room with a large bow window and a central dome; both rooms are finished in impressive, if a rather gaudy, plasterwork. The generous compensation negotiated in the 1840s for allowing the South Devon railway to disrupt the view to the east paid for the building of a new forecourt and banqueting hall on the castle's western side.

Powderham Castle

(Open daily, except Saturday, 10am to 6pm between Easter and end-September.)

Midway between Exeter and Dawlish on the A379 and adjacent to Powderham Castle is **THE DEVON ARMS,** an old coaching house dating from 1592. It offers comfortable accommodation with six bedrooms, some with en-suite bathrooms, and colour television and tea and coffee making facilities. The lounge bar has a full range of wines, spirits and beers including real ales and a dining area where an extensive range of snacks and meals to suit all palates are served both lunchtime and evenings. A special table d'hôte Sunday lunch is served and children's meals are catered for too. Outside is a barbecue area, pets' corner, children's play area and large car park.

The Devon Arms, Kenton, Near Exeter, Devon.   Tel: 01626 890213.

KENTON, on the western edge of the Powderham estate, is a sizable village with an exceptional late-14th-century red sandstone church. The tower stands over 100ft tall and is decorated with a wonderful assortment of ornate carvings; inside, there is more rich carving in the south porch and in the white Beer stone arcades of the nave. The pulpit is a 15th-century original which was rescued and restored after it was found in pieces in 1866, and the massive rood screen, one of the finest in Devon, is a magnificent testimony to the 15th-century wood-carver's art.

EXMINSTER, three miles to the north, is an ancient village which is now a dormitory for Exeter. The church of St Martin contains an unusual 17th-century plasterwork ceiling whose fifteen panels depict the apostles and the four evangelists.

KENN and KENNFORD, to the southwest of Exminster, are twin villages set amongst rich red farmland at the foot of Haldon Hill. St Andrew's church at Kenn dates from the early 14th-century and has an excellent interior, with a broad rood screen and a Purbeck marble font.

The Exeter and Devon Racecourse stands in a pleasant wooded position at the point where the busy A38 reaches the top of Haldon Hill.

CHUDLEIGH, three miles further on, is another ancient settlement whose modern role is dormitory town. In the centuries prior to the completion of the dual-carriageway in the early 1970s, it had been a busy market and coaching town on the main Exeter-Plymouth road. The church has a good interior, and the 17th-century former grammar school next door has a fine Georgian façade (it is now a private house). At one time, Chudleigh was a destination for day trippers who would travel the nine miles from Exeter to enjoy a picnic beneath the dramatic Chudleigh Rocks or top of the Iron Age hill fort known as Castle Dyke on the southern edge of town.

Over the ridge to the south, **Ugbrooke House** is a castellated mansion which lies within a beautiful 600-acre park designed by the 18th-century landscaper, Capability Brown; among his finest achievements were the series of long artificial lakes and the avenue of beech trees known as Dryden's Walk. The present house was built in 1760s on the site of a 13th-century predecessor; the interior was designed and furnished in sumptuous style by Robert Adam and contains an exceptional collection of paintings, porcelain and period furniture. (Open Sundays, and Tuesdays to Thursdays, 1pm to 5.30pm between mid-July and end-August.)

TORBRYAN. The labyrinth of lanes to the southwest of Newton Abbot is highly-characteristic of the landscape of rural South Devon. A wonderful example of a traditional hamlet is Torbryan, a tiny settlement consisting of half-a-dozen cottages, a church and a church house. The **Holy Trinity Church** is a gem. Almost entirely early-15th-century, it has a light spacious interior with white-plastered walls, pale Beer stone arcades, Georgian box pews and a wide exquisitely-painted rood screen.

THE OLD CHURCH HOUSE INN was an important inn in Tudor times, being located on what was the main Exeter to Plymouth coaching road. Reputedly Henry VIII and his father, Henry VII, visited the inn and Elizabethan bowling pins dating from that period can be seen hanging from the beams.

The Old Church House Inn

The inn retains its fascinating old world atmosphere with great open fireplaces, massive beamed ceilings and a superb collection of bedrooms. All enjoy en-suite facilities complete with colour TV and telephones. In addition to a full English breakfast you may enjoy a full à la carte menu, available to all customers, in one of the dining areas or bar lounges. The historic atmosphere of this wonderful old inn is particularly enjoyable and inviting. It is without doubt one of the oldest and most beautifully preserved in the country - truly "An Inn for All Seasons".

The Old Church House Inn, Torbryan, Ipplepen, South Devon
Tel: 01803 812372

DENBURY, a mile-and-a-half to the north, takes its name from the Iron Age hill fort which lies on its southwestern edge; the village contains an early-14th-century church, an inn and a substantial Elizabethan manor house with a Georgian frontage.

The lanes to the southeast of Denbury lead across the A381 Newton Abbot-Totnes road to the National Trust-owned **Compton Castle**. This imposing fortified manor house was built in three stages between the 14th- and 16th-centuries by the Gilberts, an ancient family whose descendants still live here. During the 17th-century, it was the home of Sir Humphrey Gilbert, Sir Walter Raleigh's brother who established an early settlement in Newfoundland. Among the castle's most interesting features are the great hall, chapel, solar and old kitchens. (Open Mondays, Wednesdays and Thursdays, 10am to 5pm between end-March and end-October.)

TORBAY

Torbay lies on a ten-mile stretch of sheltered east-facing coastline which tourist brochures like to refer to as the 'English Riviera'. The borough is composed of the seaside towns of Torquay, Paignton and Brixham, a loose conurbation which has a combined population of around 120,000.

TORQUAY. The origins of Torquay date back to the end of the 12th-century when **Torre Abbey** was founded on a site a quarter-of-a-mile inland from the northern end of Tor Bay. By Tudor times, the abbey had grown to become the wealthiest Premonstratensian monastery in England; however, it was forced into non-ecclesiastical ownership at the Dissolution in 1539 and fell into disrepair. The site then changed hands several times before it was acquired by the Careys in 1662, a family whose descendants built the present house of Torre Abbey in Georgian times and who continued to own the property until shortly after the Second World War when it was acquired by Torquay Corporation for use as a museum and art gallery. Over 25 rooms are now open to the public, one of which is devoted to the Torquay-born mystery writer, Agatha Christie; many contain superb pieces of period furniture and works of art. (Open daily between 1 April and 31 October.) Several impressive medieval remains can still be seen in the abbey grounds, including the late-12th-century entrance to the chapter house, the gatehouse of 1320, a section of the Abbot's tower, and the great 'Spanish' barn, a massive 124ft-long tithe barn which was later used to house prisoners-of-war from the

Armada. The grounds now form one of the many public open spaces in the town and are open daily, all year round; admission free.

As a fashionable watering place, Torquay was a relatively late developer and it wasn't the early-19th-century that wealthy patrons began to arrive in significant numbers after they were denied access to the Continent by the Napoleonic Wars. The expansion of the town was strictly controlled by two families - the Careys of Torre Abbey and the Palks of Haldon House, near Exeter - and together, they set about creating a select resort which would appeal to the rich and aristocratic. Whole new neighbourhoods were developed at a time, usually designed by the Harveys, a distinguished firm of architects whose elegant stuccoed terraces, leafy gardens and broad drives we can see contouring upwards from the edge of the bay. (Hesketh Terrace is perhaps the finest of these mid-19th-century developments.) In the fifty years between 1821 and 1871, Torquay rose from a village with less than 2000 inhabitants to a sizable coastal resort with a population of over 20,000, a tenfold expansion which was bolstered by the arrival of the railway in 1848. (Prior to that, the most efficient route from London involved taking a horse-drawn coach to Portsmouth and boarding a coastal steamer.)

The only resistance to this 'vulgar' expansion came from Torquay's third landed family, the Mallocks of Cockington, who refused to grant building leases on their land until the 1860s, and then only very sparingly. Instead, they went to great lengths to preserve their estate, with its part-Elizabethan manor house, 15th-century red sandstone church, forge and immaculate thatched village. (The only modern building in the present-day village is the Drum Inn which was designed in the 1930s by Sir Edwin Lutyens in a style which conforms to the existing rural architecture.) After seeming to be suspended in time for several centuries, **Cockington** was eventually sold to Torquay Corporation in 1935 for £50,000, and it is now a fascinating outdoor museum and public open space which can be found a mile from the sea on the western edge of the built up area.

Present-day Torquay has managed to retain a flavour of its exclusive Victorian grandeur, particularly around the steep limestone headland which fronts onto Tor Bay.

If you are looking for somewhere to stay which has all the charm of a country house hotel yet is conveniently situated for both the centre of Torquay and the beach, then you should make a point of finding the Frognel Hall Hotel.

The entrance to **FROGNEL HALL** is tucked away in Higher Woodfield Road, which is mid-way between the harbour and the lovely Meadfoot beach. The short tree-lined drive opens out into two acres of delightful secluded gardens, from where there are magnificent views over Torquay town and the bay.

The hotel itself is a beautiful and inviting Victorian mansion. A visit to the local museum revealed that the earliest recorded inhabitants were Sir Culling and Lady Eardley in 1851, and it remained a family home until it was tastefully converted into a stylish hotel in the late 1970s.

The timeless elegance of the drawing rooms, the comfortable intimacy of the dining room ,and the homely warmth of the welcome all remain; Lady Eardley would still feel at home here.

Combined with the modern leisure faclities, well equipped bedrooms and wonderful food, this is an ideal base from which the discerning traveller may explore the other hidden places of Torquay.

Frognel Hall Hotel, Higher Woodfield Road, Torquay. 01803 298339.

Just 150 yards from what is often described as Torquay's finest beach, **Meadfoot Bay**, stands the **Meadfoot Bay Hotel**. This charming, detached, family run hotel enjoys a very sheltered location and is a real sun trap at all times of the year. It has a variety of delightful bedrooms, all with private bathrooms, colour TVs and complementary tea/coffee making facilities. Some rooms boast a sun-balcony or patio and all are furnished to a high standard. The hotel offers delicious home-cooked food using fresh produce wwherever possible. A carefully selected wine list complements your meal. Well placed for a variety of activities including golf, tennis and swimming, and surrounded by beautiful walks, the Meadfoot Bay Hotel is the ideal choice for a family holiday.

Meadfoot Bay Hotel, Meadfoot Beach, Torquay, Devon. Tel: 01803 294722
Fax: 01803 292871

Situated on the main road to the beach and close to all amenities, the **Clovelly Guest House** offers a high standard of B & B accomodation. All of the rooms are comfortably furnished and have free Sattelite TV, tea making facilities and hot and cold running water. An ideal place for a family holiday.

Clovelly Guest House, 91 Avenue Road, Torquay. Tel: 01803 292286

A place which once provided rather more basic accommodation is located on the eastern side of the headland: **Kent's Cavern** is a series of caves which is believed to be one of the oldest inhabited sites in the British Isles. When the caves were excavated in the early 19th-century, they were found to contain primitive tools of the sort used by Neolithic man around 5000 years ago; they also contained the bones of animals which have long been extinct. Now easily accessible and clearly lit, they provide an interesting all-weather attraction.

PAIGNTON. Adjoining Torquay to the south, Paignton is an ancient settlement which has been rendered unrecognisable as such by the careless developments of the late 19th- and early 20th-centuries. The original village is believed to date back to Saxon times, and some late-medieval buildings can still be seen around the parish church of St John, half-a-mile inland. The finest of these is Kirkham House, a handsome 14th-century manor house which lies to the east of the church and is open daily between April and end-September. To the south, the much-restored Coverdale Tower is all that remains of a summer palace which once belonged to the Bishops of Exeter. The church itself stands on Saxon foundations and was substantially rebuilt in the early 15th-century of local red sandstone. It contains a surprisingly rich interior, with a Norman font and a 15th-century carved stone pulpit. The Kirkham Chantry in the south transept is entered by way of a remarkable stone-work screen which sadly has been modified, but nevertheless contains some of the finest late-15th-century stone carving to be found anywhere in England; inside, there is a Jacobean altar and a richly-carved and vaulted ceiling.

A short distance to the north of the church on Torquay Road stands Oldway, an extravagant late-Victorian pile which was built by Paris Singer, the heir to the Singer sewing machines empire, in 1874. Whim-sically dubbed the 'Wigwam' by its creator, its design incorporates the excesses of the Paris opera house, Versailles and Buckingham Palace. After having cost well over £100,000 to build, it was sold in 1945 to the local council for a mere £45,000. Its 120-or-so rooms continue to be used as municipal offices and function suites, and it is worth popping in just to have a look at the extraordinary entrance hall, with its monumental staircase, inlaid floors and polished marble veneers, a riot of gaudy neoclassicism worthy of Cecil B de Mille. The exterior of the building is equally excessive, most notably the east end with its immense Ionic colonnade.

Paignton had to wait eleven years for the railway to be extended the three miles from its neighbour to the north, and in the century which followed, its expansion was dramatic. Between 1859 and the outbreak of the Second World War, its population grew from under 3000 to well over 20,000, mostly in streets of villas, terraced houses and shops. Its suburbs are now filled with smart privately-run hotels and bed and breakfast establishments, and the resort is a good place to spend a good old-fashioned seaside holiday break.

PAIGNTON ZOO the largest zoological and botanical garden in Devon, lies just off the A385 Totnes road on the western edge of town. Set within large attractive grounds, the majority of the animals and birds are housed in spacious enclosures around which visitors can walk at their leisure. The zoo sets out to be educational as well as recreational, and encourages young people to take an interest in the future well-being of the world's wild animals, birds and plants. (Open daily, 10am to 6pm, all year round.)

If you travel along the Yalberton Road approximately two miles from Paignton, you will come upon the historic **KING WILLIAM COTTAGE** where Prince William of Orange lodged on his march from Brixham to London in 1688. The owner of the cottage at that time, being so proud of his royal visit placed an ornamentation on the ceiling above the place in which the Prince sat for dinner. It is from this lovely old cottage that Hilary Burns sells her attractive and well made willow and hedgerow baskets, in both traditional and modern designs; she is also happy to take on commissions and repairs by arrangement. From Easter to October unusual perennial plants are on sale from the cottage garden. A most interesting diversion and a chance to find an unusual gift.

Hilary Burns, King William Cottage, Yalburton Road, Paignton, Devon.
Tel: 01803 553144

BLAGDON. **Blagdon Barton**, a fine example of a late-medieval manor estate can be found in the lanes to the north of the A385, a mile-and-a-half to the northwest of the zoo.

Torbay Aircraft Museum at nearby Higher Blagdon contains a unique collection of aircraft built between 1924 and 1954, and there is also an exhibition on the history of flight with a section devoted to First World War air aces. (Open daily between late-March and early-November.)

STOKE GABRIEL, two-and-a-half miles to the south of Blagdon, the scattered village of Stoke Gabriel stands on a hillside above a tidal spur of the Dart estuary. A weir was built across the neck of the creek in Edwardian times which traps the water at low tide and gives the village a pleasant lakeside atmosphere. The part-13th-century church of St Gabriel has a restored late-medieval pulpit and a truncated screen with some good wainscot paintings, and to the south of the creek, two noteworthy country mansions command magnificent views of the estuary: Sandridge House, designed by John Nash in the 1800s, and Waddeton Court, built in mock-Elizabethan style in the 19th-century on the site of a medieval predecessor.

Travelling along the Brixham Ring Road and feeling ready for refreshment, look out for the **CHURCHWARDS CIDER HOUSE** located about a mile from the beautiful village of Stoke Gabriel. Here is a business established some 48 years ago though owned and run for the last 10 years by three sisters. As you approach the Cider Farm, acres of orchards surround you on both sides of the lane. The Farm produces every kind of Cider drink from dry to sweet with some more unusual blends in between. The owners are happy for you to look around the building and see the different selections available. The Cider Press can be seen next door to the original house and if you time your visit in Autumn you can see how cider is produced.

Churchwards Cider House, Yalberton Road, Paignton, Devon.
Tel: 01803 558157

BRIXHAM, the third urban area to make up the borough of Torbay, is a working fishing port with a very different atmosphere from its more frivolous neighbours to the north. Though still a popular coastal resort, the town is focussed around a picturesque fishing harbour with a long maritime history. A full-sized replica of Drake's **Golden Hind** is based here when not on loan elsewhere, and a statue on the harbourside commemorates William of Orange who landed here on 5 November 1688 while en route to London (the following year, he was proclaimed joint monarch along with his wife, Mary II).

During the 1840s, over 250 fishing vessels were based in the harbour and fish from Brixham was shipped all over the south of England. Today, this number has been reduced to a few dozen, although their presence still gives the town a sense of industrial purpose. For those with an interest in local history, there is a good museum housed in a converted sail loft and two former fisherman's cottages which gives an unusually personal account of Brixham's rich maritime past. All around the harbour, dense rows of pastel-painted cottages rise steeply from the water's edge. To the south, the land climbs onto **Berry Head**, a striking limestone promontory which has been designated both a Country Park and a Site of Special Scientific Interest. The remains of a two defensive installations occupy this spectacular site overlooking Tor Bay, the first an earthwork cliff-fort dating from the early Age Iron age and the second a massive fortification built at the beginning of the 19th-century when a Napoleonic invasion seemed a real possibility; the latter remains surprisingly intact and is now a listed building.

There are few locations to match that of **THE BERRY HEAD HOTEL**. The hotel is steeped in history, built as a military hospital in the Napoleonic Wars and later the home of the Reverend Lyle who wrote the famous hymn, 'Abide with me'. It nestles at the water's edge with panoramic views of the bay and beyond - the perfect backdrop, whatever the occasion.

The restaurant offers both table d'hôte and à la carte menus. Chef, Alastair Howe, and his team ensure that the magnificent views are complemented by a fine selection of foods from interesting and varied menus.

Winter or Summer there is always something of interest to view from The Berry Head Hotel, not least from the Napoleon Bar where an excellent range of beers and lagers are served, including an especially fine draught beer.

The Napoleon Bar menu is designed to appeal to all tastes and ages and offers a wide variety of food from a light snack to a substantial three course meal. Families are always welcome and vegetarians are well catered for.

In the summer, the large terrace on the water's edge, is the ideal place to enjoy morning coffee, lunch, a cream tea or relaxing evening drink.

Weddings and functions are a speciality of the hotel and there can be few settings so ideal. The hotel can cater for up to 160 people and all can be assured of friendly, professional service and a day to remember.

The hotel has recently undergone extensive refurbishment and provides comfortable and relaxing accommodation combined with the very warmest of welcomes. So if you want service with views to match, try The Berry Head Hotel.

The Berry Head Hotel, Berry Head Road, Brixham, Devon Tel: 01803 853225

The original parish church, St Mary's, is a handsome red sandstone building dating from the 14th-century which lies one mile to the south-west at Higher Brixham, the site of the first Saxon settlement.

Although the railway now terminates at Paignton, at one time the line continued southwards to Kingswear with an onward connection to Dartmouth by way of a passenger ferry across the Dart estuary (a loss-making spur to Brixham was also built in 1868). The five-mile section beyond Paignton was closed by British Rail in the 1960s; however, it was reopened some years later by the **Dart Valley Light Railway** plc, who now operate a regular steam train service along this highly scenic stretch of track. Painted in the original livery of the Great Western Railway, trains run daily between June and September, and also over the Easter weekend.

KINGSWEAR itself is a pleasant arrangement of Georgian and early-Victorian villas which rise steeply from the eastern bank of the Dart estuary. For centuries, it has been connected to Dartmouth, its larger neighbour across the water, by passenger and vehicle ferries, and the recent addition of a marina has given it fresh impetus. **Kingswear Castle**, at the mouth of the estuary, was built at the end of the 15th-century to defend the strategically important deep-water moorings of Dartmouth Harbour. Its dramatic position on a rock above the waterline was so exposed to wind-blown rain and salt water that its iron canons had to be changed for brass. The new long-range guns which were installed on the Dartmouth side in the middle of the 17th-century rendered Kingswear castle redundant (no doubt, this came as a great relief to its weatherbeaten garrison) and the building remained abandoned until the 1850s when it was converted into a summer 'cottage' by Charles Seale-Hayne, a wealthy local benefactor who founded the agricultural college near Newton Abbot, now a branch of the University of Plymouth.

To the east of Kingswear, the local slates and grits have been eroded by the sea into a series of rocky promontories and cliffs, the most impressive of which rise above Long Sands and Man Sands. A surprising discovery in this formidable landscape is the National Trust-owned **Coleton Fishacre Garden**, a delightful twenty-acre oasis which is sheltered from the coastal gales by a deep stream-fed combe. The garden was created between 1925 and 1940 by Lady Dorothy D'Oyly Carte, an enthusiastic amateur who introduced a wonderfully imaginative variety of rare and exotic trees and shrubs. (Open Wednesdays, Thursdays, Fridays and Sundays, 10.30am to 5.30pm between end-March and end-October; also Sunday afternoons in March.) Coleton Fishacre House, a small country residence designed by Oswald Milne in the 1920s, can be viewed by written appointment with the leaseholder.

Totnes, Kingsbridge and the South Hams

TOTNES is an ancient town on a hill above the highest navigable point on the River Dart. According to local legend, the town was founded by the ancient Trojans, although the first confirmed evidence of its existence doesn't appear until the mid-10th-century when a small mint was established by King Edgar.

The Saxons built a defensive earthwork rampart around a 10-acre site at the top of the hill which was refortified by the Normans shortly after they took over in the 11th-century. The Normans also built an impressive motte and bailey castle at the northwestern corner of the Saxon *burh* which originally had a timber stockade; this was replaced between the 12th- and early-14th-centuries by a tall circular stone keep with massive 6ft walls, high battlements and a steep-sided moat. Now probably the best-preserved motte and bailey castle in Devon, **Totnes Castle** is open daily, 10am to 6pm, all year round (closed Mondays in winter). A substantial section of Totnes' medieval town wall can also be seen around the east and south of the old centre. The superb **East Gate**, with its unique 16th-century clock tower, straddles the main street leading up from the Dart; sadly, it had to be virtually rebuilt after being severely damaged by fire in 1990.

In the late Middle Ages, Totnes was a cloth-making town which was second only to Exeter in importance. The town's merchants grew rich during this prolonged period of prosperity, and in the mid-14th-century they began electing a local council to look after their interests. A list of mayors dating back to 1359 is kept in the 16th-century **Guildhall**, a remarkable little building with an unusual granite colonnade which stands behind the parish church on the site of a former Benedictine priory. The council chamber contains an impressive plasterwork frieze dated 1624, and on the lower floor, the old town goal retains its dank medieval character. (Open Mondays to Fridays between Easter and end-September.) Totnes Town Council retains many of its original traditions and it is now one of the oldest institutions of its kind in the country.

The parish **church of St Mary** is an ostentatious structure with an imposing red sandstone tower which was entirely rebuilt in the 15th-century, the period when Totnes' cloth industry was at its most confident. Its most impressive internal feature is the carved Beer stone rood screen which was built to rival the one in Exeter Cathedral. Sadly, the rood loft was removed when the church was 'restored' by George Gilbert Scott in the 1860s, although the original rood stair remains as a curious stairway to nowhere. The church also contains a striking stone pulpit and an interesting collection of tombs and monuments.

The walk up Fore Street, under the **East Gate,** and on up the High Street into the old town centre passes a delightful assortment of early buildings, some of which date from the 15th-century. Of particular interest is **70 Fore Street**, an attractive half-timbered Elizabethan structure with overhanging upper floors which now houses Totnes Museum; the display includes a room on Totnes-born Charles Babbage, the inventor of the first computer. (Open Mondays to Fridays between 1 April and 31 October.) Further up the hill, the **Butterwalk** and **Poultrywalk** are two ancient covered shopping arcades whose upper storeys are held up on pillars of granite, timber or cast iron.

Just off the Plains in the centre of Totnes is a real find for lovers of good food.

The whimsically named Ticklemore Street is home to an enterprise run by Robin Congdon and Sarie Cooper in the form of **THE TICKLEMORE CHEESE SHOP**.

This is no ordinary retail outlet, as the couple produce their own cheese in a dairy outside the town, using milk from local farms.

The Ticklemore Cheese Shop

Drawing on 15 years of experience, Robin and Sarie have produced a selection of hand made cheeses from cows, goats, and sheeps milk, each with its own character and flavour.

To supplement their own range of produce, the shop also sells quality cheeses from around the country, with a definite bias towards West Country cheese. From further afield, there are French artisan cheeses; and yogurts, soft cheeses, and ice cream are also available. Well worth a visit, and an excellent opportunity to sample a quality, locally made product .

The Ticklemore Cheese Shop, 1 Ticklemore St., Totnes.
Tel: 01803 865926

At the foot of the hill, **Totnes Bridge** is an elegant stone structure built in 1828 which, until the 1980s, carried the main traffic between Torbay and the South Hams. Nearby on the Plains stands a memorial to William Wills, a native of Totnes who died of starvation when attempting to re-cross the Australian outback with Robert Burke in 1861.

During the summer, pleasure boats depart from **Totnes Quay** for the glorious seven-mile trip to Dartmouth, one of the most beautiful stretches of river in Britain. When Totnes was a busy river port, the flat strip of land beside the Dart was lined with warehouses; today, these have either been demolished or converted into smart flats. Another of Totnes' many attractions is the **Motor Museum** which can be found in Steamer Quay Road on the east bank of the river. (Open daily between Easter and end-October.)

Year round accommodation can be found at **THE OLD FORGE AT TOTNES**, a friendly and welcoming 600-year old stone building with cosy cottage-style rooms and set in a relaxing almost-rural environment. Ideal location for business people, holiday visitors and those taking short breaks. All rooms - each with its own colour theme and most with private bathrooms - have central heating, colour TV, radio alarms, hairdryers and many extras. Beverage trays provide plenty of choice and fresh milk. Ground floor and family rooms plus a cottage suite for 2-4 (suitable for semi-disabled).

The Old Forge At Totnes

The cobbled driveway leads to on-site parking and the coach arch opens into a delightful walled garden. Breakfast in the airy Tudor-style restaurant provides a wide-choice menu - traditional, unusual, vegetarian, continental and special diet. Special afternoon teas are also served in the restaurant with a good selection at reasonable prices. Evening meals are also served.

This little corner of rural paradise is just a few minutes walk from the main shopping centre and the riverside. Dogs in cars only and no smoking indoors. The building still retains an ancient prison cell and smithy workshop.

The Old Forge at Totnes, Seymour Place, Totnes, Devon
Tel: 01803 862174

Close to Totnes a warm welcome awaits you at **HATCHLANDS FARM BLUEPOST**, a luxury farmhouse set in panoramic countryside with wonderful views in such a peaceful setting.

Hatchlands Farm Bluepost, Totnes 01364 72224

There are two guest bedrooms both en-suite with colour TV, radio, tea and coffee facilities., as well as having both double and bunk beds making them suitable for up to four sharing. As well as a comfortable main lounge with real fire there is a sun lounge with snooker table and a golf practice machine, whilst out in the large garden is a barbecue which visitors are welcome to use. The more adventurous may also like to try there hand at clay pigeon shooting. Mrs Palmer is also more than happy to recommend places to eat out, many of which welcome children.

Every comfort is provided and children are most welcome, with cot, highchair and babysitting all provided free of charge Hatchlands is a 250 acres working dairy farm and guests are more than welcome to explore and join in! There are also plenty of walks around the farm which has woodlands, a lake and river, which are a haven for many species of bird and wildlife.

Hatchlands is a marvellous place to centre a holiday with all the delights of the Torbay Riviera and the wild tors of Dartmoor close to hand

Totnes is also associated with a singularly bizarre episode in Devon's history. On 9th February 1855, following a heavy fall of snow during the night, people awoke to find a strange trail of footprints that began in the town and led off across the countryside. Meandering this way and that for a distance of almost 100 miles, the trail finally petered out at Littleham. Immediately christened 'The Devil's Footprints', they were said to resemble those of a donkey - one, however, with two legs as opposed to the standard four! The trail wended its way through gardens and over walls, gates and roofs, sometimes scorching the frozen snow as if made by fiery cloven hooves. Although many believed this to be a gigantic hoax, no one ever admitted responsibility and a lot of local people refused to venture out of their homes at night for a long time.

Around Totnes

BERRY POMEROY. This historic village lies in the lanes between the A381 and A385, two miles to the east of Totnes. The local estate has been in the hands of only two families since the Norman invasion: the first, the de la Pomerais, occupied it for nearly 500 years before selling it in 1548 to the Seymours, a distinguished political family who, despite transferring their main residence to Wiltshire at the end of the 17th-century, continued to own it for several hundred years.

In the early 14th-century, the Pomeroys built a castle in a superb position on a wooded promontory above the Gatcombe Brook, one mile to the northeast of the village. Substantial remains of **Berry Pomeroy Castle** can still be seen, including sections of the curtain wall, the 14th-century gatehouse, and the shell of a three-storey Tudor mansion which was built inside the medieval fortifications by the Seymours. (Open daily, 9.30am to 6.30pm during summer months only.) Berry Pomeroy church is a handsome late-15th-century building with a high tower, a good rood screen and a number of impressive monuments to the Pomeroys and Seymours.

Half-a mile to the northwest of Totnes, a lane leading north off the A385 runs beside the serene waters of the Dart before reaching **Dartington Hall**, a once-dilapidated medieval manor which was given new life in the 1930s when it was acquired by Leonard and Dorothy Elmhirst, wealthy benefactors who set about reviving the local rural economy in line with the ideology of the Indian philosopher, Rabindranath Tagore. The original hall was built in the 14th-century as a palace for the Dukes of Exeter; it incorporated some earlier buildings erected by the Martin family and was arranged around a large quadrangle, with a semi-fortified entrance porch at one end, and a magnificent great hall at the other. It was later acquired by the Champernowne family who, despite making a number of cursory alterations, gradually allowed the manor to fall into disrepair.

By the time the Elmhirsts took over in 1925, the great hall was open to the elements, and so one of their first tasks was to reconstruct the massive hammer-beam roof using timber from locally-felled oaks. Other buildings were similarly restored, and the beautiful Dartington Hall Gardens re-landscaped and stocked with sculptures by such artists as Henry Moore and Barbara Hepworth. The Elmhirsts' Trust was also responsible for founding a college of art and drama, a co-educational school, and several enterprising rural businesses, including a sawmill, building contractor and dairy farm. (They also had a hand in founding Dartington Glass and the Beaford Centre in North Devon.)

The Trust's offshoot, Dartington Arts, continues to arrange a lively programme of music, drama and arts events, and each year the Hall hosts the famous International Music Summer School. The Hall gardens, with their sculptures and giant grassed steps, are breathtaking at any time of the year, and there is also a pleasant bar, the White Hart, in the corner of the quadrangle. A number of other interesting eating places and retail outlets can be found at the **Shinner's Bridge Centre**, three-quarters-of-a-mile to the southwest.

COTT. 500yds further on at **Cott**, there is an excellent, late-medieval inn whose immense thatched roof had to be replaced in the 1980s following a disastrous fire.

RATTERY. In the village of Rattery can be found the **CHURCH HOUSE INN**, said to be the oldest Inn in England dating back to AD 1028 when it was a rest home for the monks and a hostel for church builders. Situated close to the church, the Inn offers many items of interest for the visitor which include a massive oak screen, spiral stone staircase, great open fireplaces, and in the bar a list documents evidence of an unbroken line of 'Vicars' since the year 1199.

Here can be found a good, solid atmosphere in keeping with the age of the Inn offering a very high standard of food and drink where the traveller could, for example, select roast pheasant accompanied by real ale and finish perhaps with a selection from over 40 malt whiskies. Recommended.

Church House Inn, Rattery, South Brent, Devon.   Tel: 01364 642220

STAVERTON. Three-quarters-of-a-mile to the northwest of

Shinner's Bridge, a lane leading north off the A384 Buckfastleigh road leads down to **Staverton Bridge**, one of the finest late-medieval bridges in Devon whose six graceful arches span the deep green waters of the Dart. The station on the north bank is a halt on the **South Devon Railway**, the privately-run steam train service which runs in summer between Buckfastleigh and Totnes. Staverton village is a pleasant community in a delightful Dart valley setting.

Its largely 14th-century church has a Georgian pulpit, a restored 15th-century rood screen and some unusual monuments and brasses. There is also a good pub, **the Sea Trout**, which looks as if it may once have been the old church house.

To the south of Totnes, the fertile rolling countryside to the west of the Dart estuary contains some exceptional old settlements.

HARBERTON. The Church of St Andrew, Harberton, has been a chapel since about 1100, though little remains of the original building except the Norman font which you will see on your left as you enter. The tower is 78 feet high, tapering toward the top and having a semi-octagonal stair turret in the middle of the south wall, a characteristic feature of many South Devon churches, and holds a peel of six bells. The church also contains a superb example of a 15th-century wooden screen and the pulpit is one of the last remaining medieval stone pulpits in Devon.

The Church House Inn, Harberton, Nr. Totnes, Devon Tel: 01803 863707

THE CHURCH HOUSE INN is delightfully situated beside the village church in this picturesque village, just over 2 miles from Totnes off the main Kingsbridge road. Originally built to house the masons working on the church around 1100 it later became a Chantry House for monks and the present bar comprises the Great Hall, Chapel and Workshop where the monks would have gathered for a glass of wine. In 1327 the Abbot handed the property over to the poor and in 1950 it passed out of the Church's hands altogether. It was also around this time that plaster was removed to reveal massive beams of fluted mellow oak and a fine medieval oak screen, acclaimed as one of the oldest in the country. A Tudor window frame and latticed window containing panes of 13th-century hand-made glass can still be seen.

In addition to an extensive menu, daily specials are offered throughout the week including a traditional roast on Sundays. A wide choice is available from a humble sandwich to charcoal grilled steaks and Cordon Bleu specialities. Vegetarians are catered for and there is a family room for children. Up to four real ales are usually available behind the bar.

ASHPRINGTON, in the lanes on the opposite side of the A381 Kingsbridge road, also has a fine church with a lofty tower, a Norman red sandstone font and a lych gate in the churchyard. 300yds further on, the eleven-acre Avenue Cottage Garden is a delightful 18th-century land-scaped garden which is still in the process of redevelopment. (Open Tuesdays to Saturdays, 11am to 5pm between 1 April and 30 September.) Sharpham House, to the northeast, is a privately-owned Georgian mansion with gardens by Capability Brown which was built in 1770 in a magnificent position above a bend in the Dart.

TUCKENHAY. To the southwest of Ashprington, the road drops sharply to Bow Bridge, the site of another fine pub, the Waterman's Arms.

THE WATERMAN'S ARMS nestles beside the River Harbourne and has a long and illustrious history. It was once a smithy, a brewery, a prison during the Napoleonic Wars and a haunt of the Dartmouth 'press-gangs'. Today this award winning Inn offers beautiful accomodation, superb food, traditional ales and cider, and has a wonderful atmosphere. This is a 'hidden place' not to be missed.ETB Three Crowns Highly Commended. AA QQQQQ. RAC Inn **. A West Country Tourist Board Member.

The Waterman's Arms, Bow Bridge, Tuckenhay, Totnes.
Tel: 01803 732214

In a side creek to the south lie the remains of **TUCKENHAY MILL**, an ambitious self-contained industrial development with its own corn and paper mills which was founded by a Mr Tucker in the 1800s; after being abandoned for decades, it has recently been refurbished as private flats and holiday apartments.

CORNWORTHY. The road to Cornworthy, three-quarters-of-a-mile to the east, passes a 14th-century gatehouse which is all that survives of an Augustinian nunnery. The village itself rises steeply towards the parish church of St Peter, a striking building with a sturdy buttressed tower and a surprisingly light Georgian interior; its noteworthy internal features include a simple, but unmutilated, early-15th-century rood screen and a Norman red sandstone font, a seemingly obligatory fixture in this part of the world.

The South Hams District of South Devon is a marvellous place for a holiday as it boasts some of the best beaches in the country backed by mellow Devon countryside.

Right in the heart of all this at the head of its own wooded valley, lies **GITCOMBE HOUSE**, a Grade 2 listed Georgian Manor whose outbuildings have been sympathetically converted into the most charming self catering cottages .

This is truly a first class place for a relaxing break with each cottage featuring a high level of comfort with fully fitted kitchens, direct dial telephones, dishwashers, microwaves and colour T.Vs. in each cottage, and with open fires or wood burning stoves for the chillier days.

All these modern comforts have, however, been incorporated in the buildings without losing the feel of the place.

There is an impressive list of facilities for all guests to enjoy which include both indoor and outdoor heated pools, a games room with snooker and pool tables, and an all-weather championship size tennis court. No excuses for not keeping fit as even raquets and balls are supplied!

If you prefer not to fend for yourself, B & B arrangements are also available in one of the cottages or in the manor itself. A credit to Paul and Lynnie Jolly. Phone or fax for a brochure. Recommended.

Gitcombe Country Cottages, Cornworthy, Totnes.
Tel: 01803 712678. Fax: 01803 712209.

DITTISHAM, two miles to the east, lies on the neck of a small headland which slopes steeply down to a quay on the Dart from where a summer passenger ferry connects with Greenway on the east bank. The surrounding area is known for its plum orchards and contains an unusual number of old manor houses and farms. The part-15th-century church of St George contains some familiar internal features (Norman red sandstone font, truncated rood screen) and two exceptional ones: a set of stained-glass windows in the north aisle by Pugin, and an extraordinary 15th-century stone pulpit which is shaped like a wineglass. The latter's crudely-carved vine-leaf design is interspersed with a number of tall cavities, each of which contains a religious figure resembling a strange petrified marionette.

THE DITTISHAM FRUIT FARM AND CAPTON VINEYARD at Dittisham offers much for a good day out for all the family. Children will be fascinated by an interesting exhibition describing the prehistoric hill settlement. Adults may wish to sample some of the exquisite fruit liqueurs or dry white wine produced from fine fruit grown on the farm and produced in its own winery. Follow signs for 'Prehistoric Hill Settlement Museum'.

Dittisham Fruit Farm and Capton Vineyard, Dittisham, Nr Dartmouth
Tel: 01803 712452

DARTMOUTH. This ancient nautical town stands in a dramatic position on the steeply-sloping west bank of the Dart estuary, a mile inland from its mouth.

This sheltered deep-water port has long been used as an assembly point for departing naval forces: the Second and Third Crusades set sail from here in the 12th-century, and in more recent times, part of the D-Day invasion force congregated here before setting out for the beaches of Normandy in 1944. During the late Middle Ages, Dartmouth grew rapidly to become the fourth largest town in the county (after Exeter, Plymouth and Barnstaple), partly as a result of Henry II's marriage to Eleanor of Aquitaine in 1152. This link with the southwestern France led to dramatic upturn in the wine trade, an activity which was balanced with the export of woollen cloth from Totnes and Ashburton.

Dartmouth's subsequent rise as a commercial port was largely due to one man, John Hawley, an enterprising merchant and seafarer who was elected mayor seven times during the 14th-century. Geoffrey Chaucer met Hawley in 1373 when visiting the town in his official capacity as a customs' inspector, an encounter which is thought to have provided the inspiration for the character of the Shipman in *The Canterbury Tales*. Hawley was responsible for building **Dartmouth Castle**, the imposing fortification guarding the entrance to the Dart estuary which was specifically constructed as an artillery emplacement.

Most of the present remains date from the 15th-century when a special winding mechanism was added to provide the harbour with a second line of defence: a heavy chain stretched across the estuary to Kingswear Castle. (Castle open daily, except Mondays in winter, 10am to 6pm, all year round.) Standing within the castle grounds, the church of **St Petrock** was built in the 17th-century on the site of and early Christian minster; inside there is Norman font and some good monumental brasses. The remains of a 17th-century Civil War redoubt known as **Gallants Bower** can be seen further up the hillside.

Another ruined fortification, one built as part of Henry VIII's coastal defences, can be seen near the site of the **Old Quay** on the southern edge of Dartmouth town centre.

Also situated here is the old **Custom House**, a handsome building of 1739 which has some fine internal plasterwork ceilings. Before the New Quay was constructed in the late 16th-century on land reclaimed from the estuary, ships used to tie up against the wall of St Saviour's parish church, a part-14th-century building with an impressive stone pulpit, good parclose and rood screens, and a striking monumental brass to John Hawley and his two wives; the south door also features some remarkable early ironwork in the design of a tree and two leopards.

For nearly two centuries, Dartmouth's fleet of ocean-going trawlers departed from the New Quay for the rich cod-fishing grounds off Newfoundland. However, when the fishing and textile industries started to decline at the end of the 17th-century, Dartmouth declined with it. A further blow was dealt in 1689 when the admiralty decided to locate its new naval dockyard at Devonport, thanks to the greater availability of land. In the 19th-century it was hoped that Dartmouth would become a terminus for transatlantic steamers; however, the lack of a main line railway meant this also came to nothing.

The one major development which did go Dartmouth's way was the construction of the mighty **Britannia Royal Naval College** between 1899 and 1905; this sprawling red and white building continues to dominate the town from its position on the hillside to the north.

The centre of present-day Dartmouth is a very attractive combination of narrow lanes, historic buildings and picturesque waterfront parades. The quay is much loved by makers of TV costume dramas, it has an undeniable charm. The town has a couple of interesting museums, including one in a shed near the Butterwalk which houses an engine designed by Thomas Newcomen, a native of Dartmouth who began as a local blacksmith and ironmonger, and went on to invent an early version of the industrial steam engine in 1712.

Why not take a thoroughly enjoyable cruise along the River Dart or out to sea on one of **THE RED CRUISERS**. A range of cruises is available including an Evening Cruise, a Wildlife Cruise, circular cruises from Dartmouth, and scheduled sailings between Dartmouth and Totnes 1st Apr to 31st Oct. Winter cruises are also available. On all boats, tea, coffee, bar, toilet facility and a full commentary is given.

NOTE: Hidden Places readers are entitled to a 20% discount on production of this book when purchasing tickets! Booking kiosks are on the North and South Embankments and Boatfloat Corner (opp. Lloyds Bank), Dartmouth. Steamer Quay Totnes, look for the Red Cruisers sign.

The Red Cruisers. 4 Broadstone, Dartmouth, Devon. Tel: 01803 832109

The 100 year old **VICTORIA HOTEL** is ideally located just a short walk from the River Dart, with its boat and fishing trips, and within a short drive of Dartmoor and all of the other places of interest described in this chapter. The standard of accommodation is exceptionally high, all eleven bedrooms having been refurbished in 1993. The Victoria Hotel now offers three twin bedrooms, one large family room and one single bedroom; all but two rooms have en-suite shower or bathroom. All have colour television and tea and coffee making facilities. Each bedroom is elegantly decorated with fine paintings and prints, antique timber head boards adorn comfortable beds and great detail has been paid to the quality of furnishings and lighting which embellish each room's individuality.

A laundry service is also available if required. The Hotel is situated on level ground near to the Market Square in the centre of Dartmouth. Free car parking is available in the market square

The Victoria Hotel, 27-29 Victoria Road, Dartmouth.
Tel: 01803 882572 Fax: 01803 835815

Around Dartmouth

BLACKAWTON. There is a place to take the family here called **WOODLANDS LEISURE PARK** which has a variety of attractions including a farm, adventure playground , and a cafe.

Woodlands Leisure Park Tel : 01804 421598

The village is also known for its odd ritual of worm charming. This involves trying to see who can charm the greatest number of worms out of the ground over a specified period of time.
Competition to win the coveted "Worm Trophy" is fierce and the actual location is kept secret until the last moment to prevent cheating! Sounds like great fun and the proceeds go to charity.
A wonderful example of harmless British eccentricity at its best.
Talking of superlatives, **THE SPORTSMAN'S ARMS** is known by the locals as THE eating place of the area and can be found at Hemborough Post, 3 miles outside Dartmouth on the A3122 road.

The Sportsman's Arms

The Sportsman's has always been a pub and the smart traditional decor and friendly staff make this a very welcoming place indeed and proprietors Jon and Kim Shiner are working hard to improve the already excellent reputation for food.
Good food is the watch-word here and the service in the large restaurant is excellent, There is a comprehensive menu and a specials board - also Chinese, Indian, Thai, Mexican, French and traditional English dishes - all freshly prepared using local produce whenever possible.
Jon and Kim put every effort into achieving their aim of excellent food at realistic prices, and the food is complemented by a select wine list and a good range of real ales and beers.
Unlike many pubs these days, children are very welcome here. There is a lovely family room with toys and a blackboard, a play area in the

spacious garden and special children's portions can be ordered throughout the bars.

The Sportsman's Arms is smart and well-presented without being pretentious. The atmosphere is friendly and cosy - especially in winter with real fires blazing.

The Sportsman's Arms, Hemborough Post, Blackawton.
Tel: 01803 712231

STOKE FLEMING. Two miles to the south of Dartmouth, the church at Stoke Fleming can be seen from miles out to sea; inside, there are some interesting brasses, including one of Thomas Newcomen's great-grandfather.

Close to the village of Stoke Fleming you will find eleven purpose built holiday bungalows at **PPARK WEST**. Set in lovely gardens, the bungalows are close to Blackpool Sands and make a peaceful place to base a family holiday.

Park West, Stoke Fleming, Dartmouth. Tel:01548 580072

A little further on, the A379 passes unwittingly around the northern rim of a good secluded beach, **Blackpool Sands.**

Within walking distance of Blackpool Sands, the elegant, Georgian style of **SOUTHFIELD HOUSE** offers a high standard of B & B accomodation. The double or twin rooms have en-suite or private facilities with televisions, beverage trays and central heating. The food is delicious. You can be sure that a stay here will be relaxed, enjoyable and comfortable.

Southfield House, Stoke Fleming, Nr. Dartmouth. Tel: 01803 770359

SLAPTON. To the south of Stoke Fleming, the A379 runs for two-and-a-half miles along the top of a remarkable sand and shingle bank which divides the salt water of Start Bay from the fresh water of Slapton Ley. This extraordinary natural causeway is bordered a long expanse of beach known as **Slapton Sands**, a shoreline which is lovely on a calm summer's day, but which is wild and windswept for much of the year. During World War II, the whole area was requisitioned as a training ground for the Normandy landings. The local villagers were compulsorily evacuated and the beach sealed off to the outside world in a veil of secrecy which led to one of the worst Allied disasters of the War going virtually unreported. During a major D-Day rehearsal in April 1944, one of the principal vessels responsible for protecting *Operation Tiger* developed a fault and was forced to return to port, an occurrence which allowed an enemy E-Boat to attack the Allied landing forces with impunity and resulted in the deaths of over 600 servicemen, most of them American. Today, a lone Sherman tank stands on the beach as a memorial to this little-publicised military tragedy.

Slapton Ley, the largest natural lake in Devon, is a remarkable freshwater lagoon which is separated from the sea by Slapton's shingle bar. Continually supplied by three small rivers, this shallow body of water is a designated nature reserve which is home to large numbers of freshwater fish, insects, water-loving plants and native and migrating birds. The administrators of the **Slapton Ley Field Study Centre** in Slapton village have laid out a delightful circular nature trail which traverses the northern edge of the Ley.

Whether you choose an afternoon on the sands or a more in-depth investigation of the village, **THE QUEENS ARMS** will offer you a welcome resting place and supply your needs of refreshment. In keeping with other parts of the village, this 14th Century Inn has its historical background too. Sir John Hawkins lived here and no doubt patronised the Inn which was renowned for its White Ale once brewed by many Inns in this area; the rainwater tank used for this process remains in the cellar under the bar today. Nowadays, the Inn sells a fine selection of Real Ales and is featured in Good Beer guides. Home cooked food is served in congenial surroundings including the sun-trap walled gardens.

The Queens Arms, Slapton Village, Devon. Tel: 01548 580800

A short walk from the popular stretch of Slapton Sands and tucked away in the delightful historic village of Slapton is the **TOWER INN** with its white painted walls of local stone, and situated adjacent to the Chantry Tower. Dating back to the 14th century, the Inn originally formed part of the Collegiate Chantry of St, Mary which was founded in 1373 and is thought to have then housed the workers involved in the building of the Monastery. Today, the Inn offers a traditionally warm welcome to visitors from all parts of the world and boasts one of the widest selections of Real Ales and local brews in Devon. Accommodation is offered with en-suite facilities throughout the year, and with a good selection of home cooked fare available, the Tower Inn makes a most interesting location for a break.

The Tower Inn, Slapton Village, Devon. Tel: 01548 580216

TORCROSS is a windblown, yet strangely appealing, settlement at the southern end of Slapton Ley which scratches a living as a small holiday resort and fishing village. The impressively-situated slate quarry which supplied local builders for centuries lies on National Trust-owned land to the south of the village, just below Limpet Rocks.

STOKENHAM, on the A379, one mile inland, is a sizable village with some attractive thatched cottages built of local slate and roofed with reeds from Slapton Ley. The parish church contains an unusually wide rood screen and a Victorian pulpit which is painted with a series of curious symbols and figures.

STOKELEY BARTON is a large fruit and vegetable farm comprising a farm shop and a pick-your-own facility. Set in a charming location near Torcross, it has its own lake, and from the confines of Stokeley Barton it is possible to enjoy spectacular views of the sea and the nearby village. A visit to the farm can be incorporated into a full day out as there are lovely coastal walks and beaches nearby.

Stokeley Barton

The farm shop offers an extensive range of fruit and vegetables including fresh home-grown and locally-grown produce. The product

228

range is quite extensive and includes wholefoods, conserves, local dairy produce, honey from Stokeley's own beehives and a selection of gifts. The plant section includes home-grown bedding plants and an interesting range of patio plants for pots, tubs and hanging baskets. Roses, perennials, shrubs, conifers, cut flowers and pot plants are also available. The pick-your-own includes strawberries, raspberries, gooseberries, red and blackcurrants, plums, apples, beans and sweetcorn, when in season. At the coffee shop there are refreshments, cream teas and a choice of homely fayre.

Stokeley Barton, Stokenham, Kingsbridge, Devon
Tel: 01548 581010

BEESANDS, on the the coast to the south of Torcross, is a pleasant old fishing village which was badly damaged by enemy bombers in a 'tip and run' raid during World War II.

One mile further on, a collection of ruined walls on a rocky ledge above the sea is all that remains of the fishing community of **Hallsands**. In January 1917, a severe storm washed away over twenty buildings and the hamlet was abandoned save for one woman who lived on in the only habitable cottage until her death in 1964. The demise of Hallsands was blamed on offshore dredging: for centuries, the hamlet had stood on safe ground above the waves, then during the 18th- and 19th-centuries, millions of tons of sand and gravel were extracted from Start Bay for use in the construction of the new naval dockyard at Devonport.

However, no connection was ever proved and the inhabitants of Hallsands remain uncompensated for their loss as their homes gradually submit to the wind and the waves. The rugged and spectacular stretch of coastline between Start Point and the Kingsbridge estuary is best explored on foot along the South Devon coastal path. The lighthouse at **Start Point** was built in 1836 in a dramatic position on the cliffs above Ravens Cove, and four miles to the west, another lonely headland, **Prawle Point**, is an ancient lookout station which is the most most southerly point in Devon.

THE FORGE ON THE GREEN. Picturesque views over East Prawle to the sea make the position of this delightful old stone cottage unique.

Luxurious tasteful accommodation including an en-suite SPA BATH, emperor size bed, TV/Video and all other facilities expected for a really comfortable relaxed stay. The elegant lounge/dining, where a full Buffet breakfast and gourmet dinners are served - is furnished with antiques which have been passed down the familiy for the past 200 years. TV and video, books and games are also placed for use. A variety of Cordon Bleu dinner menus are for your choice and can be booked by prior arrangement. Pre-dinner aperitif at 7.15pm.

This is a very friendly place with a pleasant atmosphere and a high standard of service. Patrick, a retired airline flight engineer and enthusiastic golfer, and Ruth who has travelled world wide in the music entertainment business will give you a genuine welcome. Exceptional value tariff with bed and breakfast from £18.00 per person. Evening meal £12.50. Deposit.

E.T.B. HIGHLY COMMENDED

The Forge on the Green, East Prawle, Kingsbridge, South Devon.
Telephone/fax: 01548 511210

KINGSBRIDGE is a pleasant little town which stands at the head of the tidal Kingsbridge estuary, a classic drowned valley, or *ria*, which was formed many thousands of years ago when the land on the southern edge of South West peninsula tilted into the sea. (Similar drowned valleys can be seen at the mouths of the Exe, Dart, Avon, Yealm, Tamar, Fowey, Fal and Helford, although unusually, there is no significant river to speak of here.)

An important crossing place by the 10th-century, Kingsbridge was a prosperous medieval market town which became the capital of the rich agricultural lands of the South Hams. The quay was once an important boat-building centre and mooring place for seagoing vessels, but over the centuries it has gradually become the domain of seabirds and pleasure craft.

Most of the town's interesting buildings can be found in Fore Street, the main street rising northwards from the waterfront. The oldest is **St Edmund's parish church**, a part-13th-century building with a good parclose screen and some noteworthy monuments, including one by John Flaxman. **The Shambles** is an Elizabethan market arcade whose late-18th-century upper floor is supported on six sturdy granite pillars, five of them original.

A little further down the hill, the Town Hall is an early Victorian structure with imposing triple doors above which a curious slate-hung ball clock projects on an arched neck. Above the church, the old Kingsbridge Grammar School of 1670 now houses the **Cookworthy Museum of Rural Life**, a section of which is dedicated to Kingsbridge-born William Cookworthy, an 18th-century Quaker who was the first to manufacture English porcelain from china clay discovered in Cornwall.

Elsewhere in Kingsbridge, there are many fine Georgian and Victorian houses and inns which give the town a relaxed agreeable atmosphere.

All year accommodation with a difference in a rural position yet conveniently on the edge of Kingsbridge. **WASH A BROOK MILL** offers comfortable B & B with the neighbouring stone cottage available for self catering stays.

Wash A Brook Mill, Kingsbridge, Devon. Tel: 01548 852058

Just about a mile outside the village of Kingsbridge lies**COOMBE FARM**. Set in lovely gardens which includes three fishing lakes and offering a typical Farmhouse style welcome to all including children over the age of 12 years. Mr & Mrs Robinson have offered accommodation in the main house for the last six years but also run a working farm. There is a very nice atmosphere here with good-humoured people who obviously lead busy lives. The three letting rooms are large and have en-suite facilities. The customary breakfast will set you up well for the day. Clearly worth seeking out.

Coombe Farm, Kingsbridge, South Devon. Tel: 01548 852038

Fine B & B accommodation can be found near Kingsbridge at **ESTUARY VIEW FARM**, a busy, working farm set in wonderful countryside. This modern, spacious and well furnished bungalow has three double rooms, one with an en-suite bathroom, the other two with a private bathroom.

The atmosphere is very friendly. Joan, who runs the guest house prides herself on the hospitality and warm welcome extended to guests, together with their children. Take the old Salcome Road (Rope Walk) out of Kingsbridge, Estuary View Farm is situated three quarters of a mile along this road, on the right hand side.

Estuary View Farm B & B, Kingsbridge, Devon. Tel: 01548 856487

SOUTH POOL, THE MILLBROOK INN, situated in this lovely village, is reached along the winding lane from Frogmore Bridge, passing rolling farmland. If you park your car at the Millbrook Inn and walk past the wayside cottages you can have a look at the bridge and the ford.

When back at the inn, outside it you will find plenty of benches and tables in the beer garden, beside the brook which gave the inn its name. While you are having your drink and food you may even be joined by the white Aylesbury ducks which live at the inn.

The inn has a very high reputation for its food and is Egon Ronay recommended. On the Specials Board are numerous seafood dishes to tempt you - the famous crab sandwich is excellent - and there is also an impressive selection of desserts. The bars have that pleasant, old-fashioned feel about them and the ceilings are low. There is a draught Bass from the barrel, a selection of guest ales changed regularly, Ruddles Real Ale, a very good Churchwards Cider, and a good selection of wines.

When there is a high tide visitors can travel up the creek from Salcombe and moor at the pontoon and head for the inn. Around the village there are may walks to be enjoyed especially around the estuary where you can see a large collection of wildlife.

Millbrook Inn, South Pool, Nr. Kingsbridge. Tel: 01548 531581

MALBOROUGH. An outstanding example of a historic Devon barton can be found half-a-mile to the east of Malborough, just off the A381 Salcombe road. **Yarde** is a Grade 1 listed Tudor manor farm with an Elizabethan bakery and a Queen Anne farmhouse which is still run as a family farm. (Open Sundays, Wednesdays and Fridays, 2pm to 5pm between Easter and 30 September)

Nestling in a peaceful valley between the Salcombe estuary and Malborough village is **OLD WALLS,** a truly delightful 17th century thatched cob cottage, Grade11 listed and surrounded by pretty gardens complete with a babbling brook running through. Furnished in traditional style, with antiques and patchwork quilts, scented linen and soft towels, all bedrooms are en-suite, with TVs, hot drinks trays with home made shortbread, fresh flowers and spring water. Candle-lit dinner is professionally prepared by the chef proprietor using only fresh, seasonal and where possible organic and local produce; bread is baked daily and Muesli and preserves are home made. Barry and Michelle strive to extend the same comforts to their guests which they enjoy themselves - and they definitely succeed.

To see and appreciate the best of this very unspoilt area of England, guests are advised that travel is best undertaken by foot and ferry. **The National Trust Overbecks House and Gardens** are located at Sharpitor on Bolt Head (15 mins walk) and affords spectacular views along the coast and up the estuary. The area is latticed by footpaths in all directions, including the South Devon Coast Path. In Summer or Winter, whether you are a sailor, a walker, a beachcomber or just want to take life easy for a few days, you can be sure of a very warm welcome at 'Old Walls'. ETB. Listed - Highly Commended.

"Old Walls" B & B, Combe, Nr. Salcombe, Kingsbridge, Devon.
Tel: 01548 844440

HIGHER COLLATON HOUSE, near the lovely town of Salcombe, provides luxury accommodation in a quiet valley. This fine Georgian farmhouse is full of character and stands in 8 acres of beautiful gardens and grounds. All of the bedrooms enjoy superb country views, they are

233

well furnished and each has its own bath/shower and toilet. A sunny walled garden provides a perfect spot in which to relax, the guest lounge has colour television and a log fire for cooler evenings.

The food is excellent, guaranteed to keep you going all day, prepared using fresh eggs and additive-free bacon & sausages. A no smoking house. From A381 follow signs for Collaton. The House is situated on a sharp right-hand bend at Lower Collaton.

Higher Collaton House, Collaton, Malborough, Nr Kingsbridge, South Devon. Tel:01548 560826

SALCOMBE. A delightful former fishing village and yachting centre which occupies one of the loveliest coastal settings in the West Country. The resort lies a mile inland from the sandy bar at the mouth of the Kingsbridge estuary and is sheltered from the prevailing west winds by a steep hillside.

As a result, it has one of the mildest climates in the country, and it is not unusual to see mimosa, palms, and even orange trees in the terraced gardens which rise from the water's edge. Salcombe's long association with the sea is brought to life at the **Museum of Maritime and Local History** on the Custom House Quay.

Cars are banned from the central area and in summer, the narrow streets throng with visitors, many of whom arrive by yacht or pleasure craft from the marinas of Southeast England and continental Europe.

A plethora of small shops and eating places have sprung up to satisfy their demand for the modish and expensive, and at certain times of the year, the town takes on the atmosphere of an exclusive resort which has more in common with the South of France than the South Hams.

THE WOOD HOTEL in Salcombe enjoys spectacular views from an outstanding location and offers 4 star service for 1 star prices. Salcombe's mild microclimate makes this hotel the ideal base for a sailing or walking holiday, not only in the summer, but also during the quiet spring or autumn months.

The hotel has a friendly family atmosphere and excels in every respect. The five clean and bright bedrooms are of a high standard and are completely equipped.

The food can only be described as excellent, being expertly prepared from homegrown vegetables, local fish and meats, and served from bone china with silver cutlery. Breakfast can best be enjoyed on the hotel's magnificent terrace. Pat and Malcolm, the owners, are very proud of their hotel and you can be sure that you will receive a warm welcome and completely enjoy your stay in this lovely 'hidden place'.

The Wood Hotel, de Courcy Road, South Sands, Salcombe.
Tel: 01548 842778   Fax: 01548 844277

The estuary itself is an ideal place to learn to sail and there are many small boats moored here. You will doubtless notice a large ferry moored here which is in fact The Egremont, a former Mersey ferry. Now home to a sailing school.

If you are looking for a place to stay which takes full advantage of the beauty which the Salcombe estuary affords, then The **SUNNY CLIFF HOTEL**should fit the bill.

The Sunny Cliff Hotel

It is ideally located only a few minutes from the town centre and occupies a prime water front location with oustanding views across the estuary and beyond.

There are 18 comfortable and well appointed rooms of which 11 are en-suite, each room has T.V and tea and coffeee making facilities with a view of the estaury. Meals are served in the dining room which has picture windows where you can enjoy your breakfast and watch the many small craft that are drawn to this particularly beautiful part of the country.

For the more active among you there is a landing stage and moorings available, whilst within the grounds on a terrace cut into the cliff is a sea water swimming pool. A small bar and lounge complete the picture of a well run and friendly hotel, ideal for families.

The Sunny Cliff Hotel, Cliff Road, Salcombe. Tel: 01548 842207.

For those wishing to avoid the peak season hustle and bustle , relief lies within a few hundred yards. To the south, a pleasant lane runs along the western edge of the estuary past a series of small headlands and sandy coves.

ALSTON FARM CAMPING AND CARAVAN SITE near Salcombe is set in lovely countryside, has very good facilities, including ample toilet blocks equipped with showers and wash facilities with free hot water, and electrical hook-up points. The camping area is spacious, flat and well drained. This is a great site for a camping or caravan holiday.

Alston Farm Camping and Caravan Site, near Salcombe.
Tel: 01548 561260

On a rock beside North Sands stand the remains of **Salcombe Castle**, or **Fort Charles**, a fortification which was built in Tudor times as part of Henry VIII's Channel-coast defences. During the English Civil War, its Royalist garrison was the last in Devon to hold out against the Parliamentarians (indeed, it is claimed the Royalists only agreed to surrender in return for the castle being renamed Fort Charles). Sadly, the structure has since fallen into disrepair and now only a tower and some shattered walls remain.

Originally an Admiralty coastal lookout, **Rickham Coastguard Station** at **Gara Rock** has a long and interesting history. Constructed in 1847, its original purpose was to safeguard shipping from the infamous smugglers and wreckers operating in the area. In 1909 the station was disbanded and the building was purchased to begin its career as a private hotel. At the outbreak of the Second World War however, Gara Rock was requisitioned by the armed forces and occupied as an HQ for nearby West Prawle radar station. Following the war Gara Rock returned to private ownership once more and was purchased in 1961 by Mr & Mrs Leslie Richards. Today **GARA ROCK HOTEL**is owned and run by their son Colin and his wife Suzanne. The hotel has an enviable reputation, with its spectacular views of the coastline, clifftop walks across National Trust land, deserted beaches, secluded coves and welcoming oak panelled interior complete with roaring log fires, it is easy to see why.

The hotel operates differently to other hotels, here a large choice of different types of accommodation is available all year to suit your individual requirements and budget.

Some suites have self catering facilities, whilst others are traditional hotel rooms. The majority of suites enjoy superb coastal views, the others look across the hotel's tennis courts and swimming pool to countryside beyond. All are comfortable and well equipped.

You will enjoy the wide variety of home cooked English and Continental Cuisine which includes home made desserts, puddings and pies, scones with clotted cream, with local produce and vegetables grown in the hotel's gardens. Parents can participate in the many leisure facilities available at the Gara Rock Hotel whilst their children are entertained by the Clown or are enjoying activities in the 'mini-club'.

For those looking for a chance to 'de-stress' and unwind, a range of relaxation therapies are provided by Nicholsons Complementary Health Practice at Kingsbridge, who offer Shiatsu, Theraputic massage & Aromatherapy, Alexander Technique, Reiki Healing, Reflexology, Homeopathy and Mc Timoney Chiropractic on the premesis.

From Totnes take the A581 to Kingsbridge, then follow the A379 heading towards Torcross and Dartmouth. At Frogmore turn right over the bridge and follow the signs for East Portlemouth and Gara Rock.

Gara Rock Hotel, East Portlemouth, Salcombe, South Devon. Tel: 01548 842342 Fax: 01548 843033

The striking promontory known as **Sharpitor** is the location of a charming National Trust-owned museum and garden, **Overbecks**. This handsome Edwardian house stands in a breathtaking position above the Kingsbridge estuary and enjoys one of the finest views in South Devon. The six-acre gardens are famous for their collection of rare and tender plants which thrive in these mild coastal conditions. The museum contains a secret children's room, an exhibition on the natural history of Sharpitor, and a room devoted to the clipper schooner, Salcombe's traditional sailing ship; also on show are special collections of shipbuilding tools, model boats, toys and old photographs. (Museum open daily except Saturdays, 11am to 5.30pm between end-March and end-October; Gardens open daily, all year round.)

The coastline to the south and west of Salcombe, some of the most magnificent in Britain, is now largely owned by the National Trust. Here, great slanting chunks of gneiss and schist tower above the coastal path to form a breathtaking, if somewhat demanding, clifftop walk. At **Bolt Head**, the rock forms a jagged promontory which protrudes into the western approaches to the Kingsbridge estuary, and further west, the spectacular cliffs between Bolt Head and Bolt Tail are interrupted by a steep descent at **Soar Mill Cove**. After rounding Bolt Tail, the footpath drops down to the sheltered sandy beach and tourist shops of **Hope Cove**.

Nestling in its own secluded valley within the National Trust Coastal Park, just a short walk from the sea, **HOPE BARTON BARNS** is an exclusive group of sensitively restored traditional stone barns available for relaxing, affordable time share holidays all year round. Every cottage is unique in character, but all are superbly furnished and equipped to the highest standards. Guests have free access to a beautiful indoor heated swimming pool, sauna, multi-gym, play room, bar/lounge, table tennis, En-Tout-Cas tennis court, boules terrain and, for those wishing to catch their own supper, a well stocked trout lake. If you don't feel like cooking, you can have delicious Farmhouse Fayre delivered directly to your cottage. Sea fishing trips are also available.

Hope Barton Barns, Hope Cove, South Devon.
Tel: 01548 561393 Fax:01548 560938

GALMPTON. Just inland from Hope Cove is the village of Galmpton and a little further down a cul - de -sac is a gem of a place tucked away in **Maypool**.

Converted from Victorian cottages and part of a country estate, **The MAYPOOL PARK HOTEL** enjoys a wonderfully tranquil setting overlooking the River Dart with magnificent views of the Paignton and Dartmouth Railway's steam trains heading towards Dartmouth.

The hotel's 'Taste of Taylor's' restaurant has a fine reputation for its imaginative gourmet cuisine, prepared from the finest of fresh local ingredients.

The ten well furnished bedrooms all have spacious bathrooms, direct-dial telephone, colour TV, radio, hairdryer and other amenities. A no smoking establishment.

From Galmpton, follow signs for Maypool, after one mile, turn left into a narrow lane marked 'no through road', the hotel is a half mile down on the left.

The Maypool Park Hotel, Maypool, Galmpton, Devon, TQ5 0ET
Tel: 01803 842442

THURLESTONE. A lovely beach can be found a couple of miles to the north at Thurlestone, one of the most attractive coastal villages in the South Hams. In fact, there are two beaches here, divided by a headland on which a grandiose between-the-wars hotel stands alone.

Both beaches are recommended, especially the one to the south with its fine view of the holed, or *thyrled*, stone, the offshore rock from which the settlement takes its name. The village itself is situated on a long flat-topped ridge some distance away from the beaches. Despite the influx of summer visitors, it has managed to retain a slightly genteel air and is an attractive mixture of flower-decked cottages, old farm buildings, and long-established shops and inns. The part-13th-century parish church of All Saints is worth a look for its early-15th-century south porch, Norman font and Lady chapel.

Only 400 yds from **South Milton Sands** is a delightful place to stay that shouldn't be overlooked,**THE LITTLE ORCHARD HOTEL**enjoys wonderful views and offers high standards of accomodation including private bathrooms, colour TVs and excellent food. Two comfortable guest lounges, one with a welcoming log fire, help to make a stay here an enjoyable one.

The Little Orchard Hotel, Thurlestone Sands, Kingsbridge.
Tel: 01548 561279

With direct access to the coastal path and enjoying breathtaking cliff top views of Thurlestone Rock, The **SEAMARK HOLIDAY APARTMENTS**, at Thurlestone Sands, are popular with walkers and families alike. The self-contained apartments are fully furnished and equipped, the grounds are spacious and safe for children to play in. Follow signs to Thurlestone Sands.

Seamark Holiday Apartments, Thurlestone Sands, Kingsbridge, South Devon. Tel: 01548 561300

BANTHAM. One mile to the north as the crow flies, another fine sandy beach can be found on the east side of the Avon estuary at Bantham.

For such a relatively small village there is a surprising wealth of history about the area pointing to evidence of Bantham being a centre of early tin trading between ancient Britons and Gauls.

By the 8th century Anglo - Saxons were well established here, farming the fertile soil. The surrounding water too provided a great source of income in the form of pilchard fishing. A small armada of boats would be kept busy during the boom years and the humble pilchards were cured and even exported. There must have been some interesting aromas in the air around the village at times!

The village continued to be a busy little port until around 100 years ago with sailing barges bringing building stone and coal for the surrounding area.

Bantham has also seen its fair share of shipwrecks and the waters aound here have yielded some fascinating finds over the years, some of the timbers from these wrecks are incorporated in buildings in the village. A fine example of this can be found in neighbouring Thurlestone where timbers from a wreck from the Spanish Armada have been incorporated in the Village inn.

Widcombe House

Situated close to the village of Bantham, only 2 miles from the sea, **WIDCOMBE HOUSE** provides superb B & B accommodation and enjoys spectacular views across a wide valley down to the sea.

All of the tastefully furnished rooms have en-suite facilities, colour

TV, radio, refrigerator and tea & coffee facilities.

The food is excellent, a fine breakfast will set you up for the day, evening meals, vegetarian dishes or snacks are available on request. There is ample parking on site. A non-smoking establishment, not suitable for children under 14 or pets. AA Premier Selected QQQQQ.

Widcombe House B & B, Bantham, Devon. 01548 561084

There is an excellent view from here across to **Burgh Island**, a rocky offshore islet which is connected to the mainland by a tidal causeway. (Although only three-quarters-of-a-mile away across the mouth of the Avon, the journey by road involves an eight-mile diversion via Aveton Gifford.) The island is dotted with a handful of buildings, including an inn and a large hotel. Look out also the extraordinary, long-legged bus which is used for transporting over enthusiastic revellers back to the mainland after the tide has cut off their retreat. Burgh Island is thought to have provided Agatha Christie with the setting for her murder mystery, *Ten Little Indians*.

RINGMORE is another mile to the north. Here the bungalows and buckets and spades of Bigbury-on-Sea and Challaborough give way to ancient farmsteads and thatched stone cottages. This delightful old village lies half-a-mile inland at the head of a steep combe down which there is a pleasant walk to Ayrmer Cove. The parish church of All Saints is a pleasing 13th-century building with a curious spire. The dramatist, R C Sherriff, wrote his celebrated play about World War I while staying at Ringmore's medieval inn, a fine establishment which, in his honour, was renamed *The Journey's End*. Further along the coast to the west, **Wonwell Beach** at the mouth of the Erme is another good sandy beach which almost disappears at high tide. More reliable and sheltered is the beach on the opposite side below **Mothecombe**; lying within the Flete estate and virtually unspoiled as a result, this delightful south-facing cove lies at one end of a spectacular stretch of the coastal footpath.

HOLBETON. From Mothecombe, there is a superb riverside walk along the wooded bank of the Erme estuary to Holbeton, an attractive village with a good pub, an unusual row of restored almshouses, and an imposing 14th-century church with a soaring 112ft spire. The church some exceptional carved woodwork and an extraordinary 17th-century monument to Sir Thomas Hele of Flete consisting of 22 figures kneeling in rows above his armour-clad effigy.

Flete House lies within a pleasant landscaped park, one mile to the north of the village. Originally an elegant Elizabethan manor house, it was extensively remodelled in ostentatious neo-Gothic style on two occasions during the Victorian era. (Open Wednesdays and Thursdays, 2pm to 5pm between 1 May and 30 September.)

ERMINGTON and UGBOROUGH To the north of Flete, these two sizable villages, both with fine churches and pubs, lie to the north of the old B3210 Totnes road.

Ermington Church

The former is built to an ancient Saxon plan and the latter around an open square. The imposing church at Ugborough stands on top of a substantial prehistoric earthwork making it clearly visible from Ugborough Beacon on the northernmost limits of the parish; inside, there are some exceptional features, including a rood screen with a set of 32 painted panels, an unusual monumental brass of an unknown 15th-century woman, and a carved roof boss in the north aisle depicting a sow and her litter, as at Braunton (see chapter two).

Established in part in 1392, the delightful traditional Devon inn, **THE ANCHOR**, can be found adjacent to the village square in Ugborough. This attractive village has regularly won awards in the "Best Kept Village" Competitions, and is conveniently located either for touring holidays in South Devon and Dartmoor, or for business trips to Plymouth which is only 12 miles distant.

The bar offers a wide selection of both National and local real ales, some of which are served in the traditional way straight from the barrel. The popular restaurant offers an extensive à la carte menu which is both imaginative and varied, featuring dishes from around the world prepared by Sheelagh Jeffreys, the owner.

She takes great pride in buying the freshest produce available and this is reflected in the Fish and Game board which changes continually depending on the availability from the markets, the fishermen's catches, and with the seasons. Vegetarian dishes are also listed together with an interesting Bar menu. Each Autumn, The Anchor holds a "Game Festival" where they feature unusual meats such as alligator, ostrich and bison and each month there is a "Gourmet Evening". Additionally, there is live music every Monday and Saturday nights.

En-suite accommodation is provided with a choice of single, double, twin or family rooms. All of the rooms have TV and tea/coffee making facilities.

The Anchor Inn, Ugborough, South Devon Tel/Fax: 01752 892283

MODBURY. This handsome old market town of lies in a steep-sided valley, two miles to the east of Flete. Yet to be rerouted, the busy

Modbury

A379 Plymouth-Kingsbridge road descends between rows of elegant 18th- and early-19th-century town houses before rising again on the other side. Now a quiet and prosperous residential town, Modbury was once an important agricultural centre in its own right.

At one time, it could boast ten pubs (now there are two), and each year it hosted a great fair which lasted nine days. The part-14th-century parish church of St George, with its distinctive 130ft spire, reflects the town's former glory; it stands proudly on the hill at the west end of town, a landmark which can be seen for miles around. Inside, the south transept is filled with monuments to the Champernowne family, local lords of the manor who once owned a great mansion nearby. (During the English Civil War, this was the site of major skirmish when 2000 Royalist troops were routed by a force of Devonshire clubmen.)

A number of fine early buildings have survived in the centre of Modbury, including the 18th-century **Assembly Rooms and the half-timbered Exeter Inn,** a handsome part-Elizabethan building with elegant bay windows. A truly hidden place can be found in the lanes to the south of the Dartmouth road, four miles east of Modbury: **Hazelwood House** is an enchanting arts, music and study centre which lies hidden in the steep wooded valley of the River Avon.

Heading west on the A379 once more towards Plymouth brings you to Yealmpton.

YEALMPTON Pronounced 'Yampton', straddles the River Yealm and claims to have been the home of Old Mother Hubbard.

Sarah Martin, who wrote the nursery rhyme at nearby Kitley in 1805, based her character on the housekeeper there. Whether or not Kitley's housekeeper really did live at 'Old Mother Hubbard's Cottage' in Yealmpton, this thatched and ivy-clad dwelling (now a restaurant) is a sheer delight and certainly looks as if it belongs in a fairytale of some kind!

The National Shire Horse Centre can be found one mile east of the village, and is well worth a visit for its exhibitions and displays by these marvellous creatures, including three daily parades during the summer season. The term 'Gentle Giants' is apt indeed; even the smallest child seems unperturbed by their immense size. Opened in 1978, this is now the leading centre in the country for the breeding and preservation of these magnificent horses. The 200-year-old farm has some fine old buildings and the resident blacksmith, wheelwright and saddler can be seen practising their traditional skills. Other attractions are the vintage farm machinery museum, an adventure playground, a crafts centre, displays by birds of prey, and a butterfly house. The Centre is easy to find, just look out for the brown and white signs - and remember that last admissions are at 4pm.

South of Yealmpton are **Kitley Caves**, where visitors can explore the illuminated passages and marvel at the rock formations. Well laid out information boards give you plenty of insight into the origins of the strange shapes of the rocks and the geographical history of this area, while back on the surface there is a giftshop, a museum and a children's play area.

NEWTON FERRERS. A picturesque fishing village of white-washed cottages that slopes down to the river. One of many Devon villages that came into the possession of Henry de Ferrieres after the Norman Conquest, it is now one of the South Coast's best loved yachting centres.

NOSS MAYO When the creek dries out at low tide, it is possible to walk across to this equally delightful village on the other side.

St Peter's Church stands in the village itself, built in 1882 for the convenience of the local worshippers, who previously had to take the long trek one and a half miles to the south-east of the village to reach the old 14th century church. This now stands in picturesque ruins on an isolated spot on the cliffs near Stoke Point, and from here you can walk along a spectacular stretch of the South Devon Coast Path, round the headland to Erme Mouth and Mothecombe.

NETTON FARMHOUSE is located about one mile south of the pretty village of Noss Mayo in the heart of unspoilt countryside surrounded by National Trust land which ensures the protection of this beautiful area.

The Devon Coastal Path is only minutes away where the views are quite breathtaking.

The Farmhouse was built over one hundred years ago and has been sympathetically upgraded over a number of years to modern standards. The en-suite bedrooms are nicely decorated and furnished and provide tea and coffee making facilities, there's a separate television lounge, and guests can enjoy the luxury of the heated swimming pool, tennis court and games room.

Lesley Ann's welcome is a most friendly one, she will be delighted to prepare any meals you may wish to take "at home" in addition to the traditional farmhouse breakfast; local fish and 'roasts' being two particular specialities. Children are most welcome but there are no facilities for pets. Ask about out of season bargain breaks. AA 4 Q's and ETB Highly Commended.

Netton Farmhouse, Noss Mayo, Devon. Tel: 01752 873080

WEMBURY .As the crow flies, lies just a couple of miles to the north-west of Noss, but to reach it we had to make our way back to the A379 and take a left hand turn after Brixton. In the village, only 400 yards from the sea and surrounded by National Trust land, you will find **BAY COTTAGE** in Church Road. Views of Wembury church and the famous Mew Stone rock are just some of the lovely sights to be enjoyed on this beautiful stretch of coast. Sue and Andrew Farrington are the sort of hosts who will not object if you just wish to sit in the garden and enjoy home-made lunches and cream teas - the emphasis here is on peace and relaxation.

However, with all that wonderful countryside around you, we feel sure you will leap out of bed at dawn every day to set off on your rambles! In addition to a substantial breakfast, Sue is happy to provide her guests with an evening meal by arrangement, which can be enjoyed in the charming dining room. She will tempt you with her delicious recipes for crab and mussels, and can also cater for special diets and vegetarians. Plenty of information on the local area is supplied, and Sue and Andrew will be glad to lend you books and maps from their large collection, if you need further inspiration. To put it in a nutshell, Bay Cottage can offer you a holiday by the sea without the crowds, in comfortable, informal surroundings.

Bay Cottage, 150 Church Road, Wembury, Plymouth 01752-862559

The Great Mew Stone (presumably so called to distinguish it from the much smaller rock known simply as The Mew Stone, near Bayard's Cove back round the coast at Dartmouth) stands a mile offshore in Wembury Bay. This lonely islet was apparently once inhabited, but is now the home of seabirds and is also used for training purposes by the HMS Cambridge gunnery school on Wembury Point. Wembury church makes a dramatic landmark as it stands isolated on the edge of the cliff, and the coastal path offers spectacular views of the Yealm estuary to the east and Plymouth Sound to the west. The path is, however, occasionally closed to walkers when the firing range is in use, so look out for the red warning flags. After you have explored the area thoroughly, you can make your way down to the old water mill on the beach - beautifully restored by the National Trust - for a much needed cup of tea.

DOWN THOMAS There can be no better combination than staying on a farm that also happens to be situated in an area of outstanding natural beauty, on one of the finest stretches of coastline in England. This experience can be enjoyed at a delightful bed and breakfast establishment at Down Thomas, which can be found just over a mile to the north-west of Wembury.

Mrs MacBean is your host at **GABBER FARM**, where country ways mean courteous and friendly service. We found this to be a very relaxing family home, unpretentious and comfortable. This is very much a working farm, so be prepared for a bit of straw and mud! However, the accommodation itself is spotless and children are made very welcome. The farm was originally owned by one Stephen le Gabber around 1230 and he also owned the surrounding land. The MacBean family has occupied and worked this land for 40 years, and they are happy for children (under parental supervision) to have a close look at how a farm functions. Mrs MacBean provides good home cooking, and there are two lounges for guests to use, one with a piano if you fancy a sing-song. It is unlikely that any guests will feel they are intruding here, as is sometimes the case when accommodation is offered in a family home. On the contrary, we can happily recommend this as a very hospitable place to stay.

Gabber Farm, Down Thomas, Wembury, Plymouth 01752-862265

PLYMOUTH. With around a quarter-of-a-million inhabitants, Plymouth is the largest centre of population in the South West peninsula. Compared to many settlements, however, its development has been relatively recent.

It wasn't until the end of the 12th-century that the site was recognised as having any potential as a military and commercial port, and it wasn't until the 1500s that it established itself as the main base for the

English fleet guarding the western Channel against a seaborne attack from Spain.

The best way of becoming acquainted with this historic city is to approach **Plymouth Hoe** on foot from the main shopping area along the now-pedestrianised Armada Way.

As the grassy thoroughfare rises onto a broad limestone ridge, a magnificent vista opens up across Plymouth Sound, one of the finest natural deep-water harbours in Europe.

The inlet is framed on either side by wooded hills which curve into the sea and more often than not, the surface of the water is sprinkled with a fascinating assortment of marine craft ranging from tiny sailing dinghies to huge naval frigates and cross-Channel ferries. The Hoe itself is a wide, partly-paved open space which combines the functions of promenade, public park and parade ground.

It was here that in 1588, Sir Francis Drake completed his leisurely game of bowls before sailing out to defeat the Spanish Armada; his statue, a copy of the one by Boehm at Tavistock, looks proudly towards the horizon.

Just offshore, the striking shape of **Drake's Island** rises like Alcatraz from the deep swirling waters at the mouth of the River Tamar. It its time, this stark fortified islet has been used as a gunpowder repository (it is said to be riddled with underground tunnels where the powder was stored), a prison and a youth adventure centre.

Two miles from the Hoe, Plymouth's remarkable **Breakwater** protects the Sound from the destructive effects of the prevailing southwesterly winds.

Built between 1812 and 1840, this massive mile-long construction required around four million tons of limestone which was ferried out in barges from quarries on the mainland.

The surface was finished with enormous dovetailed blocks of stone and the structure was rounded off with a lighthouse at one end and a raised cage to protect marooned sailors at the other. Twelve miles further out and visible on a clear day, the famous **Eddystone Lighthouse** warns shipping of the treacherous group of rocks which rise up from the floor of the English Channel. The present lighthouse is the fourth to be built here: the first, a fragile timber structure, was swept away in a huge storm in 1703 taking its builder, the ship-owner Winstanley, with it. The third was built in 1759 by John Smeaton to a revolutionary design using dovetail-jointed blocks of granite. It lasted for 120 years before the rocks on which it stood began to collapse and the lighthouse had to be dismantled; however, it was soon rebuilt on Plymouth Hoe and today, it is still one of the city's most rewarding tourist attractions.

The view to the west from the top of Smeaton's Tower takes in **Millbay Docks**, Plymouth's busy commercial port which was once a terminus for transatlantic passenger liners; today, the docks handle a variety of merchant shipping, including the continental ferry services to Brittany and northern Spain. The view to the east is dominated by the

Statue of Sir Francis Drake, Plymouth Hoe

Citadel, a massive fortification which was built by Charles II to guard the seaward approaches to Plymouth. Although ostensibly built as a defence against seaborne attack, the presence of gun ports facing the town suggest an ulterior motive. (During the English Civil War, the town declared for Parliament and held out for four years against the forces of Charles' ill-fated father.) The Citadel is still a military base, but can be visited between 1 May and 30 September on a guided tour basis (charge payable). The magnificent baroque gateway on its northern side is particularly worthy of inspection.

Plymouth's oldest quarter, the **Barbican**, lies below and a short distance to the northeast of the Citadel. Now a lively entertainment area filled with restaurants, pubs and an innovative small theatre, the Barbican, it was here that 15th-century merchants began trading in wine and wool with their opposite numbers in continental Europe. The influence of Drake helped to establish the port as a naval base in Elizabethan times, and in 1620 the Pilgrim Fathers set out from the **Mayflower Steps** on their historic voyage to Massachusetts; the names of the Mayflower's company are listed on a board on nearby Island House, now the tourist information office. Plymouth's Sutton Harbour became a major departure point for migrants seeking their fortune in the colonies and as a result, there are now around forty Plymouths in the English-speaking world. A number of interesting old buildings around the Barbican have survived the combined ravages of time and the Luftwaffe, including the **Elizabethan House** in New Street, the **Merchant's House** in St Andrew's Street, and **Prysten House**, a 15th-century priest's house which is hidden behind St Andrew's church, off Royal Parade; all now contain delightful specialist museums.

The increased threat from France which came at the end of the 17th-century prompted the admiralty to build a new naval dockyard at the western end of the Channel. Plymouth was chosen, but instead of extending the existing port at the mouth of the Plym, a new deep-water site was developed on the Tamar estuary, which here is known as the Hamoaze (pronounced *Ham-oys*). Over the following two centuries, the **Devonport Dockyard** grew to cover 240 acres along a two-mile stretch of riverside, and the surrounding town grew to outstrip its parent to the east. The massive **Royal William Victualling Yard** was added in the early 19th-century on a partially reclaimed site at the end of Durnford Street in Stonehouse; here, all the foodstuffs and supplies required by the western fleet were manufactured and packed in watertight barrels.

The best way to view the Devonport Dockyard is to take a trip on board one of the many pleasure craft which depart from the Mayflower Steps in the Barbican. A good view of Royal William Yard can also be had from the passenger ferry which plies back and forth between the Admiral's Hard in Stonehouse and Cremyll on the Cornish side of the Tamar. This trip is well worth taking for the delightful walk which leads through **Mount Edgcumbe Country Park** to the ancient smuggling village of **Cawsand** (in summer, a return ferry service connects directly with the

Barbican). At Cremyll, the Tudor-style Mount Edgcumbe House stands in a dramatic position overlooking Plymouth Sound; its interior had to be completely restored after the building was hit by incendiary bombs during the Second World War. (Open Wednesdays to Sundays and Bank Holiday Mondays, 11am to 5.30pm between 1 April and 31 October.)

Although Devonport is not noted for its architectural merit, it contains an extraordinary group of mock-classical buildings dating from the 1820s. John Foulston's 'experimental' civic centre in Ker Street includes a town hall modelled on the Parthenon, a civil and military library, and a massive column which was intended to support a statue of George IV had the necessary funds been forthcoming. Prior to 1914, Plymouth, Stonehouse and Devonport were three separate civic areas linked by a single road, **Union Street**. This long straight thoroughfare continues to be a centre for bawdy entertainment of the kind which typifies a naval town, and on Friday and Saturday nights, its pubs and clubs attract revellers from miles around. A superb old musical hall has survived at one end, although now it is in need of renovation.

Although the Barbican area managed to escape serious damage during the Blitz, much of the rest of Plymouth was devastated by a succession of enemy air raids during the spring of 1941. The naval base and dockyard at Devonport made the city an important strategic target, and its location on the South West peninsula meant that it was both difficult to defend and easy to reach from northern France. On the night of 21 March, the entire centre of the city was razed to the ground by the combined effects of high-explosive and incendiary bombs. (It was recorded that at one point, the heat grew so fierce that shop windows melted and were seen to flow down the streets in rivers of molten glass). Many of the city's most important civic and residential buildings were destroyed, including much of the early-19th-century work of John Foulston, the architect who was to Plymouth what Nash was to London. The 15th-century parish church of St Andrew had to be almost totally rebuilt; however, it was decided that the nearby Charles' church would be left as a burned out shell as a memorial to the 1000 who died and 5000 who were injured in air-raids during the course of the War. A powerful and poignant audio-visual presentation on Plymouth's Blitz can be seen at the **Dome**, an award-winning museum which is located on the southern side of the Hoe.

Even before the end of World War II, plans were being drawn up for Plymouth's resurrection. The renowned town planner, Sir Patrick Abercrombie, was commissioned to come up with a bold scheme which would sweep away the largely-Victorian street plan and create a modern and vibrant city centre. Despite most of the rebuilding being carried out in the 1950s (not the most celebrated era for architecture) his scheme has gradually taken on a pleasant distinguished air, and today Plymouth has the character of a prosperous regional capital. The present-day city has some excellent facilities, including a first-rate **Museum and Art Gallery** near Drake Circus, the **Theatre Royal** with its two auditoriums in Royal

Parade, the **Arts Centre** with its art-house cinema in Looe Street, and the **Pavilions** concert hall, leisure pool and skating rink at the foot of Western Approach.

PLYMPTON   Four miles to the east of Plymouth and now incorporated within its city boundaries, the ancient settlement of Plympton predates its much larger neighbour by several hundred years. A small ecclesiastical community was established here in the 9th-century which grew into an Augustinian priory that was second in size only to the great abbey at Tavistock. The Normans built a motte and bailey castle at Plympton St Maurice (the remains of the keep can still be seen), and in 1328, Plympton was made one of Dartmoor's four Stannary towns. The part-14th-century parish church of St Mary has a striking 108ft granite tower and contains some impressive monuments and tombs, and the Guildhall is a handsome late-17th-century building constructed of local granite and slate. However, the town is perhaps best known for being the birthplace of the 18th-century portrait painter, Sir Joshua Reynolds. He was educated at Plympton Grammar School where his father was head teacher, and it is a remarkable occurrence that three other notable artists, James Northcote, Benjamin Haydon and Charles Eastlake, were also educated at this small Devon school in the three-quarters-of-a-century which followed. Hardwick Hill above Plympton was the site of an admiralty shutter telegraph station, one of thirty such stations built in the late 18th-century to link Plymouth with London (another stood on Telegraph Hill near Exeter).

A number of Reynolds' paintings can be seen at **Saltram House**, one of the most impressive country mansions in Devon which lies on the southern edge of Plympton. Now under the ownership of the National Trust, it occupies a glorious site overlooking the Plym estuary, along which there is a delightful circular walk. The present building is largely 18th-century and was built by John Parker on the site of a Tudor predecessor. In the 1760s, the dining room and 'double-cube' saloon were decorated at great expense by Robert Adam, with an outstanding collection of period furniture and ceilings painted by Zucchi. Other attractions are the great kitchen with its fascinating assortment of period kitchenware, the orangery in the grounds, and old chapel with its gallery of West Country art. (Open daily except Fridays and Saturdays, 12.30pm to 5.30pm between end-March and end-October.)

From Saltram, a footpath and cycle track follows the route of the old railway up the beautiful wooded valley of the River Plym (another place to join it is at Plym Bridge, two miles upstream). The track leads northwards past Shaugh Bridge, the site of the famous 400ft Dewerstone Rock, and on to the moor near Clearbrook, a village with an excellent pub, the Skylark. The church at **Shaugh Prior** contains a massive elaborately-carved oak font cover which was discovered abandoned in a nearby farm building in 1870. The road to the east skirts the enormous china clay quarries which have been eating away at the landscape of

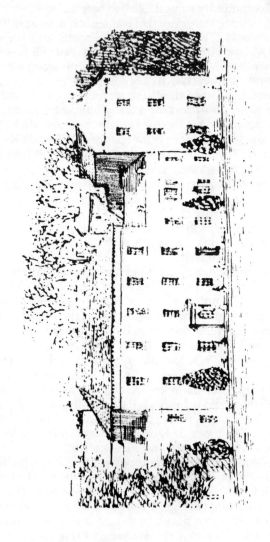

Saltram House

Shaugh Moor since 1840.

CORNWOOD, a couple of miles to the southeast, is a pleasant village on the River Yealm which is a good base for discovering the many Bronze Age and industrial remains which litter this attractive fringe of southern Dartmoor.

The indented coastal strip to the east of Plymouth contains a number of places of interest. **Mount Batten Point**, the headland at the mouth of the Plym estuary (which here is known as Cattewater), has been a fortified site since the time of the ancient Romans. It was used during World War II as a base for seaplanes and it is soon to be released by the Royal Air Force for redevelopment as a recreational facility; Mount Batten Tower is now under the ownership of English Heritage and is occasionally open to the public.

We thought that this was the perfect place to end this particular chapter, and indeed our exploration of Devon. For us, it neatly summed up the main delights of this lovely county; friendly people, magnificent scenery, an unspoilt coastline, and most definitely a place to return to time and time again. We have only been able to scratch the surface of all that Devon has to offer, but we hope that this will make it all the more exciting for our readers when they set off to discover its many other charms for themselves.

The View from Gara Rock

CHAPTER SIX

EAST & NORTH CORNWALL

The Old Post Office, Tintagel

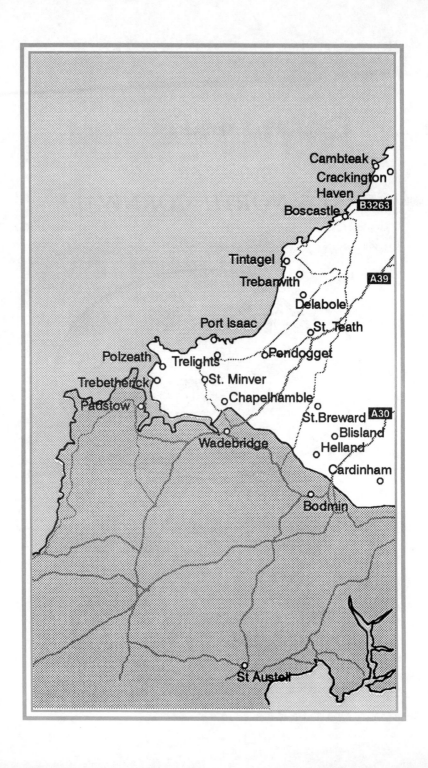

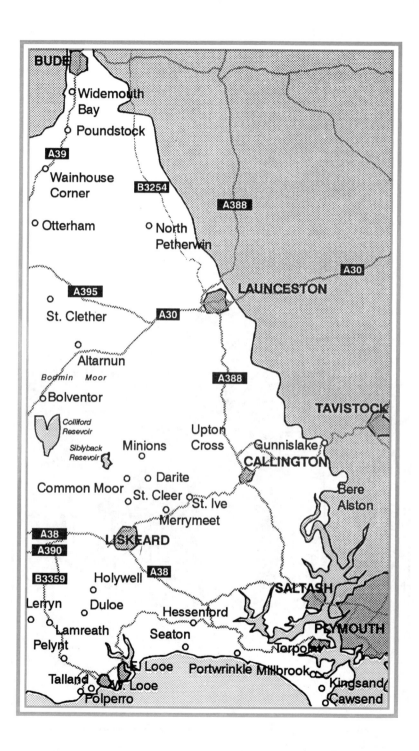

Boscastle

CHAPTER SIX

EAST AND NORTH CORNWALL

Liskeard and Southeast Cornwall

LISKEARD. Standing on an undulating site between the valleys of the East Looe and Seaton rivers, Liskeard is a pleasant old market town which was one of Cornwall's five medieval Stannary towns (the others are Bodmin, Lostwithiel, Truro and Helston). The town has a long history as a centre for mineral extraction: for centuries, the medieval Cornish tinners brought their smelted tin down from Bodmin Moor for weighing, stamping and taxing, then in the early 19th-century, great quantities of copper ore from the nearby Caradon mines and granite from the Cheesewring quarries were loaded onto barges here and despatched to the coast along the newly-constructed Looe canal. In the 1850s, the canal was replaced by the Looe valley branch of the Great Western Railway, a scenic stretch of line which still operates today although its industrial cargoes have long been replaced by passenger holiday traffic.

Thankfully now bypassed by the busy A38 Plymouth to Bodmin road, Liskeard's narrow streets contain a number of interesting old buildings, including the curious Italianate guildhall and Stuart House, a handsome Jacobean residence in which Charles I is believed to have stayed for a week during the English Civil War. The surprisingly large parish church, one of the most substantial in Cornwall, reflects the town's former importance as a centre for agriculture and mineral extraction, and there are also a number of elegant Georgian houses and coaching inns. Perhaps Liskeard's most unusual feature can be found in Well Lane where an arched grotto marks the site of **Pipe Well**, a medieval spring which is reputed to have curative powers.

ROSECRADDOC HOLIDAYS are situated in an area of rolling farmland nestling in a valley at the foot of Caradon Hill, two miles from Liskeard; an ideal location for exploring North and South coasts. Near at hand are lakes and reservoirs for watersport; riding and pony trekking centres and Bodmin Moor.

The modern though traditionally built bungalows are set in seven acres of gardens and woodland giving a quiet and delightful setting for your holiday. All facilities are provided and each bungalows is fully fitted out and carpeted in the main living areas. Kitchens have cookers, refrigerators and all equipment and utensils needed. One of the bungalows has been specially adapted for wheelchair users. Children and pets under control are welcome. A really first class holiday!

Rosecraddoc Holidays, Rosecraddoc Lodge, Liskeard, Cornwall.
Tel. & Fax: 01579 346768

DOBWALLS. Three miles to the west of Liskeard, the popular **DOBWALLS THEME PARK** can be found on the northern edge of the village from which it takes its name. The park contains a number of contrasting attractions, including the Forest Railway, a two-mile-long miniature steam railway whose locomotives and rolling stock are based on the old North American railroad. There is also an indoor railway museum, an extensive adventure playground, and a permanent exhibition on the life and work of the English wildlife artist, Archibald Thorburn. (Open daily between Easter and end-October.)

Two miles further west, the famous **CARNGLAZE SLATE CAVERNS** lie in the lovely wooded valley of the river Loveny, a mile to the north the A38. Slate for use in the building trade was first quarried in these vast manmade caverns in the 14th-century. The largest chamber is over 300ft high and was once used by smugglers as a secret rum store. The lichen on the cavern walls is covered with minute droplets of water which reflect the available light in the most magical way. Visitors can see the remains of the tramway which was built to haul the stone to the surface from the lower levels, and at the deepest level, there is a sub-terranean pool which is filled with the clearest blue-green water. (Open daily between Easter and end-September.)

MERRYMEET is a small hamlet where you will find **BUTTERDON MILL HOLIDAY HOMES**, a small privately owned family run concern, with homes nestling in a delightfully sheltered valley three miles from Liskeard just off the A390 Callington Road. The holiday homes combine the advantage of peace and natural beauty of the Cornish countryside whilst being no great distance from the beaches, fishing villages and many places of interest. Twelve detached brickbuilt homes provide top quality accommodation for all the family and are fitted out with all the facilities to make your stay a pleasure. Children are very welcome and will find lots of amusement here including a large all weather pool, tennis court, snooker, table tennis, pitch & putt golf and lots more for the little ones. There's a most friendly atmosphere at Butterdon and the amenities are excellent. Regret no pets.

Butterdon Mill Holiday Homes, Merrymeet, Liskeard, Cornwall.
Tel: 01579 342636

ST CLEER. Two miles due north of Liskeard, this sizable village lies in the heart of bleak former mining country on the southern fringes of Bodmin moor. The settlement is arranged around the parish church, a largely 15th-century building with a striking granite tower and a Norman doorway which has survived from an earlier building. To the northeast of the churchyard, another 15th-century granite structure marks the site a holy well whose waters are reputed to have restorative powers. Visitors to such holy wells commonly leave a personal item such as a handkerchief behind them, and these can sometimes be seen hanging from nearby branches. Half-a-mile to the east of the village centre stands **Trethevy Quoit**, a massive enclosed megalithic chamber which originally formed the core of a vast earthwork mound. The largest structure of its type in Cornwall, it is believed to be around 5000 years old and has much in common with those found in west Penwith. On the opposite, western side of the village, **King Doniert's Stone** is a tall stone cross which was erected as a memorial to King Durngarth, a Cornish king who is thought to have drowned in the nearby river Fowey around 870 AD. Sadly now broken into two pieces, it is carved with a Latin inscription which, when translated, reads, 'Erected for Doniert for the good of his soul'. A little further west, the River Fowey descends for half-a-mile through dense broad-leaved woodland in a delightful series of cascades known as **Golitha Falls.**

ST KEYNE. The B3254 to the south of Liskeard leads to the small village of St Keyne, home of the fascinating **Paul Corin Musical Collection.** This unique museum of mechanical instruments is housed in a lovely old mill which stands near the bridge over the East Looe river, half-a-mile east of the village centre. Exhibits include street, café and fairground organs, all of which are kept in working order and played on a regular basis. (Open daily between early-May and end-September, also at Easter.)

One of the more unusual episodes in St Keyne's history took place during the reign of the Catholic Mary Tudor when the local rector and his wife (they had married during the reign of Protestant Edward VI) were dragged from their bed in the middle of the night and placed in the village stocks.

Another famous holy well lies a mile to the south of the village beneath a great tree which is said to bear the leaves of four different species. According to local legend, the first member of a newly-married couple to drink from the spring will be the one who wears the trousers, a notion which captured the imagination of Victorian newly-weds and brought them here in their thousands.

DULOE, south of here, the B3254 passes to the west of a Bronze Age circle of eight stones in the village of Duloe.

TREMADART FARM is in the village of Duloe, three miles from the picturesque town of Looe, and offers self catering holidays for up to twelve guests plus a cot. The accommodation provided is in the front half of the large farmhouse which is part of a 320 acre mixed farm. There is a television lounge with a wood burning stove, a large dining room with open fire, and a kitchen with cooker, fridge, washing machine, dishwasher and microwave. The bedrooms are large family size and have duvets and bed linen. A pleasant lawned garden surrounds the house, with garden furniture and a swing and slide for children. A variety of attractions and activities are nearby including golf, fishing, sailing and horse riding. ETB 4 keys commended. Sorry, no pets.

Tremadart Farm, Duloe, Liskeard, Cornwall. Tel: 01503 262855.

WATERGATE. Situated in its own gardens with waterfalls and old stone bridges over a swiftly running stream in the secluded and picturesque wooded valley of Watergate, is **HARESCOMBE LODGE**, an ideal spot for nature lovers, honeymooners or those who simply wish to "get away from it all". The nearby estuaries of the East and West Looe rivers gives an abundance of interesting wildlife. The Lodge is tastefully restored and modernised offering a high standard of comfort; all the bedrooms are individually furnished and have en-suite bathroom or shower facilities. Jane and Barry are the resident proprietors who give their personal attention to ensure guests are happy and comfortable. AA Selected. Idyllic setting.

Harescombe Lodge, Watergate, Nr. Looe, Cornwall. Tel: 01503 263158

LOOE. At the mouth of the rivers East and West Looe stands the bustling coastal resort and fishing port of Looe. Originally two separate towns facing each other across the estuary, East and West Looe were first connected by a bridge in the early 15th-century and officially incorporated in 1883. (The present seven-arched bridge dates from the 19th-century and is wide enough to carry the A387 Polperro road.) In common with many other Cornish coastal settlements which have had to scratch a living by whatever means available, Looe has always been something of a jack-of-all-trades. As well as having a long-established pilchard-fishing fleet, it has also served the mineral extractors of Bodmin moor as a port for exporting tin and, later, copper ore.

As early as 1800, a bathing machine was constructed at the top of Looe's sandy beach, and when visitors began to arrive in numbers with the coming of the railway in 1859, the town began to develop as a resort. More recently, Looe has established itself as Britain's premier shark-fishing centre which regularly hosts an International Sea Angling Festival.

Over the years, Looe has evolved into a small seaside resort which has managed to retain a good deal of its original character, despite the annual invasion of holiday-makers. The old quarters on either side of the river are mazes of narrow lanes lined with old stone fishermen's cottages and inns, some of which are partially-constructed from old ships' timbers. The 16th-century guildhall in East Looe is now an impressive local museum, and there is also an interesting **Cornish Folk Museum** in Lower Street.

In summer, pleasure boats depart from the quay for trips along the coast to Polperro and Fowey, and boat trips can also be taken to ST GEORGE'S ISLAND half-a mile offshore. Now a privately-run bird sanctuary, this was once the refuge of the notorious pirate and smuggler, Black Joan, who along with her brother Fyn, terrorised the population of this lonely stretch of coast.

TRELASKE COUNTRY HOTEL AND RESTAURANT is the ideal location for a holiday in the country, whilst being only three quarters of a mile from the beach. This superb Country Hotel is set in lovely countryside two miles equidistant from the historic fishing villages of Looe and Polperro. Its four acres of magnificent lawns and gardens are quite delightful with an abundance of colourful plants and shrubs and surrounded by established trees and hedges.

The hotel is personally owned and managed by Mr. & Mrs. Rawlings who have forty years experience behind them which is reflected in the high quality of their standards of personal service a comfort for their guests.

Each bedroom is charmingly furnished and decorated with its own character and displays meticulous care for detail and luxury touches. The rooms vary in size and aspect and each room has its own colour television and telephone. The spacious executive suites have additional luxuries such as Jacuzzis.

Full English breakfast is served in the restaurant or continental breakfast is served in your room if preferred. The restaurant is certainly one of the best in the area drawing its produce from all over the world; the finest salmon from Scotland and other fresh fish from one of the best European fish markets, on their own doorstep in Looe. The restaurant is open to non-residents and maintains consistently high standards of food and wine.

Trelaske Country Hotel & Restaurant, Polperro Road, Looe, Cornwall.
Tel: 01503 262159   Fax: 01503 265360

Those looking for holiday accommodation in the picturesque fishing village of Looe can contact **ALLEN COTTAGES** who have a number of quaint and cosy cottages very conveniently situated for the beach and harbour. They are comfortable, well equipped and include central heating and hot water 24 hours a day inclusive in the charge. Colour television is provided and for a small charge, video recorders are available. Milk, papers and groceries can also be delivered by arrangement. Many recommendations have been left by satisfied guests, and given the attractions of this area, Allen Cottages make an ideal holiday base. Sorry, no dogs.

Allen Cottages, Newlyn, Bridgend, West Looe, Cornwall. Tel./Fax: 01503 262695

You can enjoy the best of both worlds at **COMMONWOOD MANOR AND COTTAGES,** with a choice of top quality accommodation, Set in six acres of grounds on the side of a wooded valley overlooking the East Looe River with unrivalled views of the soft rolling hills and woodland, yet only ten minutes from Looe town, Harbour and Beaches. The Hotel boasts views from all bedrooms which have been furnished with imagination and care and include en-suite facilities, central heating, colour television, telephone and hospitality trays.

Commonwood Farm Cottages

The peaceful sitting room has panoramic views and the restaurant offers a menu of fine cuisine and an excellent choice of wines. The three detached cottages offer the final word in luxury, quality and facilities. Everything has been thought of including fridge/freezer, washer/dryer

SKY television, central heating and superb furnishings. All guests can enjoy the hotel's heated swimming pool built into a sheltered terrace above the main lawns. Hotel: 3 Crown Commended, AA & RAC 2 star. Cottages: English Tourist Board 5- keys, Highly Commended.

Commonwood Manor and Cottages, St. Martins Road, East Looe, Cornwall.Tel: 01503 262929 Fax: 01503 262632

Over at West Looe there is a place to stay which was the runner up in the S.E Cornwall " Warmest Welcome " awards with a mere 99%.

John and Hazel Storer run this home from home and the rates are very reasonable. The house is called Kantara, and they have even produced a poem to describe their premises, part of which is below.

KANTARA

Convenient for town and beach
A short walk from the sea
A thousand times you've read those words
In guides to B & B.
Kantara's adverts say the same
But what sets us apart
is what we give to every guest
service from the heart.

We aren't 5 star, We,ve no ensuite
no round the clock reception,
But - no red tape, no penguin suits, no " Extra Charge "
deception.
We'll wash your clothes and dry them too
(No need to waste your day)
So you can wear your favourites twice, with nothing more to pay.

Kantara   7 Trelawney Terrace, West Looe,   01503   262093

HANNAFORE. To the west, just 15 minutes walk away from the centre of Looe, in the area of Hannafore, you will find the 200 year old **STONEROCK COTTAGE** which offers a very high standard of B & B accommodation, excellent breakfast and a warm, friendly atmosphere. This is a lovely place to base your holiday, many guests return year after year.

Stonerock Cottage B & B, Portuan Road, Hannafore, West Looe.
01503 263651

PELYNT. The village of Pelynt on the B3359 is just about three miles from Looe, well known for its quaint architecture, narrow streets, Banjo Pier and location as a splendid holiday centre.

It is here you will find **COLWELLS** bed & breakfast. The detached residence has panoramic views, and offers traditional hospitality combined with courteous and personal attention.

Christine Harvey has twelve years of experience in this business and is a most welcoming hostess.

The bedrooms have television, tea/coffee making equipment, cotton sheets and heating; some have private bathrooms.

You will enjoy a full four-course English breakfast, a separate lounge for guests, large garden and easy parking. A non-smoking household.

Colwells, Pelynt, Nr. Looe, Cornwall. Tel: 01503 220201

POLPERRO. Three-and-a-half miles along the coast to the west of Looe, this lovely old fishing community of is many people's idea of the archetypal Cornish village. It stands at the point where a steep-sided wooded combe converges with a narrow tidal inlet from the sea. Its steep narrow streets and alleyways are piled high with white-painted fishermen's cottages, many of which have now been converted into art galleries and specialist shops.

All routes seem to lead down to Polperro's highly-photogenic double harbour, a working fishing port which normally contains an assortment of attractive inshore fishing vessels. The mouth of the inner harbour was fitted with movable timber gates after a southeasterly storm destroyed over twenty boats which were sheltering here in the early 19th-century (they have now been replaced by a modern tidal floodgate). At one time, the smell of Polperro pilchards was so overwhelming that outsiders renamed the village 'Polstink'!

Polperro has a long association with smuggling: the practice was so rife in the 18th-century that almost everyone in the village was involved in shipping, storing or transporting contraband goods. To combat the problem, H M Customs and Excise established the first 'preventive station' in Cornwall here in the early 1800s. The atmosphere and events of those days are brought to life in a fascinating **Smugglers' Museum** which can be found near the inner harbour. (Open daily between April and end-October.)

Another attraction is a model village of old Polperro which is set within pleasant flower-filled gardens. (Open Sundays to Fridays between March and end-October.)

Modern Polperro has had to succumb to the holiday industry and in summer, cars are banned from the narrow streets.

Occupying a commanding view over the harbour and village of Polperro, **BRENT HOUSE HOLIDAY FLATS** are uniquely situated facing due south with sunbathing terrace and wonderful views. A variety of seven flats offer spacious rooms with good accommodation and catering facilities; some have a private terrace.

Brent House Holiday Flats

Bed and breakfast accommodation is also available for up to four people. With twenty years experience behind them, John and Rosemary have everything well organised. A good selection of delicious home

West Looe

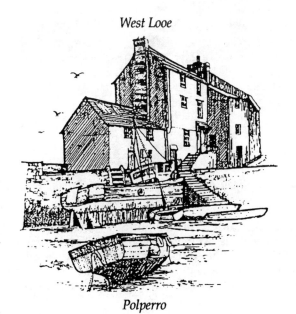

Polperro

made oven-ready dishes are available and can be delivered to your flat timed for your return after an enjoyable day out. The village is two minutes walk away and offers an interesting array of shops restaurants and pubs. You should have no trouble enjoying this Cornish holiday spot.

Brent House, Talland Hill, Polperro, Cornwall, Devon.
Tel: 01503 72495

LUCKMAUREE HOLIDAY ACCOMMODATION has been established letting cottages in Polperro since 1974 and their properties occupy some of the best locations overlooking the harbour, indeed, one such has the tide lapping beneath the windows and boats just a few feet way. An ideal spot to while away the hours watching the day-to-day life of the working harbour. The aim of the owners is to provide guests with a good standard of comfort at sensible prices and with many clients returning regularly, they clearly succeed. The area around Polperro provides many facilities including sailing, windsurfing, pony trekking, golf, fishing, historic Country Houses and Gardens, lovely walks and lots more. The directors of the company are resident in the village and the properties are maintained under their personal supervision. ETB. 4-Keys Commended. No facilities for pets.

Luckmauree Holiday Accommodation, Osprey, Talland Hill, Polperro, Cornwall. Tel: 01503 72819

CRUMPLEHORN. This delightfully named hamlet, on the outskirts of Polperro, is well worth visiting, for here you will find **CRUMPLEHORN INN AND MILL**, a restored complex of historic buildings surrounding a water mill which have a fine restaurant and bar and offer a range of hotel and self catering accomodation of an exceptional standard.

The Crumplehorn Inn, Polperro. Tel 01503 272348

Much of the coastline around the village is owned by the National Trust: to the west, the coastal path twists upwards onto the clifftops, and to the east it skirts around the edge of **Talland Bay.**

TALLAND The charming 13th-century church in this hamlet of was once the parish church for West Looe.

THE TALLAND BAY HOTEL is a lovely, part 16th century country house standing in beautiful landscaped gardens 150 feet above the sea and has magnificent views over the surrounding coast and countryside. The bay is framed by two dramatic headlands, and the beach, which is sandy at low tide, provides safe sea bathing.

Barry and Annie Rosier are the resident owners of the hotel. They and their staff provide guests with truly friendly and professional service. Morning coffee or Cornish tea can be brought to you on the terrace or in one of the elegant sitting rooms, and dinner is served in the oak-panelled dining room. Menus are jointly designed by the head chef Paul Kingswood and the owners to include as much fresh local produce as possible - in particular local seafood from Looe, including lobster, crabs and scallops. Mr. Rosier is responsible for the reasonably priced wine list which includes an interesting and balanced selection from both the "old" and "new" world.

The hotel has nineteen individually designed bedrooms which have views of the sea or surrounding countryside. All are furnished to a very high standard and have private en-suite bathrooms, however, the hotel has an on-going programme of extensive refurbishment - especially in respect of the hotel bedrooms. There is an outdoor swimming pool which is heated in summer and other outdoor activities include walking, tennis and croquet. Enquire about special interest breaks which include landscape painting, bridge, archaeology and 'murder mystery' weekends. This is an ideal location for visiting Cornwall's sub-tropical gardens, especially lovely in springtime, also walking the Cornish coastal path at the hotel's doorstep.

Talland Bay Hotel, Talland-By-Looe, Cornwall.
Tel: 01503 72667 Fax: 01503 7294

MURRAYTON. To the east of Looe, the main road curves inland; however, by following the minor roads it is possible to reach the famous monkey sanctuary at Murrayton, one mile to the west of SEATON. This sheltered wooded valley is the home of the world's first protected breeding colony of Amazonian woolly monkeys. The monkeys are allowed to roam freely and visitors are able to view them, along with a variety of other animals and birds, at close quarters. (Open Sundays to Thursdays between early-May and end-September, also at Easter.) Seaton itself has a good sandy beach which was once a favoured landing place for smugglers. The coastal footpath to the west provides some fine clifftop walking.

The most impressive stretch of beach in southeast Cornwall can be found along the shore of WHITSAND BAY, a few miles to the east of Seaton. More a series of coves than a continuous expanse of sand, the bay runs between Portwrinkle and Rame on the southwestern side of the Rame peninsula. To gain access to the beach, visitors should park in one of the car parks which are arranged at intervals along this highly scenic stretch of coast road, and then descend by way of a steep footpath. Lifeguards are on duty at busy times.

RAME. At the southeastern end of Whitsand Bay it's worth making the detour through Rame village and on to the spectacular **Rame Head**. As the road enters the village, it curves around the 13th-century church of St Germanus, a handsome structure with a tall west tower and spire which for centuries has served as a mariners' landmark. On the headland itself, visitors can park near the coastguards' station and walk over to the ruined 14th-century chapel which is perched dramatically on top of a cone-shaped promontory. The **Eddystone Lighthouse** lies ten miles offshore and can be seen on a clear day; the English fleet had their first encounter with the Spanish Armada to the southwest of here in July 1588.

CAWSAND and **KINGSAND.** One mile to the northeast of Rame village, these adjoining communities are former fishing villages which owe much of their past prosperity to the smuggling industry. In the late 18th- and early 19th-centuries, thousands of barrels of brandy, silk and other contraband were landed here and carried though the narrow streets in the dead of night. For centuries, the small stream running into Cawsand Bay formed the county boundary between Saxon Devon and Celtic Cornwall, an administrative quirk which placed one half of the village in Cornwall (Cawsand) and the other in Devon (Kingsand).

Before the Plymouth Breakwater was completed in 1840, the Royal Navy fleet used to shelter from southwesterly gales by anchoring in Cawsand Bay, another factor which added to the prosperity of the place and left it with a surprising number of inns. There is an unusual end-on view of the breakwater from here, and to the east, there is some good easy coastal walking around the bay to **Mount Edgcumbe House** (see chapter four), from where the Cremyll passenger ferry crosses to Plymouth.

TORPOINT. For those wishing to cross the Tamar estuary (here called the *Hamoaze*) by car, a 24-hour vehicle ferry plies back and forth between Devonport and Torpoint. The latter stands on the northern arm of the Rame peninsula and is a small industrial, boat-building and dormitory town which faces the naval dockyard across the estuary.

The atmosphere is very different at **Antony House**, a delightful National Trust-owned property which lies between the A374 and the estuary of the river Lynher, one-and-a-half miles to the northwest. Considered be one of the finest early-Georgian country mansions in Cornwall, it was constructed between 1718 and 1729 of pale silver-grey stone which was brought in by sea from Pentewan, near Mevagissey.

The design is neoclassical in feel and consists of a forecourt enclosed by brick colonnades, with east and west wings also of red brick. The interior is noted for its tapestries, panelling and fine 18th-century furniture, the most impressive of which can be seen in the dining room and library. (Open Tuesdays to Thursdays, and Bank Holiday Mondays, 1.30pm to 5.30pm between end-March and end-October; also Sundays in June, July and August.)

CRAFTHOLE. Just outside the nearby village of Crafthole is the **LISCAWN INN**; Liscawn is the Cornish for 'valley of the Elder' and, as you might imagine, there are some outstanding views, particularly of Dartmoor. This fourteenth century inn is approached down a meandering drive and is set in 8 acres of grounds which ensures peace and tranquillity for all its visitors. Your hosts, Paul and Fiona Ingall have several tastefully decorated and comfortable en-suite bedrooms, one with a four poster bed for that special occasion, and are happy to welcome children and pets. Lunches, dinners, bar snacks and traditional cask ales are available. A super place to stop that is off the beaten track.

Liscawn Inn, Crafthole, Torpoint Tel: 01503 230863

ST GERMANS, three miles to the northwest, gives little indication of its former standing. For half-a-century before the Anglo-Saxon diocese of Cornwall was incorporated with Exeter in 1043, this quiet backwater was, in fact, a cathedral city.

Its present church, the largest in Cornwall until Truro cathedral was completed in 1910, dates from the Norman times and was built as the great church for an Augustinian priory which was founded here in 1162.

Its west door, a series of seven receding arches, is considered to be one of the finest examples of Norman church architecture in Britain. The twin towers date from the 13th- and 15th-centuries, and inside there are a number of striking monuments, most notably that to Edward Eliot, which is considered to be one of the most impressive 18th-century examples of its kind in Cornwall.

The Eliot family, now the Earls of St Germans, acquired the priory shortly after the Dissolution of the Monasteries in 1539 and renamed their new estate 'Port Eliot'. The present house, with its Gothic-looking turrets, is largely 19th-century, although it incorporates fragments of the medieval monastic buildings. The grounds were laid out in the late 18th-century by Humphry Repton but are not open to the public.

Another of St Germans' exceptional buildings, Sir William Moyle's almshouses, can be seen on the approaches to the village. Constructed in 1538 and carefully restored in the 1950s, the row is built to an unusual design, with prominent gables and a long first-floor balcony which is reached by a sturdy external staircase. A good view of the massive thirteen-arched viaduct which carries the main London-Penzance line over the estuary of the river Tiddy can be seen from the former Victorian river port of St Germans' Quay.

A group of interesting hidden places can be found within a few miles of each other, half-a-dozen miles upstream from the spectacular twin bridges over the river Tamar at Saltash. One of the most appealing National Trust properties in England can be found buried in the lanes to the east of the A388 Saltash to Callington road. **Cotehele House** is a low granite manor house set around three courtyards which was largely built in Tudor times by Sir Richard Edgcumbe and his son, Piers. In the 1550s, the family moved their main residence southwards to Mount Edgcumbe, a more accessible site overlooking Plymouth Sound, and since then, Cotehele has been left relatively unaltered, except for the addition of the semi-fortified northwest tower in 1627. Inside, the Tudor great hall contains a remarkable collection of early armour and weaponry, and there are some exceptional tapestries and period furniture in the other rooms. The house incorporates some charming individual features, including a secret spy-hole to the great hall, a private chapel, and a tower clock with a bell, but no face or hands, which is believed to the be the oldest working example of its kind in Britain. (Open daily except Fridays, 12 noon to 5.30pm between end-March and end-October.)

The grounds of Cotehele House are some of the most delightful in the West Country. Above the house, there is an enclosed formal garden with a wide shallow pond, and below it, the ground falls away in a steep-sided combe which contains a spectacular collection of mature rhododendrons, azaleas and other flowering shrubs. The garden's most enchanting feature - a medieval stone dovecote with a domed roof - stands beside a deep stream-fed pool between the house and the Tamar. At the foot of the combe, a tiny chapel stands on a promontory, 70ft above the river's edge. This was built in the 15th-century by Sir Richard

Edgcumbe, a Lancastrian, to show thanks for his escape from the Yorkist forces of Richard III who had been pursuing him through Cotehele woods. Edgcumbe avoided capture by placing a stone in his cap and throwing it into the fast-flowing waters of the Tamar, a ploy which made his pursuers think he had jumped to his death. (He then went on to fight for Henry VII at Bosworth Field and was knighted for his loyalty.)

Cotehele was once a large working estate with its own flour mill, cider press, smithy and workshops; now restored to working order, these lie in a valley half-a-mile away from the main house and are open to visitors. Similarly, Cotehele Quay was once a significant river port with its own wharves, warehouses and lime kilns. In recent years, several of its derelict 18th- and 19th-century buildings have been given new life: one now houses a branch of the National Maritime Museum and another is an excellent tearoom.

CALSTOCK. From Cotehele Quay, it's a pleasant three-quarters-of-a-mile stroll through the woods to the former mining port of Calstock. This curious small town is dominated by a mighty railway viaduct which was one of the first in the country to be constructed of concrete blocks. It continues to carry trains travelling between Plymouth and Gunnislake along the picturesque Tamar Valley line, a stretch of railway whose opening in 1907 ironically sounded the death knell for the traditional activities of the town, for prior to that, Calstock had been the place where vast quantities of tin, granite and copper ore had been brought for loading onto barges bound for the coast and beyond. The town once had a flourishing boat-building industry, and was surrounded by mine-workings, spoil heaps and mineral railways. The picturesque churchyard of the restored 15th-century parish church of St Andrew at the top of Church Hill contains the graves of many who perished in local mine accidents; inside, there are several memorials to the Edgcumbes of Cotehele, most of whom died peacefully.

GUNNISLAKE. To the north of Calstock, the Tamar bends ex-travagantly on its way past Devon's **Morwellham Quay** (see chapter four) to Gunnislake, the northern terminus of the Tamar Valley line. Like Calstock, this is a former mining centre and minor river port which rises steeply from western bank of the Tamar.

In the 1520s, Sir Piers Edgcumbe of Cotehele built Gunnislake's 'new' bridge, a striking 180ft-long granite structure which continues to serve as one of the main gateways to Cornwall. Indeed, it was the lowest bridging point on the Tamar for over 400 years until the Plymouth-Saltash road bridge was completed in 1961, a feature which made it the scene of bitter fighting during the English Civil War.

Like many of its neighbours whose prosperity depended on the output from local mines, Gunnislake suffered a century of decline before undergoing a modest recovery in the last third of the 20th-century and today, it a pleasant small town with a number of attractive houses and inns.

KIT HILL. To the west of Gunnislake, the A390 passes along the southern edge of Kit Hill, a 1090ft peak which offers an outstanding view across southeast Cornwall to Plymouth Sound. On the summit stands the dramatic outline of an 80ft chimney stack which was built in 1858 to serve one of the area's many copper mines. The 500-acre site was donated to the county in 1985 by Prince Charles, the Duke of Cornwall; it is rich in industrial remains and has recently been designated a country park.

METHERELL. In the tiny hamlet of Metherell, off the main road between Callington and Tavistock, lies THE CARPENTERS ARMS. This is a lovely old traditional pub which offers an excellent wine list to complement the delicious home cooked food on the menu. Your hosts, George and Bob Wilson, will ensure that you have a wonderful time.

The Carpenters Arms, Lower Metherell, Near Callington
Tel: 01579 350242

CALLINGTON, a mile-and-a-half to the southwest, is a pleasant old market town lying at the heart of the fertile fruit growing country which is bordered by Dartmoor to the east and Bodmin moor to the west, the very area which, for a few decades during the Victorian area, became the scene of frantic mining activity.

There is an interesting old chapel and well-house at DUPATH, half-a-mile to the southeast of Callington, and on the return journey to Liskeard, an impressive Iron Age fort known as **Cadson Bury** stands on an oval hilltop site above the river Lynher, to the south of the A390. A little further to the west, the church in the village of ST IVE was founded in the 12th-century by the Knights Templar, along with a hospice which has since been incorporated into a privately-owned manor house.

Launceston and Bodmin Moor

LAUNCESTON, pronounced locally as *Lawn-son*, is one of the most pleasant inland towns in Cornwall. For centuries, it was an important regional capital which guarded the main land route into the county, now the A30. Shortly after the Norman invasion, William the Conqueror's half-brother, Robert of Mortain, built a massive fortification on an elevated site above the river Kensey from where subsequent Earls of Cornwall attempted to govern the defiant Cornish people. An excellent example of a motte and bailey castle, it features an outer bailey, now a public park, and a round double keep whose outer wall is twelve feet thick in places. (Open daily (closed Mondays in winter), 10am to 6pm, all year round.) Towards the end of its working life, the decaying structure was used as a gaol: a fearsome place where prisoners were kept in appalling conditions, its inmates included George Fox, the founder of the Quakers.

Launceston contains an unusual number of fine old buildings and churches. In medieval times, a settlement grew up around an Augustinian priory on the northern side of the Kensey, and it is here that the original parish church of St Stephen stands; a Byzantine-style Roman Catholic church was built nearby early in the 20th-century. The oldest surviving ecclesiastical building in the town, the 12th-century church of St Thomas, lies near the southern end of the medieval footbridge over the river; ironically, this tiny building contains the largest Norman font in Cornwall.

Some of the most impressive stonework in the area can be found on the church of St Mary Magdalene, a granite structure which was built in the early 16th-century by a local landowner following the tragic death of his wife and son. In their memory, he assembled the finest stonemasons in Cornwall to create a remarkable cornucopia of ornamental carving which covers nearly every surface of the building.

Elsewhere in Launceston, the streets around the castle are filled with handsome Georgian and earlier buildings, including the National Trust-owned **Lawrence House** in Castle Street; built in 1753, it has some fine plasterwork ceilings and now houses an interesting town museum. (Open Mondays to Fridays, 10.30am to 4.30pm between early-April and early-October; admission free.)

There is also an art gallery near the medieval **South Gate**, the last remnant of Launceston's town walls, and for railway enthusiasts, a steam railway runs along the Kensey valley to the west of the town.

Those with an interest in the arts should make a point of visiting **Sterts Arts Centre** at UPTON CROSS, eight miles to the south on the B3254 Liskeard road; as well as a gallery, dance studio and café, it boasts one of the few open-air amphitheatres in the country.

Around Launceston

NORTH PETHERWIN is just off the B3254 four miles to the northwest of Launceston. Here wild otters can be observed in their natural habitat at the **Tamar Otter Park.**

EGLOSKERRY, two miles to the southwest, has a part-Norman church which contains a number of memorials to the Speccott family, 17th-century owners of the nearby manor house of **Penheale.**

LANEAST, on the other side of the A395, three miles to the southwest, contains a part-Norman church which has been left virtually untouched since the 15th-century. Inside, there is an impressive rood screen, some striking 15th-century carved bench ends, and a pair of graceful wagon roofs in the south aisle and south porch. The parish of Laneast is the birthplace of John Adams, the astronomer who first discovered the planet Neptune. A small chapel to the southeast of the church stands over a holy well, one of many such springs to be found in this part of Cornwall.

ST CLETHER. An elaborate holy well can be found a few hundred

The Cheesewring

yards to the northwest of this peaceful village, a mile-and-a-half to the west of Laneast. Standing on its own on a bracken-covered shelf above the River Inny, the well, with its adjacent 15th-century chapel, is the most enchanting example of its kind in the county. The village itself contains a part-Norman church which was heavily restored by the Victorians; however, a number of earlier features have survived, including the Norman stone pillars and font, and the 15th-century tower.

ALTARNUN. The lanes to the south of Laneast and St Clether lead to Altarnun, an exceptionally attractive village which lies in the steep-sided valley of Penpont Water.

The largely-15th-century parish church stands in a superb position on a rise above the peat-stained river. Sometimes referred to as 'the cathedral of the moor', this surprisingly-grand moorstone structure is dedicated to St Nonna, the mother of St David, the patron saint of Wales. It has a tall pinnacled tower and an unusually light and spacious interior which contains carved rood screen, a decorated Norman font and a wonderful set of over seventy Tudor bench ends whose carvings create a charming picture of 16th-century village life.

In the churchyard, there are several fine examples of the work of Altarnun-born monumental sculptor, Nevill Northey Burnard who also carved the bust of John Wesley which stands over the door of the Meeting House by the stream. Wesley often visited Altarnun when staying in the nearby village of TREWINT; his hosts' cottage, with its specially constructed prophets' room and pilgrims' garden, has been restored and opened to the public.

BODMIN MOOR. To the south and west of Altarnun, the bleak expanse of Bodmin Moor stretches out on either side of the A30 trunk route.

This eighty square-mile area of granite upland is characterised by saturated moorland and weather-beaten tors. The exposed area to the north of the main road contains the 1370ft hill known as **BROWN WILLY**, the highest point in Cornwall. (There is no truth in the story that the hill was so-named because those who were first to reach the summit had to wade up to their waists through a grimy peat bog.)

Almost as high, and standing on National Trust-owned land a little to the northwest, is **ROUGH TOR**, a magnificent viewpoint which is also the site of a memorial to the men of the Wessex Regiment who died in World War II. This dramatic area of the moor is best approached from the northwest along the lane leading up from the A39 at Camelford.

Like Dartmoor, Bodmin moor is covered in prehistoric remains. Typical of many are the scattered Bronze Age hut circles and field enclosures which can be seen on the side of Rough Tor. A little to the south lies the **Fernacre Stone Circle**: also Bronze Age, it contains over thirty standing stones and is the largest example of its kind on the moor.

Evidence of earlier occupation can be seen between the A30 and

Hawks Tor, the site of the Neolithic henge monument known as the **Stripple Stones**, but most impressive of all are **the Hurlers**, a Bronze Age temple consisting of three stone circles arranged in a line which can be found near the exposed former mining community of MINIONS on the moor's southeastern fringe. According to Cornish legend, the circles were formed when teams of local men were turned to stone for playing hurling, a Celtic form of hockey, on the Sabbath.

Half-a-mile away to the north stands the spectacular natural granite formation known as **THE CHEESEWRING**. Another local legend states that this was the haunt of a druid who possessed a golden cup which never ran dry and provided thirsty passers-by with an endless supply of water. The story was partially borne out in 1818 when archeologists excavating a nearby burial chamber discovered a skeleton clutching a golden chalice; dubbed the Rillaton Cup, it is now kept in the British Museum.

Still on the subject of cheese, this part of Cornwall is renowned for its fine dairy products, and at **LYNHER VALLEY DAIRY** you can purchase authentic Cornish cheese at its very best. Netherton Farm at Upton Cross is part of the Duchy of Cornwall estate, and the Horrell family have been tenants here since 1905. The milk used in the cheesemaking process comes from their pedigree Holstein-Friesian herd, and is also delivered to local communities on daily rounds. The unusual tangy flavour of Cornish Yarg is derived from it being wrapped in nettle leaves. This is a traditional method of coating cheeses and accounts for its distinctive pattern. Cornish Pepper and Cornish Herb & Garlic are rich creamy cheeses with a strong flavour. They are based on wholemilk soft cheese, with Pepper being pressed into small rounds with black peppercorns, and the Herb & Garlic mixed with six herbs and garlic before being rolled in parsley. Both of these prize winning cheeses would be welcome at any dining table in my opinion.

Lynher Valley Dairy

As well as buying these delicious cheese, you can visit the dairy from April to October to watch the cheesemaking and milk bottling process. You can also enjoy one of the delightful nature trails set out

Boscastle Harbour

around the farm, and peep into the old butter well - not unlike an ice store - where the butter would have been kept really cold throughout the summer months. A small herd of wild boar live in a copse and field by the stream and provide an entertaining diversion on the woodland trail.

Lynher Valley Dairy, Netherton Farm, Upton Cross, Liskeard
Tel: 01579 362244

BOLVENTOR, midway between Launceston and Bodmin in the centre of the moor is the location of the former coaching inn which was immortalised in Daphne du Maurier's novel, *Jamaica Inn*. During the 18th- and 19th-centuries, this isolated hostelry provided an ideal meeting place for outlaws and smugglers, and something of its former atmosphere lives on despite its modern role as a haven for passing motorists.

A lane to the south of Bolventor leads past the mysterious natural tarn known as **Dozmary Pool**, another place which is couched in Cornish legend. According to one, King Arthur was brought here following his final battle at Slaughter Bridge, near Camelford, and as he lay dying at the water's edge, he implored Sir Bedivere to throw his mystical sword, Excalibur, into the centre of the lake. The reluctant knight did so, and as the sword flew through the air, the disembodied hand of the Lady of the Lake rose out of the water to catch it.

Although the tarn is rumoured to be bottomless, cattle can sometimes be seen wading near its centre, and indeed, it purportedly completely dried out during the prolonged drought of 1869.

Dozmary Pool is also said to be one of the many places in Cornwall which is haunted by the Jan Tregeagle, the wicked steward of the Earl of Radnor whose many evil deeds included the killing of a mother and father so he could lay his hands on the estate of their child. As a punishment, he was condemned to spend eternity emptying the lake using only a holed limpet shell.

To the south of Dozmary Pool, the road passes along the side of **Colliford Reservoir**, an artificial lake which offers some excellent recreational and watersports facilities.

ST NEOT. This tranquil community lies a couple of miles downstream from Colliford Dam. The village is named after a diminutive 9th-century saint who spent a large part of his life immersed up to his neck in the holy well which lies a couple of hundred yards upstream from the church. (According to folklore, the pool was also occupied by a fish which would miraculously reappear each morning after it had allowed itself to be caught and eaten the day before.)

Episodes from the life of St Neot are depicted in the magnificent stained-glass windows of the parish church, a handsome 15th-century structure with a 14th-century tower. Thought to be one of the finest collections of early stained glass in Cornwall, the windows also show a selection of delicately-fashioned scenes from the Old Testament.

WARLEGGAN. Two miles to the west, a steep lane rises through the woods towards Warleggan, a remote hamlet on the southern margins of Bodmin moor.

The settlement has long been associated with the supernatural and is an acknowledged haunt of the Cornish 'piskies'. Its most notorious inhabitant, however, was a spiritual practitioner of another kind.

In 1931, the Reverend Frederick Densham took over as parish priest and immediately succeeded in alienating his flock by closing the Sunday school, erecting barbed wire around the rectory and bringing in a pack of German Shepherd dogs to patrol the grounds! The parishioners responded by staying away in droves, to the extent that one entry in the parish register reads, 'No fog. No wind. No rain. No congregation.'

To compensate, the eccentric Rev Densham made cardboard replicas of the former church rectors, placed them in the pews, and preached on! There is also evidence his kind nature; he is known to have constructed a children's playground in the rectory garden; sadly the children never came. He died alone in his rectory in 1953, a worthy model for Lennon and McCartney's 'Father MacKenzie'.

CARDINHAM, two miles further west, contains relics from almost every era in Cornwall's history. A number of Celtic standing stones are scattered throughout the parish, including one in the churchyard which is inscribed in Latin. The churchyard is also the location of a richly-decorated 10th-century cross which stands over eight feet tall.

The nearby church is dedicated to the little-known hermit, St Meubred: largely 15th-century, its interior contains some impressive wagon roofs, a Norman font, a set of carved bench ends, and a rare early-15th-century monumental brass depicting the life-size figure of Thomas Awmarle.

Although a peaceful backwater today, this was once the location of an important Norman motte and bailey castle belonging to the Cardinham family, under-lords of Robert of Mortain of Launceston. The structure was finally abandoned in the 14th-century and today, only an earthwork mound remains on which a few traces of the original keep have been preserved.

BLISLAND, on the northern side of the A30, three miles to the northwest of Cardinham, lies hidden in the maze of country lanes which 'crisscross' the western margins of Bodmin moor.

At the centre of the village stands a broad, tree-lined green which retains its original Saxon plan, an uncommon feature on this side of the Tamar. The green is bordered by some exceptional Georgian and Victorian buildings, including a manor house, rectory, school, forge and inn.

The bright whitewashed interior of the part-Norman parish church of St Protus and St Hyacinth (for some reason, it is known in the village as 'St Pratts') was a favourite of Sir John Betjeman. It has a good wagon roof, an unusual mock-Renaissance altar and some impressive monuments and tombs.

ST TUDY. Another fine church stands at the heart of this scattered village, situated just three miles away to northwest of Blisland. Mainly 15th-century, it has a rare Norman font made of Purbeck marble and some remarkably-detailed monuments to 16th- and 17th-century members of the Nicholls family.

Bude to the Camel Estuary

BUDE, with its sweeping expanse of sand and Atlantic breakers rolling in from the west, seems to change in character with every change in the weather; a winter gale can make it seem like a remote outpost clinging to the edge of the world; however, a warm summer breeze transforms it into a genial holiday town with some excellent facilities for beach-lovers, surfers and coastal walkers.

Bude's late-Victorian and Edwardian centre is sheltered from the worst Atlantic extremes by a low cliff which separates the shallow valley of the River Neet from the ocean.

The town stood at the northern end of the now-disused Bude Canal, an ambitious early-19th-century inland waterway which was intended to connect the Atlantic with English Channel by way of the river Tamar. The only stretch to be completed, that between Bude and Launceston, was largely used for transporting seaweed, sand and other fertiliser to inland farms. Finally abandoned when the railway arrived in the 1890s, the two-mile-long section at the northern end has now been restored for use as a recreational amenity. The small fort guarding the northern entrance to the canal was built in the 1840s as an eccentric private residence, and the old forge on the canalside has been converted into an interesting museum on Bude's maritime heritage.

As you approach Bude from the main road you will pass the **BENCOOLEN INN** public house. The inn is named after the Bencoolen shipwreck which occurred at the end of the nineteenth century and it is said that the ship's timbers were used in the construction of the building.

The Bencoolen Inn

This superb inn has recently been taken over by Juan Manuel Puerta Terron, a Spaniard by birth, who has worked in Bude/Stratton for over 20 years. A professional, well known and respected chef, Juan Manuel has opened the 'El Barco' (meaning ship) restaurant which serves an interesting, international menu of meals and bar snacks of his own creation. As you might imagine the inn is decorated, to a high standard, with a nautical theme and the letting rooms, some of which are ensuite, are equally inviting. A friendly and welcoming place where you can expect excellent food.

Bencoolen Inn, Bencoolen Road, Bude Tel: 01288 354694

Around Bude

STRATTON, lying a mile inland on the main A39 Bideford to Wadebridge road, is believed to have been founded by the ancient Romans. Its steeply-sloping main street is lined with fine Georgian houses and cottages, many of them thatched, and its early-14th-century parish church contains a Norman fount and some striking early memorials and monumental brasses.

During the English Civil War, the **TREE INN** was used as a centre of operations by the Royalist general, Sir Bevil Grenville, before he led his troops to victory at Stamford Hill in May 1643. The Iron Age earthwork which had been held by the Parliamentarians can be seen a mile away to the northwest. After the battle, the dead from both sides were buried in unmarked graves in Stratton churchyard. The Tree Inn was also the birthplace of the legendary Anthony Payne, a 7ft giant who fought for the Royalist cause and was offered a post in Sir Bevil's household as a reward.

LAUNCELLS. Those with a liking for country churches should make a point of visiting this picturesque village, situated one mile to the east of Stratton. Set in a delightful wooded combe, **St Swithin's** is a medieval treasure which managed to escape the attention of the Victorian restorers. The surprisingly light and pleasant interior contains one of the finest sets of early bench ends in Cornwall, over sixty in all, each of them carved with a scene or symbol from the New Testament. Other noteworthy features are a Norman font which is finished in characteristic cable carving, a Tudor mural which, sadly, is now losing its colour, and a collection of early Barnstaple tiles which can be seen on the floor of the chancel.

In the churchyard can be seen the grave of the 19th-century physician, scientist and inventor, Sir Goldsworthy Gurney, the steam pioneer and builder of the castle at the mouth of the Bude canal. A bridge over the nearby stream leads to a holy well, one of over a hundred in the county which have become associated with pre-Norman saints but whose origins often date back to pagan times.

KILKHAMPTON. Another remarkable set of 16th-century carved bench ends can be seen in the part-12th-century church at Kilkhampton, four miles to the north. Although more numerous than at Launcells (there are over 150), their craftsmanship is perhaps not so good. The church also contains several monuments to the Grenville family, a baroque organ which is said to have come from Westminster Abbey, and an ornately-carved Norman doorway which is among the finest in the West Country.

A few miles to the north of Bude, the shoreline transforms from the broad sandy coves of Bude Bay to the wild jagged cliffs of the **Hartland Peninsula** (see chapter three).

MORWENSTOW, a tiny settlement set half-a-mile inland whose agricultural income has long been supplemented by ill-gotten gains from the sea, is a good access point to this dramatic stretch of coastline.

The part-Norman church has some impressive wagon roofs, a richly-carved Norman font, and a medieval wall-painting of St Morwenna, the Celtic saint to whom the building is dedicated.

Morwenstow's most renowned former inhabitant is the eccentric vicar and poet, Robert Stephen Hawker, who arrived here in 1834 and remained amongst his congregation of 'smugglers, wreckers and dissenters' until his death 41 years later. A colourful figure dressed in a purple cloak and long fisherman's boots, Hawker would spend much of his time striding across the clifftops, or writing verse and smoking (some accounts say opium) in a tiny driftwood hut he built for himself on the cliff. He was among the first to show concern about the number of merchant vessels which were coming to grief on this perilous stretch of coastline. (Prior to his intervention, is was a common custom for the locals to use lights to lure passing ships onto the rocks.) He would often climb down to rescue shipwrecked crews from shore or to carry back the bodies of drowned mariners so they could be given a Christian burial. A distinctive ships' figurehead in the churchyard marks the final resting place of the crew of the *Caledonia* which went down in 1842.

Hawker built Morwenstow rectory at his own expense and to his own design, with chimneys representing the towers of various churches, Oxford colleges, and in the case of the broad kitchen chimney, his mother's gravestone. He is also remembered for re-introducing the annual harvest thanksgiving festival, a custom which now takes place all over the world. Some of his less worthy exploits included expelling his cat from the church for daring to catch a mouse on Sunday, taking a Berkshire pig called Gip on his pastoral rounds, and playing a practical joke by sitting on a rock by the sea dressed as a singing mermaid. His most famous poetic work is the rousing Cornish anthem, *The Song of Western Men*, which includes the stirring lines:

> *And shall Trelawny die?*
> Here's twenty-thousand Cornish men
> *Will know the reason why!*

CRACKINGTON HAVEN. To the south of Bude, a narrow undulating road runs along the coast past **Widemouth Bay**, a striking expanse of sand which is open to the elements, good and bad. Five miles further on, the lanes wind their way back to the shoreline at Crackington Haven, one of the most dramatic spots on this formidable stretch of coast. This narrow sandy cove is approached down a steep-sided wooded combe which has a few houses, an inn and village shop at the bottom.

The beach itself is surrounded by high cliffs and jagged rocks, and it is difficult to imagine that sizable vessels once landed at this unwelcoming harbour to deliver their cargoes of limestone and Welsh coal and to collect loads of locally-quarried slate. The cliffs on either side are composed of extravagantly-folded strata of volcanic rock which have given their name to a geological formation known as **the Crackington Measures**. Although impressive to look at, the rock can often be loosely packed and the cliff edges should be approached with extreme caution.

There is some stunning clifftop walking to the south of Crackington Haven, particularly above the sandy cove known as **the Strangles**; a few hundred yards further on, the footpath rises to over 700ft at **High Cliff**, one of the highest sea cliffs in Cornwall. Parts of the surrounding coastline were donated to the National Trust in memory of the RAF pilots who died in the Second World War.

ST GENNYS This isolated hamlet (pronounced with a hard 'g') lies in a spectacular hilltop position, half-a-mile to the northeast of Crackington Haven. Its tiny part-Norman church is dedicated to St Genesius, a martyr who is reputed to have picked up his head after an executioner had chopped it off.

BOSCASTLE, five miles to the southwest, is an ancient and picturesque fishing community which stands in a combe at the head of a remarkable S-shaped inlet from the Atlantic.

The village grew up around, and takes its name from, the now-demolished Bottreaux castle which was built by the de Botterell family in Norman times. Its unique natural harbour was formed by the rivers Valency and Jordan having to carve their way through a high slate cliff to the sea.

The harbour's inner jetty was built by the renowned Elizabethan seafarer, Sir Richard Grenville, when the village was prospering as a fishing, grain and slate port, and the outer one was added 350 years later when Boscastle was being developed as a seaport for the manganese and iron ore mines near Launceston. This latter structure was accidentally blown up by stray mine during World War II and had to be repaired by the National Trust at considerable expense.

The Trust owns the harbour and much of the coastline around Boscastle, and the spectacular slate headlands on either side provide some excellent, if demanding, walking. The village itself is set around a steep broad thoroughfare which is lined with attractive houses, inns and shops, most of which cater for the holiday market. A tourist information

The Old Post Office, Tintagel

centre is located in an old forge by the harbour, and there is also an interesting museum of witchcraft which contains some sinister relics of the ancient black art. The author Thomas Hardy was a regular visitor to Boscastle when he was working as an architect on the restoration of the church at St Juliot, two miles to the southeast. Indeed, the village appeared in one of his earlier novels, *A Pair Of Blue Eyes*, as 'Castle Boterel'.

ST JULIOT. Hardy's church at St. Juliot is a gem of a hidden place (he called the hamlet 'Endelstow' in his novel). It lies in the wooded valley of the fast-flowing river Valency and can be reached from Boscastle along a lovely footpath, or by road via the B3263.

It was here in 1870 that he met his wife-to-be, Emma Gifford, the rector's sister-in-law. (She later professed that the young architect had already appeared to her in a dream, and wrote how she was 'immediately arrested by his familiar appearance.') Much of the couple's courtship took place along the wild stretch of coastline between Boscastle and Crackington Haven, and when Emma died over forty years later, Hardy returned to St Juliot to erect a memorial to her in the church. (A similar memorial was erected to the writer following his own death in 1928).

Two miles to the southwest of Boscastle, the B3263 crosses the mile-long **Rocky Valley**, a curious rock-strewn cleft in the landscape which has a character all of its own. In the wooded upper reaches can be found the impressive 40ft waterfall known as **St Nectan's Kieve.** (St Nectan was a Celtic hermit whose cell is believed to have stood beside the basin, or *kieve*, at the foot of the cascade, and whose grave is said to lie beneath it.) As it winds northwards, the valley gradually becomes deeper and more gorge-like until at the end, its suddenly opens out, depositing its river directly into the sea.

The romantic remains of **Tintagel Castle** stand on top of Tintagel Head, a mile-and-a-half to the west. Prior to a series of rock falls in the 19th-century, this formidable headland was connected to the mainland by a natural stone bridge; now only a narrow isthmus remains. Many like to believe that this was the birthplace of the legendary King Arthur, or even that it was the site of Camelot, the mythical headquarters of the Knights of the Round Table (other candidates are Caerleon in Wales and South Cadbury in Somerset). Fragments of a Celtic monastic house dating from the 6th-century have been uncovered on the headland whose origins coincide with the activities of the Welsh military leader the Arthurian legends are thought to be based upon; however, the fortification we see today was founded by Reginald Earl of Cornwall, the illegitimate son of Henry I, in the 12th-century, over 600 years after Arthur would have died. Whatever the true heritage of Tintagel castle, the scramble down towards the sea and back up to its clifftop site 250ft above the Atlantic is a breathtaking experience.

TINTAGEL owes much of its popularity to the Arthurian connection. One of its most noteworthy attractions is **'King Arthur's Halls'**; these were built in the 1930s by devotees of the legend and include the 'Hall of Chivalry', a room with over seventy stained-glass windows depicting the coats of arms of the Knights of the Round Table. Elsewhere, Arthurian eating places and souvenir shops abound.

The parish church is set some distance away from the village centre on an exposed cliff. Norman in origin, it retains substantial fragments of its original fabric, including the font, windows and sections of the walls. There is also a good early-15th-century monumental brass and a rare Roman tinners' milestone from the 4th-century AD which is one of only five surviving examples in Cornwall.

Perhaps the finest building in the Tintagel is the **Old Post Office**, a small 14th-century slate-built manor house which in the 19th-century found new life as a letter-receiving station. Now owned by the National Trust, this charming and strangely organic-looking structure has recently been carefully restored to its Victorian livery. (Open daily, 11am to 5.30pm between end-March and end-October.)

A good sandy beach can be found a couple of miles to the south of Tintagel at **Trebarwith Strand**, one of the few breaks in the wild craggy cliffscape.

DELABOLE, slightly inland of Trebarwith, is the location of the most famous slate quarry in Cornwall. High-quality dark blue slate has been quarried here without interruption since Tudor times and this prolonged activity has resulted in an open cavity some 500ft deep and a mile-and-a-half in circumference, the deepest manmade hole in Britain. At one time, most of the buildings in the county incorporated roofing slates or flagstones from Delabole, and over 500 people were employed blasting and slicing the stone into the attractively-named standard sizes: 'Ladies', 'Countesses', 'Duchesses', 'Queens' and 'Imperials'. Although the introduction of less expensive substitutes have caused a steady decline in the industry, the traditional demand from builders and monumental stonemasons has been supplemented by a demand for powdered slate from the paint and cosmetics industries. The operators have built a viewing platform which offers a breathtaking panorama of the quarry workings (visitors are not allowed into the site), and there is also a visitor centre which incorporates a slate museum and showroom. (Open between April and end-September.)

CAMELFORD, a small former wool town two miles away to the east as the crow flies, contains an interesting museum of rural life, **the North Cornwall Museum and Gallery**, which is housed in a converted coach house.

Once known as the 'great slate road', the lanes to the west of Delabole used to carry vast quantities of stone to the harbours at Port Gaverne, Port Isaac and Port Quin (some slate was also exported through Boscastle).

PORT ISAAC is the most attractive of the three, a lovely old fishing community of stone and slate houses divided by narrow alleyways, or *drangs* (one goes by the charming name of 'Squeeze-Belly Alley').

At one time, huge quantities of herring were landed here, and after the arrival of the railway, these were gutted and packed in the village's many fish cellars before being despatched by train to Britain's inland centres of population by train. One of the old cellars is now an inshore lifeboat station, and others are used as boathouses or retail outlets.

ST ENDELLION, a mile-and-a-half inland, has a church built of Lundy island granite which is dedicated to St Endelienta, a Celtic saint who lived solely on milk and who passed away after her trusty cow was killed in a dispute with a farmer.

PORT QUIN. To the west, the coast road loops round to Port Quin, a picturesque coastal hamlet which is overlooked by a Regency Gothic folly on Doyden's Point.

When Port Quin's slate trade was ended by the railways, it went through such a period of decline that at one time outsiders thought that the entire population had been washed away in a great storm. The village remained deserted for decades, but was eventually bought and restored by the National Trust. Today it is a seasonal community with a very pleasant atmosphere which is arranged around a clutch of NT-owned holiday cottages. The offshore rock formations are known as the cow and calf.

To the west of Port Quin, the small peninsula of land to the north and east of the Camel estuary is a lovely stretch of country which is entirely free from through traffic.

The table-topped **Pentire Head**, in the extreme northwest, offers some excellent walking with magnificent views over the Camel Estuary. The northernmost tip, the **Rump** is a promontory of hard greenstone which has been eroded into a series of extraordinary pinnacles; this was the site of an Iron Age hill fort, one of three on the headland. The area is known for its wild tamarisk, an elegant flowering shrub more commonly found around the shores of the Mediterranean. Pentire Head was saved from commercial development in the 1930s after local campaigners raised enough funds to purchase the land and donate it to the National Trust.

POLZEATH. This small resort has a broad west-facing beach which is popular with surfers. With its fine sand, caves and tidal rock pools, it is also a superb location for families with young children.

BREA HILL, to the south, looks out over the submerged sandbank known as the **Doom Bar**, a hidden hazard which has spelt the end for many a vessel seeking shelter from Atlantic storms.

Standing in an exquisite position on the inland side of the hill, the delightful church of St Enodoc is a largely Norman structure with a squat 13th-century stone spire. On a number of occasions throughout its history, windblown sand has almost completely buried the little building, and at such times, entry could only be gained through an opening in the roof. The sand was finally cleared away in the 1860s when the church was restored. The bell in the tower came from an Italian ship which was wrecked nearby in 1875.

St Enodoc's beautiful churchyard contains many graves of ship-wrecked mariners who came to grief on this treacherous stretch of coastline. The remains of Sir John Betjeman and his mother lie here too. The fondly-remembered poet laureate spent most of his childhood holidays in the villages and coves which border the Camel estuary. He had a lasting affection for the local people, and they and the surrounding landscape provided the inspiration for many of his poems, among them, *Sunday Afternoon Service At St Enodoc's*. The churchyard stands beside St Enodoc golf course, a natural golf links which is regarded as one of the most scenic in the country.

ROCK, a little further south, was formerly a fishing village which now has a collection of Georgian, Victorian and more recent residences, most of which are occupied for just a few months each summer. A passenger ferry pies back and forth across the Camel estuary from the quay to Padstow, as it has done for centuries. In recent years, the village has become renowned as a watersports centre, with its own sailing and wind-surfing school. In common with the church at St Enodoc, St Michael's church at nearby Porthilly has had to be regularly retrieved from unwelcome sand drifts.

CENTRAL CORNWALL

St Just in Roseland Church

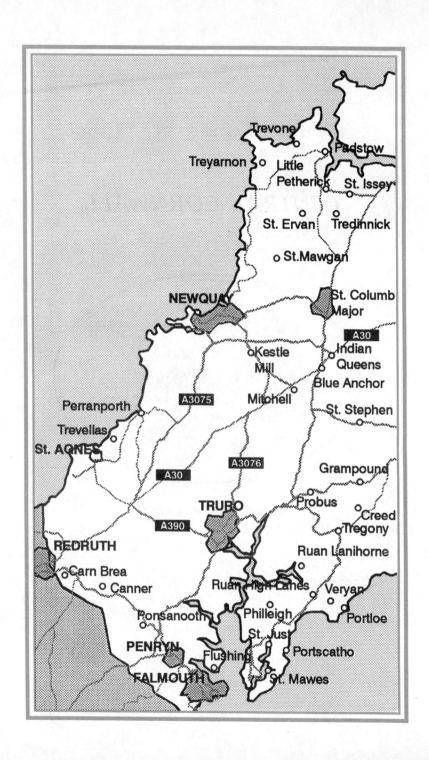

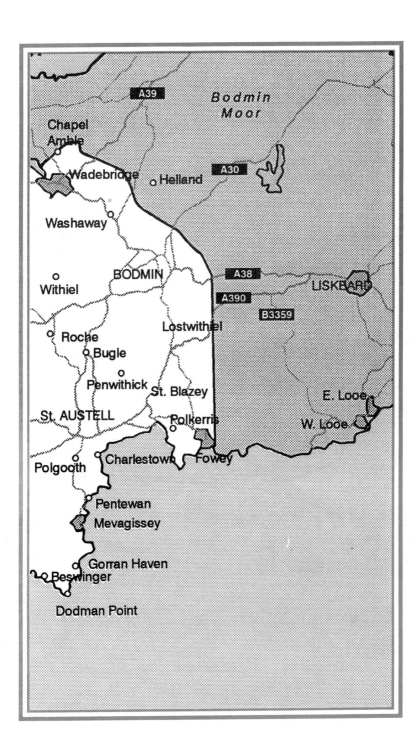

Wadebridge

CHAPTER SEVEN

CENTRAL CORNWALL

PADSTOW TO FALMOUTH

Padstow and the North Coast to Newquay

PADSTOW. For many centuries, Padstow's sheltered position on the western side of the Camel estuary has made it a welcome haven for vessels seeking shelter from the perils of the north Cornish coast. However, the silting of the river in the 19th-century created a new hazard for shipping, the evocatively-named Doom Bar, which restricted entry to the estuary mouth and effectively spelt the end for the ancient settlement as a major port.

The town's name is derived from St Petroc, the Irish missionary saint who landed here from Wales in the 6th-century. The parish church is dedicated to him, although the present building dates from the 13th- and 14th-centuries; inside there is a striking Elizabethan pulpit and some comical bench ends, one of which depicts a fox preaching to a gaggle of geese.

St Petroc also founded a monastery here, but in the 10th-century it was moved to Bodmin to protect its occupants from Viking raids.

Padstow's original monastery is believed to have stood on the site of the present-day **Prideaux Place**, a handsome Elizabethan mansion at the top of the town which was built in the 1580s by the Prideaux family.

Still occupied by the descendants of the original owners, the house is set in extensive grounds incorporating a twenty-acre deer park and formal Italianate garden. Highlights of the interior include the library, drawing room and great chamber with its fine plasterwork ceiling. (Open Sundays to Thursdays, 1.30pm to 5pm between early-May and end-September; also during Easter fortnight.) Several monuments to the Prideaux family can be seen in the parish church.

With its narrow alleyways and tightly-packed slate-hung buildings, Padstow's old quarter retains much of its medieval character. The harbour still supports a sizable fishing fleet and is enhanced by the recent addition of floodgates which retain the seawater at low tide. The area around the old port contains a number of interesting old buildings, including the 15th-century **Merchants' Guild House** on the north quay, and the 16th-century **Raleigh's Court House** on the south quay; the latter was used by Sir Walter's agents for collecting Stannary taxes.

Today, Padstow's harbour and nearby shopping streets throng with visitors throughout the summer, some of whom arrive along the beautiful Camel cycle-path which follows the course of the old railway line from Wadebridge; the long curved bridge which crosses the mouth Little Petherick creek is one of its highlights.

Those amongst you who are devotees of good food will be pleased to learn that this is the home of **RICK STEIN'S SEAFOOD RESTAURANT**. He has had a television series and continues to produce first class, imaginative food. If you want to make a night of it you can stay here too. Booking essential.

Rick Stein's Seafood Restaurant Tel: 01841 532485

There are many other alternatives however, and there are several good pubs and restaurants in the town.

One of Padstow's great traditions is the festival of the 'Obby Oss', a boisterous street celebration with origins going back to pagan times whose modern observance still makes little concession to outsiders. (The Obby Oss is a ferocious black figure with a primitive mask, tall conical hat, flat circular body and sailcloth skirt.) Throughout the day on May 1, rival Osses are led on a wild dance through the narrow thoroughfares of Padstow by a staff-wielding 'Teaser' to the accompaniment of traditional music and singing. This ancient ritual, with its strong undertones of pagan fertility rites, is believed to be one of the oldest celebrations of its kind in Europe.

Around Padstow

ST ISSEY In the church at St Issey, three miles to the south along the A389, the altar canopy incorporates a striking collection of carved Catacleuse stone figures which are thought to have once formed part of a chest tomb. There is also a remarkable early photograph of 1869 showing the church tower collapsing with a top-hatted policeman looking haplessly on.

WADEBRIDGE. Four miles further on, the ancient port and market town of Wadebridge stands at the historic lowest bridging point on the Camel (a bypass to the north now carries the A39 over the river). At 320ft, the town's medieval bridge is one of the longest in Cornwall.

Originally composed of seventeen arches, it was built in the 15th-century by the local priest to convey his flock across the river in safety. It is still known by its traditional name, the 'Bridge on Wool', for reasons that are unclear: either it was paid for by wealthy local wool merchants, or its foundations were laid on bales of raw wool, an absorbent material which solidifies when soaked and compressed. Once a thriving river port and railway town, Wadebridge is now a tranquil place with a good selection of shops. Each June, the Royal Cornwall Show is held in the county showground, a mile to the west of the centre.

One of the loveliest country manor houses in the West Country can be found on the eastern side of the A389 Bodmin road, three miles to the southeast of Wadebridge. **Pencarrow House** lies hidden in a 50-acre wooded estate which encompasses an Iron Age encampment and a beautiful woodland garden with a lake, ice house, Victorian granite rockery, and American and Italian gardens.

The grounds also contain an internationally-renowned collection of conifers and over 500 species of rhododendron. The interior of the Georgian house is furnished with some outstanding 18th-century paintings, period furniture and china. (Open Sundays to Thursdays, 11am to 5pm between Easter and mid-October.)

ST COLUMB MAJOR.To the west of Wadebridge, the A39 leads up onto the St Breock Downs, the site of such striking Bronze Age remains as the ancient St Breock Longstone and Nine Maidens stone row. Three miles further on and thankfully now bypassed by the main road, the small town of St Columb Major was once considered as the location for Cornwall's cathedral (it lost out to Truro). The parish church of St Columba is unusually large, with a four-tier tower and a wide through-arch; inside there are some fine 16th- and 17th-century monumental brasses to the Arundell family. The church is adjoined to the south and east by handsome old residential buildings which create something of the atmosphere of a cathedral close.

The Red Lion inn is renowned for its former landlord, James Polkinghorne, a famous exponent of Cornish wrestling who is depicted in action on a plaque on an external wall. Another of St Columb Major's inns, the Silver Ball Hotel, marks the town's other great sporting tradition, 'hurling the silver ball'.

This rowdy medieval game is played twice a year, on Shrove Tuesday then on the Saturday eleven days later, and involves two teams of several hundred people (the 'townsmen' and the 'countrymen') who endeavour to carry a silver-painted ball made of apple wood through goals set two miles apart. Once a common pastime throughout the county, this ancient Cornish game is now only practised here and, in a less rumbustious form, at St Ives.

Such is the passion for the St Columb event that windows of houses and shops in the locality have to be boarded up for the occasion. Two miles southeast of St Columb Major, the land rises to 700ft above sea level on Castle Downs, site of the massive Iron Age hill fort known as Castle-an-Dinas whose three earthwork ramparts enclose an area of over six-acres. The climb to the gorse-covered summit is rewarded with panoramic views over the leafy Vale of Lanherne to the northwest, and towards the unearthly landscape of the china clay spoil heaps to the south.

ST. MAWGAN. The beautiful village of St Mawgan lies submerged in the mature trees of the Vale of Lanherne, midway between St Columb and the coast. The restored church has one of the finest collections of monumental brasses in the county; most are of the Arundell family whose former 13th-century manor house, Lanherne, was taken over by the closed Carmelite order of nuns in 1794. The churchyard contains a richly-carved lantern cross dating from around 1420 and an extraordinary timber memorial in the shape of the stern of a boat which is dedicated to the ten souls who froze to death in their lifeboat after being shipwrecked off the coast in 1846. The village inn, the Falcon, is reputed to have been named during the Reformation when it was the practice to release a bird into the air to signal that a secret Catholic Mass was about to take place. On the coast at **Mawgan Porth**, the remains of a Saxon settlement can be made out which once supported a small fishing and herding community. Various 9th- to 11th-century dwellings can be identified near the beach, along with the foundations of a larger court-yard house and the outline of a cemetery.

The coastline between Mawgan Porth and Padstow is among the most rugged and impressive in Cornwall.

Near Park Head, the sea has pounded the volcanic cliffs into a series of spectacular shapes known as the **Bedruthan Steps** after the ancient Cornish giant who is said to have used them as stepping stones.

At high tide, the steps are lashed by the waves, but at low tide the water recedes to reveal a superb sandy beach which can only be accessed via a steep and perilous cliff path which is often closed due to subsidence.

PORTHCOTHAN. Much of the cliffscape around this former smugglers' haunt is owned by the National Trust, and further north, the view of the Atlantic is particularly dramatic around Constantine Bay and **Trevose Head**.

NEWQUAY. To the south of Mawgan Porth, the coast road traverses the beach at Watergate Bay before arriving in the popular seaside and surfing resort of Newquay.

A settlement since ancient times, evidence of an Iron Age coastal fort can be seen among the cliffs and caves of Porth Island to the northeast of the centre. In common with many Cornish coastal communities, this was an important pilchard fishing centre in the centuries leading up to the industry's decline early in the 20th-century.

An original 'huer's' hut can still be seen on the headland to the west of the harbour; this was where a local man would keep a look out for shoals of red pilchards and alert the fishing crews when one was sighted close to shore by calling 'hevva' through a long loud-hailer. He would then guide the *seine* boats towards their quarry with semaphore-style signals using a pair of bats known as 'bushes'.

The town takes its name from the new harbour which was built in the 1830s by Joseph Treffry of Fowey for exporting china clay, a trade which continued for several decades until the purpose-built port facility was completed on the south coast at Par.

The decline of Newquay as a port was tempered by the arrival of the railway in 1875, and before long, train loads of visitors were arriving to enjoy the town's extensive sandy beaches, scenic position and mild climate. Over the years, a number of popular attractions have been constructed to satisfy tourist demand, including Trenance Garden with its boating lake, miniature railway and zoo. Towan Beach is a good sheltered beach with a tidal paddling pool which is ideal for children; this can be found at the base of the 'Island', a detached outcrop which is

Newquay Harbour

connected to the mainland by an elegant suspended footbridge.

In recent decades, Newquay has also acquired a reputation as one of the finest surfing centres in the British Isles. Throughout the year, thousands of keen surfers arrive in Volkswagen campers and the like to catch the waves of Fistral Beach, or to watch the increasing number of national and international competitions which are held here each season.

Along with the cafés and gift shops, the streets of the town are lined with a refreshing variety of shops offering everything for the surfer, both for sale or for hire. Another colourful summer attraction involves Newquay's fleet of traditional pilot gigs, 30ft rowing boats which race each other over a six-mile course in the bay.

Around Newquay

ST COLUMB MINOR, which adjoins Newquay to the east, has an impressive church whose 15th-century pinnacled tower rises to 115ft.

The exceptionally attractive small Elizabethan manor house, **Trerice**, lies hidden in the lanes to the west of the A3058, three miles southeast of Newquay.

Built in 1571 on the site of a medieval predecessor, it was the family home of the influential Arundell family for several centuries. The structure has a characteristic E-shaped front and unusual curved gables, a possible Dutch influence, and stands within fourteen acres of beautiful landscaped grounds. The interior is noted for its striking plasterwork ceilings, huge fireplaces and fine walnut furniture.

Most impressive is the great hall with its delightful minstrels' gallery and remarkable window containing over 500 panes of glass, most of them original. An unusual small museum in one of the outbuildings is dedicated to the history of the lawn mower. The property is now under the ownership of the National Trust and is open daily except Tuesdays, 11am to 5.30pm between 1 April and 31 October.

NEWLYN EAST. A mile to the south at Newlyn East, the Lappa Valley narrow gauge steam railway carries visitors along an attractive section of the former GWR Newquay to Chacewater line. The short ride ends at a leisure park containing a number of historic attractions, including the imposing old engine house and chimney stack of East Wheal Rose, Cornwall's richest lead-producing mine until a flash flood brought disaster in July 1846.

Reopened the following year, it finally closed altogether in 1885. (Open daily 10am to 5pm between Easter and end-October.) Lying beside the A30 three miles to the east, **Summercourt** is worth a visit for its interesting country life museum.

MITCHELL. Eight miles outside the Cathedral city of Truro is the village of Mitchell just off the A30.

MITCHELL FARMHOUSE, a Grade 11 listed building, offers comfortable bed and breakfast accommodation with a homely atmosphere.

John & Louise are sympathetically developing their organic small-holding with conservation in mind. The guest facilities include tea making facilites in the bedrooms, a Guest dining room and a lounge with colour television. Children are especially welcome for whom lower rates apply.

A separate entrance allows guests to come and go at their own convenience. Vegetarian and special diets are catered for and other meals are available at the pub in the village. Registered with Tourist Board. Pets by prior arrangement.

Mitchell Farmhouse, Mitchell, Cornwall. Tel: 01872 510657

PERRANPORTH. This popular summer holiday centre lies on the coast, five miles to the southwest of Newquay.

Formerly a mining community, all signs of its industrial heritage have long since disappeared, either as a result of encroaching sand or encroaching tourist development. The resort's main asset is its three-mile beach, a beautiful stretch of golden sand which is popular with bathers and surfers, although respect should be given to the inshore currents which at certain stages of the tide can be hazardous.

PERRANZABULOE. The local parish, Perranzabuloe, means 'St Piran in the Sand', for it is here that the 6th-century missionary saint, St Piran, is reputed to have landed having sailed from Ireland 'on a millstone'.

His landing place on **Penhale Sands** is marked by a tall granite cross which is one of only two three-holed Celtic crosses in the county. St Piran, the patron saint of tinners, founded a church and oratory half-a-mile inland, but by the 11th-century it was entirely engulfed in sand where it lay undisturbed until the 19th-century. Now protected by a concrete shell, the delightful little building is worth making the effort to find.

According to local legend, the old mining town of Langarroc lies buried beneath the dunes of Penhale Sands. An ungodly community, it was swallowed up in a great tempest which lasted three days and nights as an act of retribution. On stormy nights, it is said that ghostly cries for help can still be heard above the sound of the wind and waves. A remarkable carved Celtic face which once adorned St Piran's oratory has been remounted in the south porch of the church.

St Austell and the Roseland Peninsula

ST. AUSTELL. This sprawling former market and mining town was transformed in the second half 18th-century when William Cookworthy discovered large deposits of china clay, or *kaolin*, here in 1755.

Over the years, waste material from the clay pits has been piled into great conical spoil heaps which dominate the landscape to the north and west of the town. These bare bleached uplands are sometimes referred to as the 'Cornish Alps', although in recent years steps have been taken to landscape their surface and seed them with grass.

This part of Cornwall is still one of the world's largest producers of china clay, a surprisingly versatile material which, as well as being the basic ingredient of porcelain, is used in the manufacture of paper, paint and pharmaceuticals.

The narrow streets of old St Austell create an atmosphere more befitting a market town than a mining community. The central thoroughfares radiate from the parish church of the Holy Trinity, an imposing structure with a tall 15th-century tower which is decorated on all four sides with carved figures and topped by impressive pinnacles and crenelations. The granite facing stones were brought from the famous Pentewan quarries, three miles to the south.

The church interior has a fine wagon roof and some interesting early features, including a rare pillar piscina and a Norman font carved with a curious assortment of human heads and mythical creatures. Elsewhere in the town centre there are some notable old buildings, including the **Town Hall, Quaker meeting house** and **White Hart Hotel**, as well as a good modern shopping precinct.

Around St Austell.

CARTHEW. Those interested in the history of the Cornish china clay industry should make for Wheal Martyn beside the B3374 at Carthew, two miles north of St Austell.

This fascinating open-air museum is set in an old clay works dating from around 1880, and features a giant restored water wheel, an exhibition of historic locomotives, and a unique collection of clothing and mining equipment used by local clay workers. (Open daily between April and end-October.) In common with the other mining communities throughout the country, there is a tradition for those in Cornwall to have their own silver band. Each year, the musicians come together to show off their skills and compete at the music festival in BUGLE, an aptly-named village lying on the A391 Bodmin road, a couple of miles further north.

ROCHE. It's well worth forking northwest onto the B3274 at Carthew to reach Roche (pronounced *Roach*), an old clay mining village whose restored parish church retains its medieval tower and a pillared Norman font.

Much more impressive, however, is the 14th-century hermitage on **Roche Rock**, the striking granite outcrop which stands beside the road to Bugle, half-a-mile east of the village. The feat of erecting this remarkable little two-storey building in such a precarious place is a testimony to the determination of its medieval builders. According to local legend, the hermitage was the cell and chapel of St Gonand, a saintly leper who survived thanks to his daughter who each day carried food and water up the hill to her invalid father. The rock is also associated with the legendary Cornish scoundrel, Jan Tregeagle (see Dozmary Pool in chapter 6), who attempted to seek sanctuary in the chapel when being pursued across Bodmin moor by a pack of headless hounds. Sadly, his torso became trapped in the window, exposing his lower body to the fury of his pursuers.

BODMIN. Bustling by day, yet quiet by night, the historic former county town of Bodmin lies midway between Cornwall's north and south coasts at the junction of two ancient cross-county trading routes.

For many centuries, traders between Wales, Ireland and the northern France preferred the overland route between the Camel and Fowey estuaries to the hazardous sea journey around Land's End. **Castle Canyke** to the southeast of the town was built during the Iron Age to defend this important trade route, and a few centuries later, the Romans erected a fort on a site above the River Camel to the west of the town, one of a string they built in the South West to defend strategic river crossings; the remains of a quadrilateral earthwork can still be made out today. The ancient crosscountry route is now a waymarked footpath known as the Saints' Way.

Bodmin's most famous early visitor is perhaps St Petroc, one of the most influential of the early Welsh missionary-saints who landed in Cornwall in the 6th-century. The monastery he founded near Padstow was moved to Bodmin in the 10th-century to protect it from seaborne Viking raids; although it survived until the Dissolution of the Monasteries in 1539, little of it remains today. Bodmin's parish church, perhaps the most impressive in Cornwall, is dedicated to St Petroc. Rebuilt in the 15th-century and renovated in the 19th, it contains a magnificent Norman font whose immense bowl is supported on five finely-carved columns, and a priceless ivory casket in which the remains of the saint were placed in 1177 after they had been recovered from a light-fingered Augustinian monk.

Bodmin is also renowned for its holy wells - eleven in all. Some, such as Eye Water Well, are known for their restorative properties, and some, such as St Guron's Well opposite the church, for being ancient places of baptism.

Bodmin was the only market town in Cornwall to be mentioned in the Domesday Book, and at one time it boasted its own mint and, later, the county assizes. However, the 19th-century rise of Truro as Cornwall's cathedral city stripped Bodmin of its county town status.

A number of impressive relics of its former glory nevertheless remain, including the Tudor guildhall, the former court buildings, and the Turret Clock where former mayor, Nicholas Boyer, was hanged for his part in the Prayer Book Rebellion of 1549. Public executions were also held at Bodmin gaol, a once-feared place which now operates as a hotel.

Bodmin also contains two first-rate museums: the recently-refurbished town museum, and the **Duke of Cornwall Light Infantry Museum** which is housed in the old regimental headquarters. Turf Street leads up past Mount Folly to the Beacon, a scenic picnic area with a 140ft obelisk at is summit which was built to commemorate the Victorian general, Sir Walter Raleigh Gilbert. One of Britain's earliest railways was opened in 1830 to link Bodmin with the Camel estuary at Wadebridge. In recent years, the track has been reopened as a public cyclepath and walkway which runs all the way from Boscarne Junction to Padstow.

The spectacular National Trust-owned property, **Lanhydrock House**, lies two miles to the south of Bodmin, midway between the A38 and B3269. Prior to the Dissolution of the Monasteries, the 400-acre estate belonged to Bodmin's Augustinian priory of St Petroc, then in 1620 it was acquired by the Robartes family in whose possession it remained until it passed to the National Trust in 1953. The house is set in a superb position in the valley of the River Fowey and is approached along an avenue of sycamore and beech trees, some of which were originally planted over three centuries ago. Visitors pass through an imposing 17th-century gatehouse which, along with the north wing, is one of the few parts of the original structure to have escaped the fire which tore through the building in 1881.

Thankfully, the magnificent first floor gallery in the north wing survived; over 115ft long, it is illuminated by broad mullioned windows and contains a remarkable plasterwork ceiling showing scenes from the Old Testament which is believed to be the work of the Abbott family, master plasterers of North Devon.

Because of the fire, most of Lanhydrock House is a Victorian reconstruction which was built in the 1880s to the original 17th-century design.

The updated interior contains a maze of comfortably-appointed rooms, over forty of which are now open to the public. Highlights include the estate offices, servants' quarters, buttery and recently-furnished nursery, which together create a unique picture of life in an opulent Victorian country mansion. The grounds contain an attractive woodland shrubbery, and a much-photographed formal garden and parterre which is overlooked by the small estate church of St Hyderoc. (Open daily except Mondays, 11am to 5.30pm between 1 April and 31

October.)

A mile-and-a-half downstream, the imposing Norman keep of **Restormel Castle** stands on a promontory overlooking the wooded valley of the River Fowey. The fortress was built early in the 12th-century by Edmund, Earl of Cornwall, and is remarkably well-preserved for its age. The walls of the massive circular shell are 30ft high in places, and the whole structure is surrounded by a deep dry moat which is lined with flowers in spring. The castle was in use until the 16th-century, and was reoccupied for a time by Parliamentarian forces during the English Civil War. Now under the care of English Heritage, visitors can climb a series of walkways onto the ramparts. (Open daily, 10am to 6pm between 1 April and 30 September.) The road to the south passes close to the site of a disused mine which was once the largest source of iron ore in Cornwall. Material was transported from here by tramway to Lostwithiel, and then by barge to Fowey for loading onto seagoing vessels.

LOSTWITHIEL. This attractive small market town stands at the head of the Fowey estuary at the historic lowest bridging point on the river. One of Cornwall's medieval Stannary towns, tin and other raw metals were brought here for assaying and onward shipping until upstream mining activity caused the anchorage to silt up, forcing the port to move down-river to the estuary mouth. Present-day Lostwithiel is an atmospheric touring and angling centre whose long history has left it with a legacy of interesting old buildings, many of which are set in characteristic narrow alleyways, or *opes*. The remains of the 13th-century great hall which served as the treasury and stannary offices can be seen in Quay Street, and in Fore Street, there is a fine example of an early 18th-century arcaded Guildhall which now serves as the civic museum. The nearby municipal offices date from later in the century, as does the old grammar school in Queen Street, and elsewhere in the town there are some fine Georgian residences and shop fronts. **The old malt house** is worth finding for its unusual plaque declaring: 'Walter Kendal founded this house and hath a lease for 3000 years beginning 29 September 1652.'

Lostwithiel's 14th-century parish **church of St Bartholomew** has a rare octagonal spire; one of only six in the county, its style is reminiscent of the church architecture of northern France. Another unusual feature is the row of upper windows in the aisle, or *clerestory*, which is one of only four in Cornwall. The early-14th-century font is unusually large and richly carved. During the Civil War, the Parliamentarians made this the focus for their anti-Royalist feeling when they brought a horse into the church and provocatively christened it Charles 'in contempt of his sacred Majesty.'

LUXULYAN The lanes to the west of Lostwithiel lead to Luxulyan, the location of the remarkable **Treffry Viaduct**. Over 100ft high and 200 yards long, it was built in 1842 to carry mineral ores, quarried stone and fresh water to the newly-created port of Par.

The countryside to the east of the Fowey estuary contains some exceptionally attractive rural backwaters, including Lerryn, Couch's

Mill and St Veep. The church at **St Winnow** has an impressive 15th-century stained-glass window and one of Cornwall's few rood screens.

LANREATH.There is an interesting museum of rural life which contains a unique collection of antique farm engines, tractors and agricultural implements. Much of the dense lush woodland surrounding the Fowey estuary is owned by the National Trust, and it was here that Kenneth Grahame discovered the glade that was to become the Wild Wood in his children's classic, *The Wind In The Willows*. It can be found along the path which runs north from the 16th-century bridge at LERRYN

You could be forgiven for thinking you have arrived at the wrong place as you pull up at **The Old Rectory** in Lanreath, for this impresive Georgian Mansion with its beautiful secluded gardens looks straight out of the 'luxury Homes' magazines.

The property has been converted into spacious, modern holiday flats of one, two or three bedrooms. They are comfortable and fully furnished. By staying at the Old Rectory you can enjoy the best of the busy beaches or local attractions, returning to the peace and tranquillity of the gardens and swimming pool when you have had enough. The local village pub , The Punchbowl, is renowned for its atmosphere and good food. For those who enjoy sea fishing, sailing or surfing, a round of golf or National Trust houses, such facilities are within a few miles travel. ETB four keys approved. Pets by arrangement.

The Old Rectory, Lanreath by Looe, Cornwall. Tel. & Fax: 01503 220247

FOWEY. The lovely old port of Fowey (pronounced *Foy*) guards the western entrance to the river from which it takes its name.

The narrow lanes and alleyways of the old town rise abruptly from the water's edge in a pleasant mixture of architectural styles from Elizabethan to Edwardian.

The deep water harbour has been used as an anchorage for seagoing vessels since the time of the ancient Romans, and china clay continues to be exported from the whitened jetties which lie half-a-mile or so upstream.

The town's long history is closely linked with its maritime tradition. During the Hundred Years War, local mariners recruited to fight the

French became known as the 'Fowey Gallants'; some refused to disband, and instead formed a notorious gang of pirates who would attack any vessel straying too close to this stretch of coast.

Following a devastating French raid in 1457, a chain was stretched across the estuary mouth at night to deter hostile ships from entering the harbour.

Present-day Fowey is a peaceful community which is connected by vehicle ferry to Bodinnick on the eastern bank, and by passenger ferry to Polruan. The harbour is filled with pleasure craft from all over Britain and continental Europe, and there are a number of fine old buildings which are worth a closer inspection, for example the **Noah's Ark Museum**, which is housed one of the oldest structures in Fowey, the medieval town hall in Trafalgar Square, which is occupied by another interesting local museum, and **THE SHIP INN,** a part-15th-century building with a Victorian façade which was once the town house of the Rashleigh family.

Their family seat, Menabilly, lies to the southeast of the town and was subsequently the home of Daphne du Maurier who used the setting, rechristened as 'Manderley', in her famous novel, *Rebecca*. Another of Fowey's literary residents was the Cornish novelist, Sir Arthur Quiller-Couch, who lived for over fifty years at the Haven on the Esplanade.

GOLANT. A mile-and-a-half to the northwest, the B3269 passes the remarkable Tristan stone, a 6th-century standing stone which is inscribed in Latin.

The 7ft monolith is believed to come from Castle Dore, a circular Iron Age fort lying close to the turning to Golant which was occupied periodically until the 6th-century.

Golant itself is a delightful waterside community whose small early-16th-century church, **St Samson's,** contains an unusual wooden pulpit made of medieval bench ends; an ancient holy well lies beneath the south porch. The return journey to St Austell passes close to **Tregrehan,** an attractive woodland garden which has been developed since early 19th-century by the Carlyon family. Specialising in rare species from warm-temperate regions, the garden incorporates a walled garden, a series of glasshouses and a small nursery. (Open daily, 10.30am to 5pm between mid-March and end-June, and also in September.)

The east-facing shoreline to the south of St Austell shelters some exceptionally pretty coastal communities.

PENTEWAN (pronounced *Pen-Túan*) is a former quarrying village and china clay port which has found new life as a sailing and holiday centre. The enchanting **Lost Gardens of Heligan** can be found to the west of the B3273 between Pentewan and Mevagissey.

This superb 57-acre Victorian garden which has recently been beautifully restored after having been left to overgrow for over seventy years. Highlights include a subtropical valley containing the largest collection in tree ferns in Britain, an Italian Garden, Crystal grotto, and four walled gardens. The kitchen garden is being remodelled as a museum of 19th-century horticulture, and there is also a pleasant sales area stocked with rare and unusual plants. (Open daily, 10am to 6pm, all year round.)

MEVAGISSEY. Once aptly known as Porthilly, it was renamed in late medieval times after the Welsh and Irish saints Meva and Itha. The village is a renowned fishing port which was once an important centre of the pilchard industry. Each year during the 18th- and 19th-centuries, thousands of tons of this oily fish were landed here for salting, packing or processing into lamp oil.

Some were exported to southern Europe, or supplied to the Royal Navy to whose sailors they became known as 'Mevagissey Ducks'. The need to process the catch within easy reach of the harbour created a labyrinth of buildings separated by steep-sloping alleyways, some of which were so narrow that the baskets of fish sometimes had to carried on poles between people walking one behind the other.

At one time, up to 100 fishing luggers could be seen jostling for a berth in Mevagissey's picturesque harbour. Today, all but a handful of inshore fishing craft have gone, and in common with most of Cornwall's coastal communities, the local economy relies heavily on visitors, an annual influx which has given rise to a proliferation of cafés and gift shops, but which thankfully has failed to diminish the port's essential character. The part-13th-century Pentewan-stone **church of St Peter** is worth a look for its Norman font and amusingly inscribed monument to Otwell Hill, an early in-comer who died here in 1617. Elsewhere, there are a number of more modern indoor attractions, including a model village, and a folk museum containing an interesting assortment of fishing and agricultural equipment.

GORRAN HAVEN. Once a pilchard-fishing community with a history to rival Mevagissey, Gorran Haven is now a pleasant village which has the added attraction of a sheltered pebbled beach. To the southeast, the land rises onto the impressive headland of **Dodman Point**, much of which is owned by the National Trust. Sometimes known locally as 'Deadman Point', it is the site of a substantial Iron Age coastal fort whose 2000ft northern defensive earthwork can still be made out. The view to the northwest takes in the delightfully-named Porthluney Cove with its neo-Gothic flight of fancy, **Caerhays Castle**, behind.

THE ROSELAND PENINSULA. This is the name the indented tongue of land which forms the eastern margin of the Fal estuary, or 'Carrick Roads'. It can be approached along the coastal lanes or from the main A390 St Austell to Truro road. Although less scenic, the latter route also takes in a number of noteworthy places of interest.

GRAMPOUND. Although it is hard to imagine today, Grampound was once a busy port and market town at the lowest bridging point the River Fal.

A number of interesting old buildings are to be found here, including the guildhall, clock tower and toll house. The local tannery is renowned for its traditional methods of bark-tanning.

CREED. A small vilage lying due south of Grampound where there is a good place to stay, which was described as follows.

"Driving through the gate on a rainy evening, was like driving into sheer elegance" - so writes a recent guest to **Creed House,** the lovely Georgian home of Lally and William. The house is a listed building dating back to around 1730 and stands amid five acres of landscaped garden occasionally open to the public. There are three guest bedrooms, all comfortably furnished with antiques. Guests have their own sitting room with television; breakfast is served in a farmhouse style kitchen. The International Clientele have written many wonderful messages and comments about this family and their beautiful home, Book early! Well placed for all the attractions of the County.

Creed House, Creed, Grampound, Truro, Cornwall. Tel: 01872 530372

A short distance further west, **Trewithen House** is an elegant Georgian manor house which was built in the early 18th-century by the Hawkins family, in whose hands it remains to this day. The exceptionally beautiful 25-acre gardens were planted by George Johnson, an authority on Asiatic flowering shrubs, and contain a world-renowned collection of magnolias, camellias and rhododendrons which are particularly spectacular in late-spring. (Gardens open Mondays to Saturdays, 10.30am to 4.30pm between 1 March and 30 September; house open Mondays and Tuesdays only, 2pm to 4.30pm between early-April and end-July.)

The grounds of Trewithen adjoin the **County Demonstration Gardens,** a six-and-a-half acre area devoted to the study of plants grown in different soil and climatic conditions; there is also a small arboretum, nature trail and a helpful gardening advisory service.

PROBUS. The nearby village of Probus is famous for having the tallest parish church tower in the county. Built of granite in the early 16th-century and towering to over 123ft high, its three-tiered design, with its elaborate tracery, carving and pinnacles, is an outstanding example of the 'Somerset style'.

CRUGSILLICK.To the south, the A3078 leads onto the Roseland peninsula proper, where comfortable and spacious B & B accommodation can be found on The Roseland Peninsula at **THE OLD STABLES** in Crugsillick.

Set in lovely gardens, this quiet and relaxing place is the ideal base for a holiday. Two rooms are available, both are well furnished. Breakfast is super and includes freshly cooked home grown vegetables and delicious home-made jams. You can be assured of a warm welcome at this pleasant 'hidden place'.

The Old Stables B & B, Crugsillick, Ruan High Lanes, Truro.
Tel: 01872 501783

TREGONY. Like Grampound, Tregony is a former river port with some fine old buildings, including a Gothic clock tower and a row of balconied almshouses. Four miles further on, it's well worth making a short detour from the main road to visit Veryan.

VERYAN is a charming village set in a wooded hollow which is famous for its five round houses.

Set two at each end of the village and one in the middle, these curious whitewashed cottages each has conical thatched roof with a wooden cross at the apex. They were built in the 19th-century for the daughters of the local vicar, Jeremiah Trist. According to legend, their round shape is a defence against the Devil who likes to enter a house by the north wall and hide in the corners. The much-altered village church is set above a delightful water garden which doubles are a garden of remembrance.

The road to the safe sandy Pendower beach passes close to the Bronze Age round barrow on Carne Beacon, one of the largest examples of its kind in Britain.

ST JUST IN ROSELAND. To the southwest of Veryan, the A3078 meets the Carrick Roads at St Just in Roseland, an enchanting hamlet whose tiny part-13th-century church lies in one of the most superb settings in the country. Concealed in a steep wooded tidal creek and entered through a lychgate which is level with the top of the church tower, the churchyard contains a wonderful collection of trees and shrubs, including semitropical species such as the African fire bush and Chilean myrtle. Sadly, the church interior suffered a clumsy Victorian restoration, although the 15th-century font and 16th-century monumental brass survive. In 1733, a wealthy parishioner bequeathed ten shillings (50p) a year to the vicar for dedicating a funeral sermon to him on 27 December.

ST MAWES. A couple of miles to the south, the popular yachting centre of St Mawes guards the eastern entrance to the Fal estuary.

The town is dominated by its artillery fort which, along with **Pendennis Castle** on the western bank, was constructed in the 1540s as part of Henry VIII's coastal defences. Built to a characteristic cloverleaf, or *trefoil*, design around a circular central tower, its cannons were able to fire in a wide arc from a number of levels. Yet, it was destined never to

St Just in Roseland Church

fire a shot in anger and today, its gun emplacements and restored Tudor interior remain in remarkably fine condition. (Open daily, 10am to 6pm, all year round; closed Mondays in winter.) The fort is surrounded by extensive gardens which offer dramatic views of Falmouth harbour.

ST ANTHONY. On the remote southern side of the Percuil estuary, the hamlet of St Anthony contains a small church which is rumoured to have been founded after the young Jesus Christ had sheltered here from a storm at sea with his uncle, Joseph of Arimathea.

The remains of a monastery which once stood nearby have been incorporated into the 19th-century Place manor house. A good way to reach the western side of the Fal is via the King Harry vehicle ferry which lies two-and-a-half miles along the B3289 to the north of St Just.

The unusually deep water in the estuary is often used as an anchorage by ageing seagoing vessels waiting to be recommissioned or broken up for scrap - an unexpected and spectacular sight.

Truro to the Atlantic Coast

TRURO. An elegant small city which has grown to become the administrative capital of Cornwall.

Its site at the head of a branch of the Fal estuary has been occupied for thousands of years, but it wasn't until large-scale mineral extraction began in medieval times that the settlement took on any significance. One of the first Cornish towns to be granted rights of Stannary, huge quantities of smelted tin ore and other metals were brought here for weighing, taxing and shipping until the industry went into decline in 17th-century. By this time, the estuary has also begun to silt up, allowing Falmouth to take over as the area's principal seaport. A number of picturesque alleyways or opes (pronounced *opps*) have survived from Truro's heyday as a port, many of which have colourful names such as Tippet's Backlet, Burton's Ope or Squeezeguts Alley.

An increase in metal prices during the 18th-century led to a revival in Truro's fortunes; wealthy merchants and banks moved in, and the town became a centre for fashionable society with a reputation to rival Bath.

This Georgian renaissance has left a distinctive mark on the town's architecture, particularly around Pydar Street, with its handsome Assembly Rooms and Theatre, Walsingham Place, and Lemon Street, one of the finest complete Georgian streets in the country.

A few minutes walk from here is **THE MARCORRIE HOTEL.** This is a pleasantly situated former Victorian Town House set within the City Conservation Area. The Pearson designed Cathedral in the city centre is only a few minutes walk down Lemon Street, lined with its famous Georgian houses.

The twelve tastefully decorated rooms each have their own bathroom, colour television, kettle, and telephone. Two of these rooms are ground floor rooms he suitable for the less mobile.

A two bedroomed bungalow in the same quiet location is available for a self catering holiday. Sharing a peaceful garden and outdoor swimming pool.

Both Paul and Pam Treseder have their historic roots in Cornwall and are pleased to impart their wealth of local knowledge to those who wish to seek those hidden haunts of historical Cornwall. Many of the fine country houses, gardens full of abundant early spring flowers or rugged coastal walks are easily reached by car, bus or train after a substantial breakfast in the Victorian dining room.

Marcorrie Hotel, 20 Falmouth Road, Truro Tel: 01872 77374

Also worth seeing are the indoor Pannier Market and the city hall is Boscawen Street. The arrival of the railway in 1859 confirmed Truro's status as regional capital, and in 1877 it became a city in its own right when the diocese of Exeter was divided into two and Cornwall was granted its own bishop.

Three years later, the foundation stone of a new cathedral, the first to be built in Britain since Wren's St Paul's, was laid by the future Edward VII, and over the next thirty years it was constructed to a design in Early English style by the architect John Loughborough Pearson. Finished locally-sourced granite and serpentine, this graceful three-spired structure incorporates the early-16th-century south aisle of St Mary's church which originally occupied part of the site. The soaring 250ft central spire can be seen for miles around and stands are a fitting centrepiece for this elegant and prosperous shopping and administrative centre. Those with an interest in gardening should make a point of finding **Bosvigo House** which lies just off the A390 Redruth road, three-quarters-of-a-mile to the west of the city centre. This delightful series of walled herbaceous gardens is set around a handsome Georgian house which is not open to visitors; the grounds incorporate a woodland walk, Victorian conservatory and a nursery offering rare and specialist plants. (Open daily, 11am to 6pm between early-June and end-September.)

COME TO GOOD. Three miles south of Truro in this delightfully-named hamlet, the road between Carnon Downs and the King Harry

Truro Cathedral

Ferry passes a pretty cob and thatch building which is one of the oldest Quaker Meeting Houses in the country. Built around 1710 when the Society of Friends was still outlawed, it is still in use to this day. Despite its pious-sounding name, the hamlet takes its name from the Cornish phrase *Cwm-ty-quite*, meaning 'house in the wooded combe'.

A mile to the east, the National Trust-owned **Trelissick Gardens** lie on either side of the B3289 as the road descends to the King Harry Ferry. These beautiful wooded gardens were laid out in their present form by the Copelands between 1937 and 1955 in the grounds of a 19th-century neoclassical mansion which is not open to visitors. Renowned for their collections of mature trees and flowering shrubs, which include magnolias, rhododendrons, azaleas and hydrangeas, the gardens are particularly lovely in early summer. Special features include a summer house with a Saxon cross, and a Victorian water tower with a steep conical roof and 'squirrel' weather vane. A network of delightful woodland walks leads down to the banks of the Carrick Roads. (Open daily, 10.30am (12.30pm Sundays) to 5.30pm between 1 March and 31 October.)

FEOCK. The lanes to the south of Trelissick lead to Feock, a charming collection of whitewashed thatched cottages and affluent modern homes which overlook the deep-water estuary. The yew-filled churchyard contains a free-standing 13th-century tower and is entered through an unusual lychgate incorporating an upper storey hung with slates. A pleasant creek-side walk to the west follows the course of an old tramway, a sign that this tranquil place once had a bustling industrial economy. A lane to the south of Feock leads to the tip of Restronguet Point, the landing stage for a passenger ferry which once formed part of the main post route from Falmouth to Truro and beyond. On the southern side, there is an attractive inn, the Pandora, which is named after the ship which was sent out to capture the mutineers from the *Bounty*.

MYLOR and MYLOR BRIDGE stand respectively at the mouth and head of a narrow arm of the Fal estuary. Once a small dockyard and landing place for the packet sailing ships which carried mail throughout the world, Mylor is now a popular yachting centre. The beautifully-sited churchyard contains the graves of many sea captains and shipwrights who were based in the parish, some of which have amusing inscriptions. The church has two Norman doorways and a 15th-century south porch beside which stands a round-headed Celtic cross which, at over ten feet, is one of the tallest in Cornwall. Dating from the 10th-century, it was rediscovered in Victorian times after having been used for centuries to prop up the south wall of the church.

FLUSHING is another attractive yachting centre which was built by settlers from the Low Countries in the 17th-century and still retains a distinctive Dutch feel.

BUSVEAL. Six miles northwest of Flushing, the mysterious **Gwennap Pit** lies to the north of the A393 Falmouth to Redruth road near the hamlet of Busveal. This remarkable round amphitheatre and former cock-fighting pit is thought to have been formed by the collapse of a subterranean mine-shaft. Sometimes referred to as the 'Methodist cathedral', the founder of the nonconformist denomination, John Wesley, preached here on the first of many occasions in 1762. In 1806, seating terraces were cut into the banks, and the following year, an annual Whit Monday service was established which has become a focus for Methodist pilgrimage from all over the world. The nearby museum of Cornish Methodism was opened in 1982.

The southern approach to Redruth is dominated by the dramatic form of **Carn Brea** (pronounced *Bray*), a 738ft granite prominence which is the site of the earliest known Neolithic settlement in southern Britain. The legendary home of a Cornish giant, many of the hill's features are dubbed with such names as Giant's hand, Giant's cradle, Giant's head, and even Giant's cups and saucers. (The last-named are natural rain-eroded hollows which over-imaginative Victorians thought had been made by bloodthirsty Druids.) The summit is crowned by an unprepossessing 90ft monument dedicated to Francis Basset de Dunstanville, a benevolent Georgian mine- and landowner who did much to improve the lot of poor labourers. Much more attractive is the small castle on the lower eastern summit, a part-medieval building which in its time has been used as a hunting lodge and restaurant. More easily approached from the south, the whole site is strewn with fascinating industrial and archeological remains.

CAMBORNE and REDRUTH have administratively combined to form the largest urban centre of population in the county. In the mid 19th-century, the surrounding area was the most intensely mined in the world, and the district is still littered with evidence of this lost era. In the 1850s, Cornwall had well over 300 mines which together produced two-thirds of the world's copper and employed around 50,000 workers. However, most had to close in first few decades of the 20th-century when the discovery of extensive mineral deposits in the Americas, South Africa and Australia rendered the local industry uneconomic.

Camborne and Redruth have much to offer those with an interest in industrial archeology. Midway between the two at POOL, the National Trust have acquired a pair of massive old high-pressure beam engines, one of which has a cylinder over seven feet in diameter. One was built by Holmans of Camborne in 1887 as a winding engine for raising ore and delivering workers into the mine; the other was built by Harveys of Hayle in 1892 for pumping water from depths of up to 1700ft. (Open daily, 11am to 5.30pm between 1 April and 31 October.) The Trust's Norris Collection of minerals can been in the geological museum of the old Camborne School of Mines, half-of-a-mile to the west. Still one of the foremost institutes of mining technology, the School moved to new premises in Redruth in the 1970s.

The home of pioneer Cornish engineer Richard Trevithick can be seen at Penponds on the southwestern outskirts of Camborne. This little-known inventor was responsible for developing the high-pressure steam engine, the screw propeller, and an early locomotive which predated Stephenson's *Rocket* by twelve years, yet he died penniless and was buried in an unmarked grave in Dartford, Kent. Known locally as the Cornish Giant, a statue of this underrated genius and accomplished amateur wrestler can be seen outside Camborne Library; he is also commemorated in the colourful Trevithick Day procession which is held in the last week of April. Another inventor who settled in the area was Scotsman William Murdock. Responsible for such innovations as coal-gas lighting and the vacuum-powered tubes which were once a common feature in most department stores, his home in Cross Street, Redruth is now open to the public. Perhaps more architecturally pleasing than its neighbour, Redruth contains pockets of Victorian, Georgian and earlier buildings, particularly in Churchtown where there are some attractive old cottages, a Georgian church with a 15th-century tower, and a lychgate whose unusually long coffin-rest was built to deal with the aftermath of mining disasters.

The B3300 to the northwest of Redruth leads past the **Tolgus Tin Mill**, an 18th-century streaming mill where tin deposits were extracted from the river bed by a process of sifting and stamping. Prior to a quay being constructed at **Portreath** in 1760, copper ore from the mines around Redruth and St Day had to be loaded onto ships from the beach, a slow and dangerous task. Built by Francis Basset, the man whose monument stands on Carn Brea, the harbour was connected to the mines in 1809 by the first railway in Cornwall. The remains of the inclined plane which was used to lower ore-laden wagons down the final 1 in 10 gradient to the quay can still be made out. The white conical structure on the cliff above the harbour was built in the 19th-century as a daymark; known-locally as the Pepperpot, it continues to guide mariners to safety to this day. Now a pleasant small beach resort, modern housing now stands in the place of the great mounds of ore, coal and lime which once dominated Portreath harbour. The high headland to the west of the beach is known as the Wedding Cake; it was once used by the local 'huer' whose job it was to look out for shoals of pilchards and alert local fishermen (see Newquay). Much of the dramatic stretch of coastline to the southwest is owned by the National Trust.

ST AGNES. Once known as the source of the finest tin in Cornwall, the old mining community of St Agnes lies at the head of a steep valley, five miles to the northeast of Portreath. Despite having been subjected to 200 years of mineral extraction and almost 100 years of tourism, it still manages to retain its original character, especially around the narrow-spired parish church and nearby terrace of stepped miners' cottages which are known locally as the 'Stippy-Stappy'. The village is also renowned as the birthplace of the Georgian society painter, John Opie, and is known to thousands of readers of Winston Graham's *Poldark* novels as 'St Ann'. A good local museum can be found near the church, and there is also a popular leisure park to the south of the village which features a model of Cornwall in miniature and a number of themed areas, all set in seven acres of attractive landscaped grounds.

In Trevaunance Cove near St Agnes, which incidentally is one of the best surfing beaches in Cornwall, is a gem of a place called rather oddly **THE DRIFTWOOD SPARS**. This first class free house run by Gordon and Jill Treleaven takes its name from the fact that part of its construction is of huge wooden ships spars which were used in the building of what was at one time a mine warehouse and a sail loft before its conversion to the hotel and inn we see today.

It has lost nothing of its earlier character however, and there is even a wreckers tunnel which can be seen through a porthole set into one of the walls.

With something for everyone, there are 3 cosy bars with one particularly suitable for those with children, a separate restaurant upstairs and with the added bonus of overnight accommodation this is an ideal place to stop, be it by car or if you are using the coastal footpath from Perranporth which passes the front door.

The Driftwood Spars Hotel & Restaurant, Trevaunance Cove, St. Agnes.
Tel: 01872 552428

A quay constructed in the 18th-century for loading tin ore survived here until it was washed away in a storm during the 1930s; its four predecessors suffered a similar fate. The surrounding landscape is littered with abandoned pump houses and mine shafts (walkers should keep to the paths): many of the mines, such as Wheal Kitty and Wheal Ellen, were named after female members of the mine-owning families, or in the case of Wheal Freedom and Wheal Friendly, were given other romantic associations. One of the most photogenic of Cornwall's derelict pump houses stands on a narrow cliff platform 200ft above Chapel Porth, a mile-and-a-half to the west of St Agnes. Now under the ownership of the National Trust, Wheal Coates was in operation for thirty years between 1860 and 1890. A good circular walk from the car park at Chapel Porth also takes in St Agnes Head and **St Agnes Beacon**, a 628ft peak which offers outstanding views across Cornwall to Bodmin Moor in the east and St Ives in the west; it is said that over thirty church towers can be seen from here on a clear day.

CHAPTER EIGHT

WEST CORNWALL

St Michael's Mount

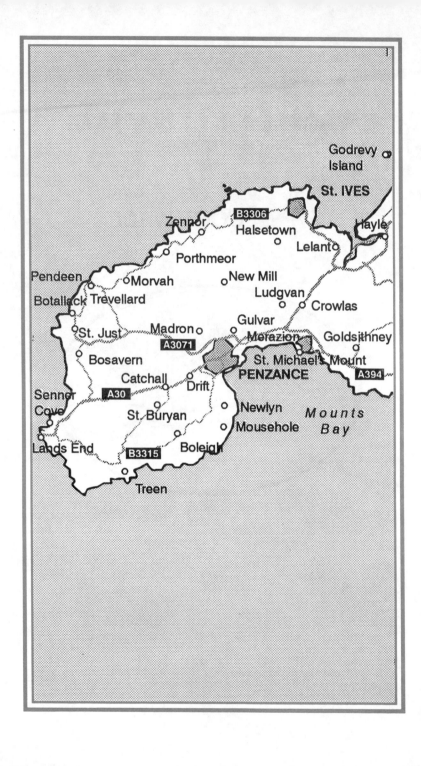

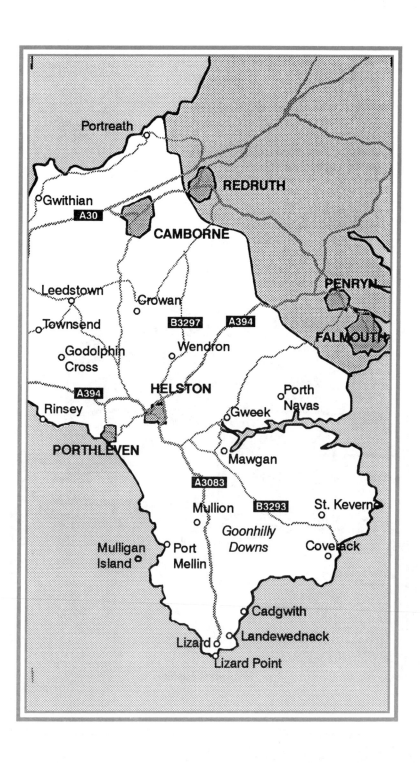

Pendennis Castle

CHAPTER EIGHT

WEST CORNWALL

Falmouth, Helston and the Lizard Peninsula

FALMOUTH stands in a magnificent position at the entrance to the Carrick Roads, a spectacular deep-water anchorage which is formed by the merging of seven river estuaries. Although a settlement has existed here for many hundreds of years, it wasn't until the 17th-century that the port was properly developed as a mail packet station which subsequently became the communications' hub for the British empire. During its heyday in the early 19th-century, Falmouth was the base for almost forty sailing ships which carried documents, personal effects and cargo to almost every corner of the globe. A few decades later, however, the introduction of steam-powered vessels heralded the end for Falmouth and by the 1850s, the packet service had moved to Southampton.

Three centuries before, Henry VIII built a pair of fortresses on either side of the estuary mouth to protect the strategically-important deep-water anchorage from attack by forces loyal to the Catholic faith. (The Pope's disapproval of Henry's marital and religious antics was well-known.) **Pendennis Castle** on the western side is superbly-sited on a 200ft promontory overlooking the entrance to the Carrick Roads. Its low circular keep has immensely thick walls and stands within a 16-sided enclosure; the outer curtain wall was added during Elizabethan times in response to the threat of a second Spanish Armada. One of the last Royalist strongholds to fall during the English Civil War, Pendennis only succumbed to the Parliamentarians following a grim siege lasting five months. The castle remained in use as a coastal defence station until the end of the Second World War and is now under the ownership of English Heritage. (Open daily, 10am to 6pm, all year round.) The spectacular viewpoint of Pendennis Point is also the location of the Maritime Rescue Centre, the operational headquarters which was opened in 1981 to coordinate all search and rescue operations around the British coastline.

That Falmouth was developed as a port at all was due to Sir Walter Raleigh, a man whose early vision was later realised by the influential local buccaneering family, the Killigrews. A monument to the family erected in 1737 can be seen in Grove Place, a short distance from the remains of their once-splendid Tudor mansion, Arwenack House. Falmouth's Royalist sympathies are demonstrated in the 17th-century parish church which is dedicated to 'King Charles the Martyr'; much altered, it retains its curious rectangular tower and arcades with Ionic plaster capitals. Elsewhere in the town there are some handsome early 19th-century buildings, including the **Falmouth Arts Centre** in Church

Street which began life as a Quaker institute 'to promote useful arts', the synagogue in Vernon Place, and the Custom House with its fine colonnaded façade. A curious chimney near the Custom House was used for burning contraband tobacco and is still referred to as the 'King's Pipe'. The area around Custom House Quay has been made into a conservation area, the centrepiece of which is the tall-funnelled steam tug, the *St Denys*. This fascinating little ship forms part of Falmouth's Maritime Museum and is open daily, 10am to 6pm between early-April and end-October.

Modern Falmouth has a dual role as a commercial port and holiday centre. The docks continue to be used by merchant shipping, and there is still an indigenous ship-repairing yard. However, these traditional activities are perhaps overshadowed by the town's increasing popularity as a yachting and tourist destination. Throughout the year, visitors arrive by land and sea to enjoy the mild climate, pleasant atmosphere and excellent facilities. For those keen to explore the upper reaches of the Carrick Roads by boat, a variety of pleasure trips depart from the Prince of Wales pier, as do the cross-estuary passenger ferries to St Mawes and Flushing. The tree-lined square known as the 'Moor' can be found a short distance inland from the pier; on one side stands the town hall and art gallery, and on the other, a steep flight of 111 steps known as Jacob's Ladder leads up to a Wesleyan chapel. An attractive sight throughout the summer months are the periodic races between Falmouth's old gaff-rigged working boats. These colourful competitions evolved from the traditional practice of racing out to newly-arrived sailing ships to tender for work. A number of these handsome working vessels, some of the last examples in the country still to operate under sail, are used for dredging oysters from the Helford estuary.

Around Falmouth

PENRYN. Before Falmouth's rise to prominence in Tudor times, the controlling port at the mouth of the Carrick Roads was Penryn, a now-tranquil place lying at the head of Penryn creek, three miles to the northwest of Falmouth. During medieval times, this was the home of Glasney College, an important collegiate church which survived until the Dissolution of the Monasteries in 1539. (All that remains of the church today is some small sections of pillar.) At one time, granite quarried in the parish was exported from Penryn docks for use in such projects as the Thames embankment and Singapore harbour. The availability of the stone has left the old town with a legacy of fine Tudor, Jacobean and Georgian buildings; now attractively restored, the centre is now a well-visited conservation area. An interesting museum of local history is housed in Penryn's town hall, formerly the parish gaol. The two well-stocked reservoirs lying to the southwest of Penryn are contained within the **Argal and College Water Park**; excellent facilities for sailing and windsurfing can also be found a couple of miles further west on the much larger Stithians reservoir.

A lane to the southwest of Falmouth leads past the little-known **Penjerrick Gardens,** an attractive garden laid out by the Quaker Fox family which contains one of the largest magnolias in the country. Penjerrick is also famous for its hybrid rhododendrons which were developed by the head gardener in the 19th-century. (Open Wednesdays and Sundays only, 2pm to 4pm between mid-March and end-September.) Another beautiful garden, **Glendurgan,** lies a couple of miles to the south in a secluded valley leading down to the Helford estuary. Created in the 1830s by another member of the Fox family, Alfred, it is known for its magnificent tulip trees, magnolias and camellias. Its attractions include the Giant's Stride and the recently-restored laurel maze. Now owned by the National Trust, Glendurgan is open Tuesdays to Saturdays (and Bank Holiday Mondays), 10.30am to 5.30pm between 1 March and 31 October. The NT-owned hamlet of DURGAN at the southern end of the valley is a gem which should not be missed.

HELFORD. During the summer, a passenger ferry operates between Helford Passage and the village of Helford on the southern bank. This exceptionally pretty community stands in one of the most lush and attractive settings in Cornwall, the secluded tree-lined estuary of the **Helford River.** Once the haunt of smugglers, this deep series of tidal creeks is also rumoured to be the home of Morgawr, the legendary Helford monster. Since his first recorded sighting in 1926, he has been seen on a number of occasions and described as a 'hideous hump-backed creature with stumpy horns'. The village itself has a charming relaxed atmosphere, with traffic being banned from the streets during the summer months.

The Frenchmen's Creek immortalised by Daphne du Maurier in her novel of the same name lies half-a-mile to the west of the village. Although best seen by boat, land access to this beautiful wooded inlet can be made via the farm at Kestle which is signposted off the road to MANACCAN another attractive village standing at the head of a tidal creek.

GWEEK. Further upstream, stands at the head of the westernmost branch of the Helford river. Although it is hard to imagine today, this was once a flourishing commercial port whose importance grew when the harbour at nearby Helston silted up in the 13th-century. Gweek eventually suffered the same fate, and the cargo vessels of old have long since been replaced by small pleasure craft and sailing dinghies. In recent years, however, the port has undergone something of a rejuvenation with the opening of the Quay Maritime Centre, the largest collection of historic small craft in Cornwall. Another of Gweek's attractions is the Cornish Seal Sanctuary which can be found a short distance from the village on the northern side of the creek. Injured seals and orphaned pups are brought here from all over the county for treatment and care before being returned to the wild.

TOLVAN CROSS. One mile to the north of Gweek, the back

garden of a cottage in the hamlet of Tolvan Cross is the unusual location of a massive Bronze Age monolith known as the Tolvan Holed Stone. Standing seven feet tall, this curious triangular stone is said to bring fertility to those squeezing their naked bodies through its seventeen-inch circular aperture.

MAWGAN-IN-MENEAGE lies a couple of miles to the southeast of Gweek. Here, **Trelowarren House** is an impressive part-Tudor country mansion which as been the home of the Vyvyan family since the 15th-century. Its main rooms and chapel are open to visitors on conducted tours. (Open Wednesdays and Bank Holiday Mondays, 2.30pm to 5pm between mid-April and early-October).

LIZARD PENINSULA. To the south of Gweek, the landscape changes dramatically from the luxuriance of the Helford River to the rugged splendour of the Lizard Peninsula. Here the land rises onto Goonhilly Downs, an area of windswept granite and serpentine heathland which is littered with Bronze Age remains and some rather more up-to-the-minute human creations, the huge saucer aerials and satellite dishes of British Telecom's **Goonhilly Downs Earth Station.** Chosen for its location on solid bedrock near the most southerly point on the UK mainland, this important international telecommunications link can be seen beside the B3293 midway between Helston and the coast. A guided tour of the station can be taken during the summer months which incorporates an informative audiovisual presentation on the development of modern satellite communications.

As well as being of interest to the Bronze Age archeologist, the Lizard is of special interest to the botanist. The peninsula's moorland and cliffs are home to a number of rare wild plants, including the pink-flowering 'Cornish Heath', and a nature reserve has been established on Predannack Downs to preserve this valuable natural habitat. The rugged and undulating stretch of the South West Coast Path around the Lizard is amongst the most spectacular in Cornwall.

COVERACK. Those who require a restful and peaceful holiday need look no further than the **BAY HOTEL** at Coverack. Occupying a superb position on one of England's finest coastlines, Coverack is a traditional, picturesque, uncommercialised fishing village on the Lizard Peninsula. This adult only, hotel sets high standards at reasonable prices. The climate is generally milder is this part of the country and what could be nicer that to sample tea on the secluded lawns or hotel patio with uninterrupted seascape views. Other amenities nearby include fishing, Golf and the famous Cornish Gardens. Your palate is well catered for with a most comprehensive menu of great variety including Lobster and Oysters. Most of the fourteen bedrooms have wonderful sea views and are furnished to a high standard of comfort. All main bedrooms are en suite with private facilities. Anyone with a disability will be well catered for and it is the owners real desire that you have a wonderful holiday at the Bay Hotel.

The Bay Hotel, Coverack, Helston, Cornwall. 01326 280464

The many picturesque settlements and coves include the former pilchard-fishing and smuggling villages of CADGWITH (which holds the record for the most pilchards caught in a single day: 1.3 million), CARLEON COVE with its disused serpentine works, the well-visited LIZARD village which supplements its living producing ornaments from the local stone, the National Trust-owned KYNANCE COVE with its sandy beach and dramatic offshore rock formations, and MULLION COVE with its remarkable little weather-worn harbour. The view to the west of Lizard Point is enhanced by the sight of St Michael's Mount, a dozen miles away across Mount's Bay.

LIZARD POINT is the southernmost point on mainland Britain. Once the location of a coastal beacon, it was from here that the alarm was raised when the Spanish Armada was first sighted entering the western English Channel in July 1588. The jagged fingers of serpentine and granite which project into the sea have long been a hazard for shipping, and as long ago as 1620, a lighthouse was erected on the headland to alert passing vessels of the danger. The original coal-fired warning light was erected by the notorious Killigrew family of Falmouth who were subsequently accused of trying to prevent shipwrecks on the Lizard so that vessels might founder nearer the Carrick Roads where they held the appropriate rights of salvage. A more dependable lighthouse was established here in 1752, which was then taken over by Trinity House in 1790. Converted from coal to oil 1815 and then to steam-driven electric power in 1878, it now has a tremendously powerful beam which can sometimes be seen from over fifty miles out at sea. The present lighthouse is open to visitors from 10am to 4pm on fine days throughout the summer.

One mile to the north of Mullion, a memorial on the cliff above **Poldhu Cove** commemorates the work of Guglielmo Marconi, the radio pioneer who transmitted the first transatlantic wireless message from

Cottage at Cadgwith

here in 1901. The previous year, he had chosen this lonely spot to build one of the largest wireless stations the world had ever seen, a complicated affair of pylons and aerials which survived until the 1930s. Marconi's achievement is commemorated by a small granite obelisk near the Poldhu Hotel which was unveiled by his daughter after the inventor's death. In 1785, a ship carrying a consignment of silver dollars ran aground on nearby **Gunwalloe Church Cove**, a place which is still popular with treasure hunters who can be seen combing the sandy beach with metal detectors. The charming little church which gives the cove its name lies protected in the sand dunes behind a cliff. Rebuilt in the 15th-century on the site of an earlier structure, it is named after a little-known 6th-century Breton abbot, St Winwalloe.

On the southern approaches Helston, the A3083 passes close to two very different places of interest: **FLAMBARDS**, a popular all-weather theme park set in attractive landscaped grounds offering a variety of attractions, including an aero park, Victorian village, 'Britain in the Blitz' feature and an assortment of up-to-date fairground rides,

CULDROSE. The Royal Naval Air Station at Culdrose is one of the largest and busiest helicopter bases in Europe. With a range incorporating several hundred miles of the British coastline and extending well out into the Atlantic, aircraft from here have been responsible for a great many successful search and rescue missions since the base was established in the 1940s. Visitors can observe the many comings and goings from a special public viewing area near the car park.

HELSTON is the westernmost of Cornwall's five medieval Stannary towns. During the early Middle Ages, streamed tin was brought here for assaying and taxing before being despatched throughout southern Britain and continental Europe. Although difficult to image today, this was a busy port until the 13th-century when a shingle bar formed across the mouth of the River Cober preventing access to the sea. Goods were then transported to a new quay at Gweek until further silting and a decline in tin extraction brought an end to the trade.

Helston's long and colourful history has left it with a legacy of interesting old buildings. The Blue Anchor Inn, a hostel for monks in the 15th-century, can be found at the lower end of the main Coinagehall Street, and further up, the part-16th-century Angel Hotel is the former town house of the Godolphin family. In the 1750s, the Earl of Godolphin was responsible for rebuilding the parish church of St Michael at the back of the town with its imposing exterior, fine plaster ceiling in the chancel, and impressive internal gallery on three sides of the nave. The church tower dates from the 1830s, its predecessor having been destroyed in a lightning storm almost a century before. The churchyard contains a memorial to Henry Trengrouse, the Helston man responsible for inventing the rocket-propelled safety line which saved so many lives around the British coast. He dedicated himself to developing the device after the frigate *Anson* ran aground on nearby Loe Bar in 1807, resulting in the unnecessary loss of 100 lives. An exhibit devoted to his life's work can be found in Helston's folk museum, a fascinating collection of historical artefacts which is housed in the old Butter Market.

Helston continues to be a market town, and on Mondays, the main thoroughfare is lined with colourful market stalls. The town's steeply-sloping streets contain a surprising assortment of Georgian, Regency and Victorian buildings which together create an almost genteel atmosphere. In Coinagehall Street there is a fine neoclassical guildhall, and in Wendron Street, a modest thatched cottage is the birthplace of 'Battling' Bob Fitzsimmons who went on to become the world heavyweight boxing champion. However, Helston is perhaps best known for its 'Furry Fair' which takes place each year in early May. This ancient pagan celebration of spring takes its name for the Cornish *fer*, meaning feast day, although in the 18th-century, it was given Roman roots and renamed after the goddess, Flora. According to local legend, what is now often referred to as the Floral Dance is performed in commemoration of St Michael's victory over the Devil who tried to claim possession of the town. (The final boulder thrown by Satan is claimed to have missed its target, ending up in the garden of the **Angel Hotel** where it remained until 1783.) Every May 8, the town is closed to traffic and formally-dressed couples and pairs of children dance through the streets, and in and out of people's houses, to the strains of traditional folk melodies.

When the shingle bar formed across the mouth of the **River Cober** in the 13th-century, the dammed river created the largest natural fresh-water lake in the county. Lying a couple of miles to the southwest of Helston and once forming part of an estate belonging to the Rogers family, **Loe Pool** is now under the ownership of the National Trust. A delightful six-mile walk leads around the wooded fringes of the lake, although the less energetic can take a shorter stroll through the woods on the western side. This tranquil body of water is a haven for sea-birds and waterfowl, and is a paradise for ornithologists and picnickers. A Cornish folk tale links Loe Pool with the Arthurian legend of the Lady of the Lake: like Bodmin Moor's Dozmary Pool, a hand is said to have risen from the depths to catch the dying King Arthur's sword, Excalibur. Another story connects Loe Bar with the legendary rogue Jan Tregeagle, who was set the task of weaving a rope from its sand as a punishment. A second monument to Henry Trengrouse, the inventor of the rocket-propelled safety line, can be seen on the cliff to the southeast of Loe Bar.

Around Helston

PORTHLEVEN, at the northern end of Loe Bar, is a small port with a good beach and a working harbour which accommodates a handful of fishing boats and a small boat-building yard. Its surprisingly substantial inner harbour was built in the middle of the 19th-century when there were ambitious plans to make Porthleven into a major tin-exporting centre. Although the scheme ended in failure, the inner basin can still be sealed off from the worst of the southwesterly gales, a periodic necessity in winter. A number of Porthleven's old industrial fixtures have been converted to craft galleries and the like, and higher up, the harbour is overlooked by an assortment of handsome residential terraces, fishermen's cottages and inns. One street is named after Porthleven-born Guy Gibson, the instigator of the famous 'Dambusters' bouncing bomb missions during World War II.

BREAGE, (pronounced *Braig*), a mile-and-a-half inland to the north of Porthleven, is renowned for its exceptional 15th-century church. Large by Cornish standards, it has a soaring three-stage pinnacled tower and contains a remarkable set of medieval wall-paintings which lay undiscovered under a layer of whitewash until the 1890s. The murals are as old as the church itself, and depict such subjects as St Christopher, and Christ Blessing the Trades. In the north aisle, there is also a rare Roman milestone from the 3rd-century AD, evidence that Cornish tin was extracted on behalf of the Roman empire. The churchyard contains a Celtic four-holed wheel cross, the only example of its kind in Cornwall to be carved in sandstone, and affords a stunning view of Mount's Bay and the western side of the Lizard peninsula.

WENDRON. One of the Romans' principal sources of tin ore was a mine near the village of Wendron, four miles to the northeast of Breage. Lying off the B3297 Helston to Redruth road, the re-dubbed **Poldark Mine** now offers visitors the opportunity to experience conditions in an underground mine at first-hand. The three-acre site incorporates a number of impressive above-ground visitor attractions, including a working beam-engine and an interesting collection of historic mining machinery and related artefacts. The Poldark Mine lies within a popular fun park containing fairground rides, cinema, picnic gardens and a variety of children's attractions. Letters posted in a unique underground postbox are stamped with a special postmark. (Open daily, 10am to 6pm between early-April and end-October.)

The exceptional part-Tudor **Godolphin House** can be found in the wooded lanes to the north of Breage, midway between the villages of Townshend and Godolphin Cross. Part early 16th-century with substantial Elizabethan and Carolean additions, this is the former home of the Earls of Godolphin, prominent Cornish entrepreneurs who amassed a fortune from their mining interests. The unique north front was completed shortly after the English Civil War and incorporates an impressive seven-bay granite colonnade. The interior is noted for its splendid King's Room, fine Jacobean fireplaces, and a painting of the famous 'Godolphin Arabian', a stallion imported by the second Earl which is said to be one of the three from which all British thoroughbred horses are descended. (Open Tuesdays and Thursdays, and all Bank Holiday Mondays, 2pm to 5pm between early-May and end-September.)

There is some excellent walking on nearby **Tregonning Hill**, a site littered with Bronze Age remains which also has an important place in industrial history for it was here that William Cookworthy first discovered china clay, or *kaolin*, in the 1740s. An Admiralty signalling station was also established here during the Napoleonic Wars. More evidence of the area's industrial heritage can be seen to the southwest of Breage: the chimney and engine house of Wheal Prosper and the ruins of Wheal Trewavas both lie beside the coastal path on Trewavas Head.

GERMOE In the church at Germoe, two miles to the west of Breage, there is a remarkable Celtic font carved with a gaunt human head which is said to have come from the baptistery founded by the Irish king and missionary, Germochus, in the 6th-century. There are good safe sandy beaches at nearby **Praa Sands**, and beyond **Cudden Point**.

Prussia Cove is so-named for being the haunt of John Carter, a notorious 18th-century smuggler who is rumoured to have modelled himself on Frederick the Great of Prussia. One story records how he used a cannon mounted on the cliff to scare off revenue cutters. The smugglers' wheel tracks can still be seen in the steep stone slipway leading up from the water's edge.

St Ives, Penzance and West Penwith

ST IVES. With its five sandy beaches, maze of narrow streets, and picturesque harbour and headland, the attractive fishing and former mining centre of St Ives manages to retain a special atmosphere, despite being deluged with visitors throughout the summer. The settlement takes its name from the 6th-century missionary saint, St Ia, who is said to have landed here having sailed across from Ireland on an ivy leaf. The 15th-century parish church near the harbour's shorter west pier bears her name. An impressive building with a soaring pinnacled tower, it contains an unusual granite font carved with stylised angels and lions. Another striking ecclesiastical building, a mariner's chapel, stands on **St Ives Head**, the promontory to the north of the harbour which is known locally as the 'Island'.

The headland is also the location of a 'huer's' hut, the viewpoint from which a local man would keep a look out for shoals of pilchards in the bay. When one was sighted, he would alert the crews of the *seine* boats (open rowing boats) by calling 'hevva' through a long loud-hailer, before guiding the fishermen towards their goal with semaphore-type signals using a pair of oval bats known as 'bushes'. St Ives was one of Cornwall's most important pilchard fishing centres until the industry went into decline in the early 20th-century. The town holds a record dating back to 1868 for the greatest number of fish caught in a single seine net. Once the pilchards were brought ashore, they were compressed to release fish oil before being salted and packed into barrels for despatch to southern Europe where the Catholic code for avoiding meat on Fridays guaranteed a steady demand. At such times, the streets of St Ives would stream with the oily residue of these once-plentiful fish, and the air would be filled with an appalling smell which would drive away all but the most determined outsiders. A local speciality, 'heavy', or *hevva*, cake was traditionally made for the seiners to returning with their catch.

As well as providing shelter for the fishing fleet, St Ives' harbour was built for exporting locally-mined metal ores. The sturdy main pier was built by John Smeaton, the 18th-century marine architect who was responsible for designing the famous Eddystone lighthouse which now stands on Plymouth Hoe. Like many parts of western Cornwall, the surrounding valley was once rich in veins of tin, copper and other minerals, and indeed the building which now houses St Ives museum began life as Wheal Dream copper mine. The town's labyrinth of narrow streets was once divided into two communities: 'Downalong', where the fishing families lived, and 'Upalong', which was inhabited by the mining community. There was much tension between the two, and fights would often break out between gangs of young rivals, a practice which ended with the closing of the mines and the steady reduction in the fishing fleet.

One of St Ives' most colourful inhabitants was John Knill, the 18th-century mayor who was responsible for constructing the unusual steeple to the south of the town, supposedly as a mausoleum. Despite being a customs officer by profession, Knill was also widely rumoured to be an energetic smuggler who built the tall monument for the purpose of guiding vessels filled with contraband to the shore (it still serves as a mariners' daymark). He was actually buried in London, but bequeathed a sum to the citizens of St Ives for holding a curious ceremony which continues to be held in the town at five yearly intervals. On 25 July in the first and sixth years of the decade, a procession led by a fiddler, two widows and ten young women sets out from the centre to dance around the steeple and sing the old 100th psalm.

St Ives' decline as a mining and fishing centre has been offset by its rise as an artists' colony. The painter William Turner visited the town towards the end of his life, and both Whistler and Sickert are known to have been attracted here by the special light of west Cornwall. In the first half of the 20th-century, Barbara Hepworth, Ben Nicholson and others began to convert the disused pilchard cellars and sail lofts around the harbour into artists' studios, and a 'St Ives School' was established which gained an international reputation. The town's artistic standing was also boosted by the arrival in the 1920s of the potter Bernard Leach who established a workshop beside the B3306 at HIGHER STENNACK which is still in operation; many examples of his work are now on show to the public. (Open Mondays to Saturdays, 10am to 5pm, all year round.)

One of the highlights of any stay in St Ives is a visit to the **Barbara Hepworth Sculpture Garden and Museum** in **Barnoon Hill**. After she died in a fire at the premises in 1975, the sculptor's living quarters, studio and garden were turned into a museum and gallery dedicated to her life and work. The garden is packed with a remarkable concentration of her work, and two particularly poignant features are the little summerhouse where she used to rest in the afternoons, and the workshop which has been left entirely untouched since her death. Barbara Hepworth's studio is now administered by the **TATE GALLERY**, the London-based institution which has also opened a large-scale annexe in the town which is dedicated to the work of the St Ives School. An imposing white-painted building which uses Porthmeor Beach as a stunning backdrop, the architecture is considered by some to dwarf the quality of the work inside. (Both galleries open daily, 11am to 7pm all year round; closed Mondays in winter.)

The narrow thoroughfares of St Ives contain an unusual number of museums and galleries. **PENWITH GALLERIES** in Back Street West is a good place to see the work of the St Ives Society of Artists which was founded by Sir Alfred Munnings, and St Ives Museum in Wheal Dream contains a unique collection of artefacts illustrating the natural, industrial and maritime history of the district, and includes a special feature on the exploits of John Knill. As the child, the writer Virginia Woolf spent most of her summers at Talland House overlooking St Ives Bay from where it is possible to see the Godrevy lighthouse, the setting which provided the inspiration for her extraordinary novel, *To The Lighthouse*.

If you are seeking Guest House accommodation in St. Ives, **'WHITEWAVES' GUEST HOUSE** offers really good quality and value, and a warm and friendly welcome is assured. Janet and David are very keen to please and rate highly the comfort of their guests. The house has excellent views over St. Ives and is easily reached on foot, free parking is available at the front of the house. The inside is bright and welcoming and the rooms are nicely furnished, each has colour TV and tea and coffee making facilities. Guests have their own keys and access to their rooms and the comfortable T.V. lounge at all times. Full English breakfast is provided.

Whitewaves Guest House, 4 Seaview Terrace, St. Ives, Cornwall.
Tel: 01736 796595

With extensive views of St. Ives Bay and the harbour, and with all local services and amenities close by, **CHANNINGS HOTEL** is a con-

338

venient and comfortable family run hotel in which to enjoy this popular resort. Roger and Dorothy are the resident proprietors who provide a very friendly atmosphere and nothing seems too much trouble to ensure their guests are well cared for. Children of all ages are very welcome and a baby listening service is provided. All bedrooms have en-suite facilities, are well decorated and tastefully furnished. Channings, under the personal supervision of Roger, is well known for its excellent cuisine, and the well appointed lounge bar is an ideal meeting place for guests to make new friends. ETB. 3 Crowns Commended.

Channings Hotel, Talland Road, St. Ives, Cornwall. Tel: 01736 795681

A good way to travel to St Ives, especially in high summer when traffic congestion and parking can be a headache, is to park and take the local train from **St Erth** or **Lelant**. The railway skirts St Ives Bay, with its five-mile long stretch of unbroken sand, and is widely regarded to be one of the loveliest coastal branch lines in Britain. The train also passes close to **Lelant Saltings**, a 500-acre tidal area at the mouth of the Hayle estuary which is now a RSPB bird sanctuary.

LELANT was once an important port which lost out to St Ives when its anchorage became clogged with silt at the end of the Middle Ages. Now a flourishing holiday centre, its renowned golf links is overlooked by a 15th-century church dedicated to St Uny, an early Celtic saint who is reputed to be the brother of Ia from St Ives. A spectacular view of St Ives Bay can be enjoyed from the summit of Trencrom Hill, the 500ft granite prominence lying a mile-and-a-half to the west Lelant. The site of a small Iron Age hill fort, excavations have revealed numerous hut circles and pottery fragments from the 2nd-century BC.

Lying beside the A3074 between Lelant and Hayle, **Merlin's Magic Land** offers a selection of popular fairground rides. (Open daily, 10am to 5.30pm between Easter and end-October.)

Another good holiday attraction, **Paradise Park**, can be found on the southern edge of Hayle. The park is a haven for rare and endangered birds including the Cornish chough, a once-common inhabitant of the local cliffs which is now extinct in the county. (The striking red-billed bird is incorporated into the Cornish coat of arms.) Several species of brightly-plumaged parrots can be seen flying freely, and there is also an otter sanctuary where the animals are bred for possible reintroduction to the wild. Displays of eagles and other birds of prey in flight can be seen at certain times throughout the day. (Open daily, 10am to 6pm, all year round.)

HAYLE was a major industrial port and engineering centre in the centuries leading up to the decline of the mining industry at the turn of the 20th-century. The great Cornish inventor, Richard Trevithick, built an early version of the steam locomotive here in the early 1800s, and not long after, one of the first railways in the world was constructed to carry tin and copper to Hayle Quay from Redruth. At the height of the industry in the 19th-century, steam-powered engines built by the famous 'Harveys of Hayle' could be found in most of the mines in Cornwall. After more than a century of decline, plans are being drawn up to comprehensively redevelop the old port area.

LEEDSTOWN. You will find a good place to stay near Leedstown. PENGELLY is a traditional 17th century Cornish farmhouse where Ken & Sylvia Britnell offer probably one of the best cream teas in Cornwall plus accommodation on a Bed and Breakfast basis. Located halfway between Helston and Hayle off the B3302 at the crossroads signposted - **Trenwheal**. Here you can enjoy a selection of home made preserves, scones, pastries, sandwiches, and rolls served in a delightful conservatory; a very quiet and relaxing atmosphere. Once sampled, visitors return again and again to this "little bit of heaven". The farmhouse offers a high standard of spacious accomodation with hand basins in each room and separate bathroom, toilets and shower room for guests. Traditional breakfast is served in the Dining or Sun room and there is a lounge and colour TV for guests. Pets will be considered by prior arrangement. A good location to reach the coast on either side of the Peninsula.

Little Pengelly, Trenwheal, Leedstown, Hayle, Cornwall. Tel: 01736 850452

The eastern side of St Ives Bay is lined with one of the finest sandy beaches in Cornwall. A popular centre for windsurfing, various competitive events are staged here throughout the season, including breathtaking demonstrations of wave jumping.

GWITHIAN This ancient village stands away from the tourist development behind the high windblown sand dunes, or *towans*, at the northern end of the beach. This picturesque community of thatched cottages and farmhouses has a good inn, a tiny early-19th-century cobwalled Methodist chapel, and a Victorian parish church with a low 15th-century tower. The churchyard is filled with the graves of sailors who came to grief on nearby Godrevy Island. A sizable prehistoric settlement is said to lie buried beneath the nearby towans, along with a 7th-century oratory founded by the Irish missionary, St Gothian. The stream passing between Gwithian and **Godrevy Point** is often stained with tin from the mines around Camborne and is known appropriately at the Red river.

MARAZION. It's well worth diverting off the A30 between Hayle and Penzance to visit Marazion (pronounced *marazion*), the ancient trading point on the mainland opposite St Michael's Mount. The village was a port as long ago as the Bronze Age, and for many centuries this was the most important settlement on Mount's Bay. Its long history has left a legacy of fine old inns and residential buildings, and there is also a long sandy beach to the west which offers magnificent views of the Mount. Marazion Marsh, on the inland side of the main road, is a protected breeding ground for many rare species of waterfowl.

ST MICHAEL'S MOUNT. A third-of-a-mile offshore, and connected by a cobbled causeway which is exposed at low tide, St Michael's Mount is a remarkable granite outcrop which rises dramatically from the waters of Mount's Bay. The steep-sided islet has been inhabited by human beings since prehistoric times, and it has been a place of religious pilgrimage since a party of fisherman saw a vision of St Michael on the seaward side of the rock in the 8th-century. Three centuries later, Edward the Confessor founded a priory here which was granted to the Benedictine monks of Mont St Michel in Normandy, the island's even more spectacular cousin across the Channel. The monastery was fortified after the Dissolution in 1539, and later passed to the St Aubyn family who incorporated the old monastic buildings into a series of 18th- and 19th-century improvements to form the striking multi-layered structure we can see today. A direct descendant of the family, Lord St Levan, donated the 21-acre site to the National Trust in 1954; his son continues to reside in the castle.

The present-day structure contains some impressive medieval remains, most notably in the Chevy Chase room, the old chapel, and the central tower which soars to a height of over 250ft above Mount's Bay. One of the more handsome recent additions is the southeast wing which was designed in the 19th-century by Piers St Aubyn, a cousin of the first Lord St Levan. The interior contains some fine period furniture, silver and paintings, including a number by St Agnes-born John Opie. (Open Mondays to Fridays, 10.30am to 5.30pm, all year round; closed Tuesdays and Thursdays in winter; also open most weekends in high summer.) At

St Michael's Mount

The Egyptian House, Penzance

times of high water, a ferry service runs from Marazion (weather permitting in winter).

PENZANCE. From Marazion, it's a short drive west to Penzance, the principal town of West Penwith which lies in the northwestern corner of Mount's Bay. For centuries, this was a remote market town which made its living from fishing, mining and smuggling. Along with nearby Newlyn and Mousehole, it was sacked by the Spanish in 1595, then at the end of the English Civil War it suffered a similar fate for being such a staunch supporter of the Royalist cause. However, the fortunes of the town were transformed by the arrival of the railway in 1859, a development which permitted the direct despatch of early flowers, vegetables and locally-caught fish to the urban centres of Britain, and which also allowed increasing numbers of holidaymakers to be carried in the opposite direction.

The main broad thoroughfare of Penzance, Market Jew Street, takes its name from the Cornish term for 'Thursday market'; it has a high stepped pavement on one side, and at its southwestern end there is a domed neoclassical **Market House** of 1837.

In front of this stands the statue of Penzance-born, Humphry Davy, the 19th-century scientist who is remembered for inventing the miners' safety lamp. A number of interesting buildings are located in Chapel Street, the narrow thoroughfare which winds southwards from the Market House to the quay.

The most unexpected is the **Egyptian House**, with its exotic 1830s façade, which has recently been restored by the Landmark Trust; the National Trust occupy the ground floor shop.

The Union Hotel opposite has an impressive Elizabethan interior which is concealed behind a Georgian frontage; the first mainland announcement of victory at Trafalgar and the death of Nelson was made from a minstrel's gallery in its main assembly room. At the rear stands the shell of one of the earliest theatres in the country where performances were first held in 1787.

Further down Chapel Street, there are two quaint old hostelries, the 13th-century **Turk's Head**, and the **Admiral Benbow Inn** with its famous figure of a smuggler on the roof.

Almost facing the latter, the **Maritime Museum** contains a unique collection of artefacts recovered from shipwrecks around the Cornish coast. Marie Branwell, the mother of the Brontë sisters, was brought up at No 25 Chapel Street, and at its lower end, the early-19th-century St Mary's church stands on a ledge above the harbour and Customs House, a reassuring landmark for returning sailors.

Elsewhere in Penzance, there is an interesting **Geological Museum** in Alverton Street, a good local history museum and exhibition of paintings by the Newlyn School in **Penlee Memorial Gardens**, and a striking collection of sub-tropical trees and flowers in **Morrab Gardens**.

Around Penzance

NEWLYN. An intriguing mixture of the elemental and the esoteric, the busy harbour of Newlyn lies short distance around Mount's Bay to the southwest. Its massive jetties were built in the 1880s to enclose some forty acres of the bay, including the existing 15th-century harbour, to create the most important fishing port in the South West. This is now the base for around 200 vessels, varying in size from open lobster boats to large beam trawlers, whose valuable catches are shipped throughout Britain and Europe in huge refrigerated trucks. But Newlyn also has another side: a highly-regarded artistic tradition which was founded in the late 19th-century by Stanhope Forbes. The 'Newlyn School' advanced the idea of working out of doors using everyday subjects in their natural light, and was a precursor to the school founded in St Ives in the first half of the 20th-century. In 1895, the Cornish-born philanthropist, Passmore Edwards presented the town with a splendid art gallery in New Road, and work by the many artists working in the area, along with those from much further afield, can be seen there to this day. (Open Mondays to Saturdays, 10am to 5pm, all year round.)

MOUSEHOLE To the west of Penzance, an outstanding circular route skirts the many beautiful coves and coastal communities of West Penwith. (Take the B3315 as far as Land's End, and then the B3306 to St Ives.) Mousehole (pronounced *Mouzel*), one-and-a-half miles to the south of Newlyn, is one of the loveliest and most characteristic fishing villages in Cornwall. Along with Penzance, it was sacked by the Spanish in 1595, and subsequently rebuilt in solid Cornish granite. The parish churchyard at Paul, one mile inland, contains the grave of the fishwife, Dolly Pentreath, who was the last person in the county to speak only Cornish when she died in 1777. Injured and oil-covered sea-birds are cared for at the Mousehole wild bird hospital on Raginnis Hill; originally founded by the Yglesias sisters in 1928, it is still run by a private charity. (Open daily, 10am to 4.30pm, all year round.) Every 23 December, 'starry-gazy' pie, a local speciality with fish heads poking up through the pastry, is prepared in commemoration of the fisherman, Tom Bawcock, who saved Mousehole from starvation by setting sail in a storm and bringing home a large catch of fish. Less fortunate were the eight-man crew of the Penlee lifeboat, *Solomon Browne*, who were lost in hurricane conditions while attempting to rescue the last four crew members from the coaster *Union Star* in December 1981; all were Mousehole men. The lifeboat station near Penlee Point has the steepest slipway in England.

THE SHIP INN is a lovely old nautical pub constructed a few years after the village was burnt to the ground by Spanish raiders in 1594, it stands facing the harbour at the foot of Mousehole's maze of narrow winding streets. The pub was once a haunt for smugglers and the interior is still divided into a number of small half-panelled rooms with stone floor and low beamed ceilings. The walls are decorated with nautical

A typical Cornish Tin Mine

memorabilia including a magnificent brass propeller and a display of over 60 fisherman's knots. The Ship offers a good selection of bar meals and has three en-suite letting rooms, two of which overlook the harbour.

The Ship Inn, Mousehole, Cornwall. Tel: 01736 731234

LAMORNA, two miles further on, is an isolated granite hamlet in a rocky cove at the end of a beautiful wooded valley. Once only licensed to sell beer, its pub, the 'Wink', got its name from the old custom of winking to the landlord to obtain something stronger from under the counter. Back on the main road, an exceptional Bronze Age stone circle can be seen in a field beside the B3315. Known as the **Merry Maidens**, its standing stones are reputed to be all that remain of nineteen young women who were turned to granite for daring to dance on the Sabbath. The nearby 'Pipers', two large menhirs one hundred yards apart, are rumoured to be the accompanying musicians who suffered the same fate.

TREEN, three miles further west, is an ancient tin-streaming settlement which shelters from the worst of the winter gales in a shallow valley in the lea of the clifftops. An attractive place with a good inn and campsite, the hamlet lies a short walk away from the spectacularly-sited Iron Age coastal fort, Treryn Dinas. Despite having been constructed over 2000 years ago, the earthwork defences on the landward side can still be made out. The distinctive arm of pinnacled granite at the opposite end of the headland incorporates the Logan (pronounced *Loggan*) Rock, a 65-ton boulder which at one time could be rocked by hand. The rock was a popular tourist attraction until 1824 when it was toppled into the sea by a group of naval ratings under the command of Lieutenant Hugh Goldsmith, the nephew of the poet Oliver Goldsmith. The officer was later instructed to replace the rock at his own expense, a task which turned out to require some extraordinary engineering skills, although sadly the fine balance of the rocking stone was not restored. Details of the recovery operation can be found outside the inn.

PORTHCURNO, one of the most dramatic and atmospheric coves in West Penwith, lies to the west of the Logan Rock. Reached by way the coast path or along a narrow no-through-road from the B3315, its brilliant white sand shelves into a turquoise sea between cliffs of weatherbeaten granite. A number of undersea cables, including one running beneath the Atlantic, come ashore here.

The famous **Minack Theatre** stands perched on the headland overlooking the cove. Based on the notion of an ancient Greek amphitheatre, this superb open-air auditorium was created in the early 30s by Rowena Cade. (It opened with an aptly-chosen production of Shakespeare's *The Tempest* in 1932.) With its precariously-positioned stage, rows of seating hewn from the rock, and azure backdrop of sea and sky, this must be one of the most spectacular theatre settings in the world. Performances take place throughout the summer months; telephone (01736) 810181 for programme details.

ST LEVAN. Above Porthcurno, the road from the B3315 curves inland before terminating in this isolated hamlet. Here there is a handsome part-13th-century parish church with a fine pinnacled tower, a simple Norman font, some unusual carved bench ends, and the remains of a 16th-century painted rood screen.

In the churchyard can be seen the mass grave of the crew of the Liverpool-based grain ship *Khyber*, which ran aground on nearby rocks in 1905. There also a tall pre-Norman cross and a curious twin boulder known as the **St Levan's Stone** which is said to have been split in two by the 6th-century Celtic saint. St Levan is also reputed to have founded the now-roofless baptistery standing on the cliff above the secluded sandy beach of Porthchapel; water from the holy well is said to cure eye complaints and is still used for baptisms. The superb stretch of the coastal footpath to the west takes in the lonely seaweed-infested **Porthgwarra Cove** and the majestic cliffs around **Gwennap Head** on its way to the westernmost point in mainland Britain.

LAND'S END is a curious mixture of natural spectacle and manmade indulgence. Here, the granite backbone of West Penwith succumbs to the Atlantic in a series of savage cliffs, reefs and sheer-sided islets. On a clear day, it is possible to see beyond the **Longships lighthouse** (one-and-a-half miles offshore) and the **Wolf Rock** (seven miles offshore) to the **Scilly Isles,** over 25 miles away to the southwest. The Land's End site has long been in private hands and over the years, various attempts have been made to create a visitor attraction worthy of this illustrious setting. Today, the 'Land's End Experience' offers a range of impressive audio-visual presentations on the natural and maritime history of the area, which since Roman times has been known as the 'Seat of Storms'. There is also a hotel with magnificent sea views and a number of children's attractions.

SENNEN. The 15th-century church a mile inland at Sennen is the most westerly in mainland Britain, and back on the coast, the wide sandy beach at **Sennen Cove** offers some excellent bathing and surfing. A lifeboat has been stationed here since 1853, and today a modern rescue vessel continues to serve one of the most perilous stretches of coastline in the British Isles. The Land's End airport is situated beside the B3306 to the northeast of Whitesand Bay; as well as a regular service to the Scilly Isles, short flights can be taken which offer visitors a spectacular bird's eye view of the surrounding coastline.

ST JUST stands at the southwestern margin of one of the most remarkable areas of industrial archeology in the country. An austere community of low granite houses and inns, this was once an important tin and copper-mining centre. Despite the demise of the industry, the streets still have a solemn working air: there are two Methodist chapels, one with a neoclassical façade and room for almost 1000 worshippers, and a solid 15th-century church which contains some fascinating early relics, including two medieval wall paintings, now restored, and a 5th- or 6th-century headstone carved with a faint inscription from the dawn of British Christianity. A shallow grassy amphitheatre can be found near the clock tower in the centre of town; known as 'Plen-an-Gwary', it was once used for performing medieval miracle plays and is now a venue for the annual carnival.

CAPE CORNWALL. A narrow road to the west of St Just leads to the National Trust-owned Cape Cornwall; often referred to as the only cape in England, it marks the supposed boundary between the English and St George's Channels.

BOTALLACK. One mile further north, a pair of the most spectacularly-sited old engine houses in Cornwall can be seen on the cliffs near Botallack. Reached via the coastal footpath or along a track from the village, these partly-restored industrial relics once delivered the workforce to, removed material from, a network of tin mines which reached out far beneath the waves. (During severe storms, miners were said to have able to hear the movement of boulders on the seabed above.) According to tradition, the Cornish pasty was developed by local tin-mining families as an easy and relatively hygienic way of preparing cooked food for consumption underground.

TREWELLARD. An engine house containing the oldest working beam engine in Cornwall has recently been restored by the National Trust at Trewellard, one mile west of Pendeen. The Levant mine was the scene of a tragic accident in 1919 when the mechanism for raising miners to the surface catastrophically failed, killing 31 men and boys. Visitors are now able to see the engine in operation after it had lain unused for over sixty years. (Open daily except Saturdays, 11am to 5pm between 1 July and 30 September; also on restricted days between Easter and end-June.)

PENDEEN. **Geevor**, the last of the twenty-or-so mines in the area to close, can be seen beside the main road in Pendeen. A lane to the north of the village leads to the strikingly-situated lighthouse on **Pendeen Watch**, which is open to the public on most fine days.

The nine-mile stretch of coastline between Pendeen Watch and St Ives is among the wildest and most spectacular in Cornwall. Here, bracken-covered and boulder-strewn moorland tumbles dramatically into the sea in a series of sharp headlands and rocky coves.

ZENNOR is one of the few settlements in this stark landscape. An ancient village skirted by the coast road which has a history dating back to the early Bronze Age, its 12th-century church of St Senara contains a wooden bench known as the Mermaid's chair which was made around 500 years ago from two carved bench ends.

One side depicts the figure of a mermaid holding a mirror and comb which resembles Aphrodite, the Greek goddess of love. A famous local legend tells of a mysterious young maiden who was drawn to the church by the beautiful singing voice of the squire's son, Matthew Trewhella. An enchanting singer herself, one night she lured him down to nearby Pendour Cove (now known as **Mermaid's Cove**) where he swam out to join her and disappeared. On a warm summer's evening some say their voices can be heard rising from beneath the waves. The village also has a fine old inn, the Tinner's Arms, and an informative local museum which gives some interesting background information on this most fascinating part of West Cornwall.

Further inland, the granite moorland of **West Penwith** is littered with a remarkable number of prehistoric remains. A mile to the south-east of Zennor village, **Zennor Quoit** is a Neolithic chamber tomb whose huge capstone was once supported on five broad uprights; two other standing stones mark the entrance to an inner chamber.

CHYSAUSTER, one of the best-preserved Iron Age settlements in southern Britain lies on an exposed hillside in the heart of the Penwith peninsula, a couple of miles to the south. Founded around 100 BC, this ancient village was occupied for around four centuries. It then lay undisturbed for over 1500 years until archeological excavations in the 1860s revealed a sizable grouping of nine courtyard houses arranged on either side of a central thoroughfare. The village is adjoined by an irregular pattern of small Iron Age fields, and also incorporates the remains of a *fogou*, an semi-underground stone-lined trench which would probably have been used for storing communally-owned provisions. (Open daily (closed Mondays in winter), 10am to 6pm, all year round.)

Half-a-mile to the east, the ground rises onto the 750ft hill occupied by the Iron Age fort, **Castle-an-Dinas**. Its still-discernible system of defensive ditches and stone ramparts are centred upon a folly of the late-18th-century from where there are magnificent views over west Cornwall. Further to the west, and reached along the narrow road which runs between Morvah and Madron is **Lanyon Quoit**, a remarkable 5000-year-old Neolithic chamber tomb which looks like a massive three-legged stone table. The thirteen-ton capstone was re-erected in Victorian times with the help the lifting gear that was used to replace the Logan stone near Treen. According to legend, King Arthur ate his last meal here before going into his final battle.

A mile-and-a-half to the north, a rough track leads to the mysterious **Men-an-Tol**, a mysterious holed stone standing between two menhirs. Probably Bronze Age in origin, it is said to have curative powers which can relieve a range of conditions from backache and rickets, to infertility

Lanyon Quoit

and impotency. Other Iron Age chamber tombs in the area include **Chun Quoit** near MORVAH, and **Mulfra Quoit** near NEW MILL

To the south of Lanyon Quoit, the road passes close by the **Holy Well of St Madernus**, another place which is claimed to have healing powers. It's an ancient custom for those making a wish here to tie a piece of cloth onto a branch which overhangs the water. Nearby, there is a roofless baptistery with a tiny stone altar.

MADRON. The part 14th-century church in Madron was once the mother church of Penzance; inside, there is a fine wagon roof, a Norman font and a 17th-century monumental brass to a former mayor of Penzance.

The National Trust-owned **Trengwainton Garden** lies on the southwestern edge of the village; it is particularly known for its large spring-flowering shrubs, walled garden and fine views of Mount's Bay. (Open Wednesdays to Saturdays, 10.30am to 5.30pm between 1 March and end-October.)

SANCREED. To the west of Penzance, several interesting prehistoric sites can be found around this ancient village.

Two Bronze Age stone monuments, the **Blind Fiddler** and the **Two Sisters**, stand within a quarter-of-a-mile of each other behind the hedge on the northern side of the A30 Land's End road. Like many Cornish menhirs, they are said to represent human beings turned to stone for committing irreligious acts on the Sabbath.

GRUMBLA. A mile to the west of the village, the Iron Age hill fort of **Caer Bran** can be reached along a footpath from this tiny hamlet. Perhaps most fascinating of all, however, is the Iron Age courtyard village of **Carn Euny**, which lies another half-mile to the west above the hamlet of BRANE. Founded around 300 BC by an early Cornish farming community, it is renowned for having the best-preserved granite-lined *fogou* in Britain. This mysterious 65ft-long underground passage leads to a circular chamber which may have been used for purposes of religion, storage or habitation.

The Isles of Scilly

Lying approximately 27 miles to the southwest of Land's End, the Scillies are a granite archipelago of around 200 islands of which only five are inhabited by human beings: St Mary's, Tresco, St Martin's, St Agnes and Bryher. The islanders' traditional occupations of fishing, boat building and smuggling have given them a fierce sense of independence from both Cornwall and the rest of Britain. However, in recent decades, the economy has grown more and more dependent on the income from visitors as increasing numbers fly in from Penzance, Newquay and St Just, or arrive aboard the *Scillonian III* from Penzance.

Most come to escape from the pressures of modern living (for example there are very few cars on the islands and only 9 miles of decent road), to visit some of the 100-or-so Bronze Age sites, to observe migrating birds, or simply to enjoy the unique flora which thrive in this exceptionally mild climate. A good time to visit is during the flower harvest in early spring, a busy season which culminates in an annual flower show in March. The origin of the Scillies' flower industry are believed to go back to 1867 when a local farmer sent some early blooms to Covent Garden in his aunt's hat box. It was later encouraged by Augustus Smith, the benevolent landlord who administered the islands in the mid-19th-century.

ST MARY'S, the main island, is the first port of call for the majority of visitors. Most arrive at the small air terminal at OLD TOWN, or step ashore in the harbour in HUGH TOWN, the main centre of population which stands on a narrow isthmus between the 'mainland' and the Garrison peninsula on the island's southwestern corner. A pleasant walk around the peninsula takes in a number of gun emplacements dating from the time the island was fortified against possible Spanish aggression in the 1590s. Star Castle was built during this era in the shape of an eight-pointed star (it is now a hotel), and the Garrison, with its imposing gateway, was completed 150 years later. The peninsula is an excellent place from which to view the other islands and the sun setting over the Atlantic.

The Isles of Scilly Museum in Hugh Town has a variety of interesting displays on the archeology, natural and maritime history of the islands. One its central features is a fully-rigged pilot gig, a forerunner of the modern open rowing boats which take part in spectacular races around the islands during the summer months.

Elsewhere on St Mary's, there are numerous beaches and interesting geological formations, particularly around Peninnis Head, the southernmost point on the island. At Porth Hellick Bay to the east, a huge rock stands as a memorial to Sir Cloudesley Shovell, the unfortunate admiral whose flagship, the *Association*, and three other warships ran aground on the Western Rocks in October 1707 with the loss of around 2000 men, the most calamitous of the islands' many shipwrecks.

A group of five ancient chambered tombs stand above the bay on Porth Hellick Down. Similar examples can be found at the northern end of the island at Innisidgen Carn and Bant's Carn; the latter is also the site of an Iron Age settlement.

TRESCO. The inter-island ferry departs from St Mary's quay at regular intervals throughout the day. A crossing to Tresco provides an opportunity to observe some of the islands' abundant wildlife, including puffins and Atlantic grey seals.

Tresco's internationally-renowned Abbey Botanical Gardens were founded in the mid-19th-century by Augustus Smith in the grounds of a ruined 10th-century Benedictine priory.

Begun as a small collection of plants from Kew, specimens from all over the world have gradually been added to create one of the finest subtropical gardens in the world. Augustus Smith also established the Valhalla Museum within the grounds of the Abbey Gardens, a unique collection of figureheads and other artefacts salvaged from ships wrecked off the Scillies.

ST AGNES. The whitewashed lighthouse on St Agnes is one of the earliest examples of its kind in the British Isles; now disused, it still serves as an effective mariners' daymark. Elsewhere on St Agnes, and on the other inhabited islands of **St Martin's** and **Bryher**, there are fine sandy beaches and some interesting prehistoric remains. The western island of **Annet** is a sanctuary for sea-birds where landing is not permitted during the breeding season.

It is here that we must regrettably finish our tour around this lovely part of the world, always full of surprises no matter how often you visit the area. We hope the book has been of use to you and that it will prompt you to discover some of the 'Hidden Places we have found on this journey.

Tourist Information Centres

AXMINSTER, The Old Court House, Church Street 01297 34386

BARNSTAPLE, North Devon Library, Tuly Street 01271 388583

BIDEFORD, Victoria Park, The Quay 01237 477676

BODMIN, Shire House, Mount Folly Square 01208 76616

BRIXHAM, The Old Market House, The Quay 01803 852861

BUDE, The Crescent Car Park 01288 354240

BUDLEIGH SALTERTON, Fore Street 01395 445275

CAMELFORD, The North Cornwall Museum, The Clease 01840 212954

COMBE MARTIN, Cross Street 01271 883319

CREDITON, Market Street Car Park 01363 772006

DARTMOUTH, 11 Duke Street 01803 834224

DAWLISH, The Lawn 01626 863589

EXETER, Civic Centre, Paris Street 01392 265700

EXETER SERVICES, Sandygate (M5), Nr Exeter 01392 437581

EXMOUTH, Alexandra Terrace 01395 263744

FALMOUTH, 28 Killigrew Street 01326 312300

FOWEY, The Post Office, 4 Custom House Hill 01726 833616

HELSTON Flambards Theme Park Car Park, Clodgey Lane 01326 565431

HONITON, Dowell Street East Car Park 01404 43716

ILFRACOMBE, The Promenade 01271 863001

IVYBRIDGE, South Devon TIC, Leonards Road 01752 897035

KINGSBRIDGE, The Quay 01548 853195

LAUNCESTON, Market House Ardade, Market Street 01566 772321

LOOE, The Guildhall, Fore Street 01503 262076

LOSTWITHIEL, Community Centre, Liddicoat Road 01208 872207

LYNTON, Town Hall, Lee Road 01598 52225

MODBURY, Poundwell Meadow Car Park 01548 830159

NEWQUAY, Municipal Offices, Marcus Hill 01637 871345

OKEHAMPTON, 3 West Street 01837 53020

OTTERY ST MARY, The Old Town Hall, The Flexton 01404 813964

PADSTOW, Red Brick Building, North Quay 01841 533449

PAIGNTON, The Esplanade 01803 558383

PENZANCE, Station Road 01736 62207

PLYMOUTH, Civic Centre, Royal Parade 01752 264849

ST IVES, The Guildhall, Street-an-Pol 01736 796297

SALCOMBE, Council Hall, Market Street 01548 843927

SALTASH, Granada Motorway Services, Carkeel 01752 849526

SCILLY ISLES, Porthcressa Bank, St Mary's 01720 22536

SEATON, The Esplanade 01297 21660

SIDMOUTH, Ham lane, 01395 516441

SOUTH MOLTON, 1 East Street 01769 574122

TAVISTOCK, Town Hall, Bedford Square 01822 612938

TEIGNMOUTH, The Den, Sea Front 01626 779769

TELEGRAPH HILL, A380 (Top), Kennford, Nr Exeter 01392 833559

TIVERTON, Pheonix Lane 01884 255827

TIVERTON SERVICES, Junc 27 (M5), 01884 821242

TORQUAY, Vaughan Parade 01803 297428

TOTNES, The Plains 01803 863168

TRURO, Municipal Buildings, Boscawen Street 01872 74555

VICTORIA, Mid-Cornwall Service Area, Victoria A30, Nr Roche 01726 890481

WOOLACOMBE, Hall '70, Beach Road 01271 870553

Index

THE HIDDEN PLACES

If you would like to have any of the titles currently available in this series, please complete this coupon and send to:

M & M Publishing Ltd.
118 Ashley Road, Hale, Altrincham, Cheshire, WA15 2UN

Ireland	£5.90	___
Scotland	£5.90	___
Northumberland & Durham	£5.90	___
The Lake District and Cumbria	£5.90	___
Yorkshire and Humberside	£5.90	___
Lancashire and Cheshire	£5.90	___
North Wales	£5.90	___
South Wales	£5.90	___
The Welsh Borders	£5.90	___
The Cotswolds (Gloucestershire and Wiltshire)	£5.90	___
Thames and Chilterns	£5.90	___
East Anglia (Norfolk, Suffolk, Cambs & Essex)	£5.90	___
The South East (Surrey, Sussex and Kent)	£5.90	___
Dorset, Hampshire and the Isle of Wight	£5.90	___
Somerset, Avon and Dorset	£5.90	___
The Heart of England	£5.90	___
Devon and Cornwall	£5.90	___
Set of any five	£20.00	___

TOTAL £

Price includes Postage and Packing

- -

Name: _

Address: _

_ _

_ _

_ _

_ _ _ _ _ _ _ _ _ Postcode: _ _ _ _ _ _ _ _ _ _

Please make cheques payable to M&M Publishing Ltd.